DISCARD

BIG BLUE BOOK
OF BICYCLE REPAIR

A Do-It-Yourself Bicycle Repair Guide From Park Tool

Big Blue Book of Bicycle Repair
A Do-it-Yourself Bicycle Repair Guide from Park Tool

Park Tool Company

Copyright © 2005 Park Tool Company

The Big Blue Book of Bicycle Repair is published by Park Tool Company. For more information or to contact us:

Park Tool Company
6 Long Lake Road
Saint Paul, MN 55115
(651) 777-6868
Fax: (651) 777-5559
http://www.parktool.com

To report errors, please send a note to info@parktool.com

For the latest on all our products and services please go to http://www.parktool.com

Written by: C. Calvin Jones
Editor: Doug Shidell
Contributing Editor: Dan Garceau
Graphic Designer: Matthew McCoy

ISBN 0-9765530-0-7

Printed and bound in the United States of America

CONTENTS

CHAPTER FOUR - WHEEL TRUING

CHAPTER FIVE - PEDALS, CRANKS, & BOTTOM BRACKET

CHAPTER SIX - CHAINS

CHAPTER SEVEN - DERAILLEUR SYSTEMS

CHAPTER EIGHT - RIM CALIPER BRAKE SYSTEMS

CHAPTER NINE - CALIPER DISC BRAKE SYSTEMS

CHAPTER TEN - HANDLEBARS, STEMS, SADDLES & SEAT POSTS

CHAPTER ELEVEN - HEADSETS

CHAPTER TWELVE - BIKE WASHING

CHAPTER THIRTEEN - ON-THE-RIDE REPAIRS

APPENDICES - A-C

Introduction

The bicycle, possibly the perfect combination of simplicity and complexity, is more than just a vehicle that transforms your muscular energy into motion. It provides transportation and exercise, a way to escape and a way to be together with others. The bicycle itself consists of numerous levers, bearings, pivots and parts that require proper care and maintenance. Without a basic understanding of these parts and how they all work together, fixing your bike can be intimidating. Knowledge of the mechanics of the bicycle can change the way you ride, giving you the confidence to ride longer and further, the skills to do trail or roadside repair and the ability to maintain your bike and get it ready for the next ride.

Whether you own a single, high-end bike or a fleet of bikes for the family, the Big Blue Book of Bicycle Repair is designed to help you, the home mechanic, keep your equipment in top-notch condition. This book is a natural for Park Tool Company. We've been designing and manufacturing bicycle tools for professional and home mechanics since 1963. With Big Blue we pull together over four decades of knowledge about bicycle repair into one comprehensive and easy-to-use manual.

With the Big Blue Book of Bicycle Repair and practice, you should be able to make most adjustments to your bike and install or upgrade many components, but Big Blue is not a substitute for a good bike shop. Bicycle shocks, for example, vary greatly in design and service procedures and therefore shock repair is best left to the professional mechanic. Wheel building involves complex procedures and component selection, such as choosing proper spoke length, and some procedures require tools that are too expensive to justify purchasing for one time or occasional use. Your favorite bike shop is a great source for information about upgrades, new products, and compatibility of components, and the most reliable source for the tools you will need to do the repairs in this book.

The service procedures outlined in this book include a list of tools and supplies needed to do the repair. Look for the Tool List, these may be general-purpose tools, such as hammers and screwdrivers, or special purpose tools such as crank removers or cone wrenches. Most bike shops carry the bicycle specific tools mentioned in the tool list.

Read through any procedure first before taking apart the bike. Also look for the warning icon. This indicates an issue of safety, such as with wheel installation or seat post installation. Pay special attention to the text and discussion on these topics.

Bicycle design has not changed from the basics of two wheels, a place to sit, and a handlebar. However, modern bikes are becoming more proprietary in their details. There are components that may fit only one bike and one model. It is very difficult for a book to include all possibilities of component service. There will be situations where it is necessary to contact the manufacturer for additional information.

The Big Blue Book of Bicycle Repair has several features that you will find useful. There are thirteen chapters in the book and three appendices. The appendices include a glossary of terms AND a table of recommended torque values. You will also see references to Park Tool's website www.parktool.com. Whenever Big Blue does not cover the service of a particular item, or we feel that more discussion of a topic will be valuable, you'll see a reference to Park Tool's website. When visiting www.parktool.com, click the "Repair Help" button on the left side navigation panel, then click the banner "Bike Repair" for a list of repair topics. You will find comprehensive coverage of many topics that are too complex to deal with in this book.

Creating a bicycle repair book is like creating a new bicycle tool. It takes time and effort and the process is never as straightforward as one would hope. I want to thank Eric Hawkins, the owner of Park Tool Company, for his continued support and patience as we worked through design changes and prototypes in the development of Big Blue. I also want to thank Dan Garceau, National Sales Manager, for his help with organizing the chapters, evaluating the repair procedures and double-checking the references to Park Tool products. Graphic designer Matt McCoy joined a process that was already well underway and did an outstanding job of pulling together the graphics and book layout and Doug Shidell's steady editorial guidance was invaluable. I want to thank all of the manufacturer's reps and technical people for providing detailed information about the proper procedures to use when preparing or maintaining their products. Finally, I want to thank my family for their understanding and support during the seemingly interminable process of writing this book.

Thanks for purchasing the Big Blue Book of Bicycle Repair. I think you will find it the most comprehensive and easy-to-use bicycle repair manual ever published.

– Calvin Jones
Park Tool Company

Forward

The year was 1956. My Father Howard and his partner Art Engstrom had just bought a small fix-it shop on the East side of St. Paul, Minnesota named Hazel Park Radio and Bicycle. Both loved to get their hands dirty, so the shop seemed to be a good fit with their skills. Along with the lawn mowers and ice skates, the shop sold bicycles, which neither knew much about. As they dug in to their new venture and bicycles evolved to include hand brakes and shifting systems, Howard and Art soon tired of working on bikes turned upside down while squatting on the floor. With the help of a longtime friend, Jim Johnson, they designed their first bicycle repair stand. Soon, they realized there was a need for other tools that could make their lives easier and a tool business was born. At first Howard and Art produced tools under the Schwinn label, then shortened Park Cycle Center Repair Stand Company into Park Tool Company, and the rest, as they say, is history.

Hazel Park Bicycle, 1958

Today, Park Tool is a worldwide company producing and supplying nearly 300 different bicycle specialty tools to over 60 countries worldwide. Go into any bike shop in America, and nearly any shop worldwide, and you'll find the world famous Park Tool Blue tools in the back room and for sale on the showroom floor. Our goal is simple: Build the best bicycle tools. We are constantly improving and expanding our line to meet the expectations of Team and Professional mechanics as well as those doing their own work at home or on the trail.

This manual, The Big Blue Book of Bicycle Repair, represents one more tool in our constantly expanding lineup. While we love to sell tools, we feel strongly that information and knowledge are the most valuable tools of all. Once you gain some of this knowledge and the confidence to use it, a whole new side of bicycling can open up to you. With a basic understanding of the bicycle and how it works you'll be free to ride longer and farther. You'll understand what makes one bike or one component better than another. You may even take apart your bike and put it back together just for fun. This manual is designed to give you a complete, well-rounded look at the mechanics of a bicycle. We've designed the BBB-1 to help guide you through a wide variety of repairs from flat tires to bearing replacement, from repairing a chain to lacing spokes and truing a wheel. Road or mountain, recumbent or kids bike, tandem or city bike, whatever you ride we've included information that can help you maintain or repair your bike.

When we decided to produce a guide for home mechanics, we knew it had to be great, full of photos and tables, up to date information featuring the latest components and tools, and an easy to use format. Our author, Calvin Jones is, without a doubt, one of the most qualified mechanics and instructors in the world today. With over 30 years in the industry, Calvin lives, eats and breathes bicycles. Here is a short list of his qualifications.

- **US Olympic Team Mechanic, Los Angles 1984**
- National Team Mechanic and Manager of National Team Mechanics at MTB World Championships 1994, 96, 97, 01, 03 and 04
- Instructor at USA Cycling Mechanics Licensing Clinics at the U.S. Olympic Training Center in Colorado Springs, Colorado since 1985
- Eight years instructor at Barnett's Bicycle Institute for Bicycle Mechanics
- Author, Park Tool School Manual. Park Tool's in-store clinic presented by your local bike shop
- Park Tool Director of Education since 1996
- Mechanical advisor for countless bicycle industry manufacturers, racing teams and retailers

We're sure you'll agree that Calvin has done his homework and created a complete and concise manual sure to be a reference for nearly any mechanical procedure you choose to tackle. A special thanks to Calvin for all his hard work, we're proud to present The Big Blue Book of Bicycle Repair.

– Eric Hawkins
Owner
Park Tool Company

Chapter 1

Basic Bicycle
Maintenance Skills

Equipment and machinery all share many commonalities. Leverage, friction, tension, material strength, and bonding are part of automobiles, coffee makers, satellites, and bicycles. Understanding some basic concepts of engineering will help you understand and service any equipment.

1-1
Threaded Fastener
Tension & Torque

Threaded fasteners are used to hold many components to the bike. Understanding threaded fasteners is an important part of bicycle maintenance. Threaded fasteners are things such as nuts, bolts, screws and threaded bicycle parts and fittings. All these fasteners are made of two parts. One is the external thread, which is the bolt or screw. The other is the internal thread, which is the nut.

Threads are made in many different sizes. The size of the thread is designated and named by the external thread diameter and pitch of the thread. The pitch is the distance from the crest of one thread to another measured along the length of the thread. Thread diameter can be measured with a caliper, and pitch is best measured with a thread pitch gauge.

The so-called "English" or SAE (Society of Automotive Engineers) threads are designated by the frequency of how many threads are counted along one inch. This is called "threads per inch," and is abbreviated as "tpi." An example of an SAE thread is 9/16" x 20 tpi (pedal threads). Metric threading uses the direct pitch measurement in millimeters from thread crest to the adjacent thread crest measured along the thread axis. An example of metric thread would be 10mm x 1mm (common rear derailleur bolt).

Threads are made to tighten as they rotate. Many threaded fasteners, but not all, tighten when turned clockwise. These are called right hand threads. Some threads on the bicycle are made to tighten when turned counter-clockwise and are called left hand threads. All threads are made at a slight angle. If the threaded bolt or screw is held vertically, it will appear to slope upward toward its tightening direction. Right hand threads slope upward to the right, and left hand threads slope upward to the left (1-1_Figure 1).

1-1_Figure 1

Left hand threads are seen on the left pedal, and right hand threads are seen on right pedal. Threads slope upward toward the direction of tightening.

As a fastener is tightened, the fastener and threads actually flex and stretch, much like a rubber band. This stretching is not permanent, but it gives force to the joint, holding it together (1-1_Figure 2). The stretching force is called "preload," or tension. Each fastener is designed for a certain range of tension. Too much tightening will deform the threads or damage the parts. A thread with too little preload will loosen with use, which in some cases can also damage the part. For example riding with a loose crank bolt will eventually damage the crank. Loose bolts and nuts are also a common source of creaking noises on the bike, as the component parts move and rub one another.

1-1_Figure 2

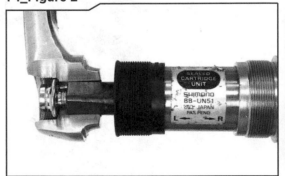

A crank bolt under tension keeps the arm pressed to the spindle

Typically it is necessary to lubricate threads. Unlubricated bolts or nuts cause threads to rub and scrape rather than tighten fully. Lubrication also aids in preventing corrosion. As a rule of thumb, if the threads are relatively small with a fine thread pitch, a liquid lubricant is adequate. If the thread size is relatively large, grease is preferred. For example, a small bolt holding derailleur cables can be oiled, but the large threads of pedals should be greased.

There are exceptions to always lubricating a thread. Either the internal or external thread may have a nylon fitting, commonly called "Nylock." The nylon in the thread prevents the screw or bolt from turning. Nylock systems are used for adjustments when there is low torque or even no torque on the fastener. For example, derailleur limit screws use plastic fittings to prevent the screws from turning and changing the derailleur adjustment. Do not lubricate the limit screws.

Generally, bolts and nuts should be tightened as tight as the weakest member of the bolt-nut-component system can withstand. For example, crank bolts are large and can take a very high torque. Cranks, however, are typically made from aluminum and cannot withstand as much pressure as the bolt could potentially generate. The crank is the weak link in that system.

To prevent over tightening and under tightening, many manufacturers provide specific torque values, best achieved by using a torque wrench (1-1_Figure 3). Torque wrenches are simply a type of measuring tool, like a tape measure or a ruler. Torque wrenches measure the amount of turning effort applied to the bolt or nut. A torque wrench should be part of the bicycle tool kit, although it is possible to work without one.

1-1_Figure 3

Torque wrench use

Measured torque may be given as Newton-meters, inch-pound or foot-pound units. This refers to the force at the end of a lever. For example, 60 inch-pounds are equal to sixty pounds of force at the end of a one-inch wrench. If the wrench were two inches long, thirty pounds of force would be required to achieve the same torque on the bolt. If force were applied at twelve inches from the bolt, only 5 pounds of effort would be required.

To convert inch-pound units into foot-pound units, divide the inch-pound number by 12. For example, 60 inch-pounds are equal to 5 foot-pounds. To convert foot-pound units into inch-pounds, multiply foot-pounds by 12. Three foot-pounds are equal to 36 inch-pounds. To convert Newton-meters to inch-pounds, multiply Newton-meters by 8.85. This book will use inch-pounds when referring to torque values. There is a list of recommended torque specifications in Appendix C. Use the component manufacturer's recommended torque when available.

With experience, a person may learn the amount of force to apply to a wrench when tightening a fastener. It may require both over tightening and then under tightening fasteners in order to learn acceptable torques. Tightening by feel relies on "perceived effort." Perceived effort is subjective and will change with the length of the tool used and where the hand holds the tool. Think about lifting a six-pack of 12-ounce beverage cans. The six-pack weights approximately 4.7 pounds. This effort applied to a wrench held six inches from the bolt is about 30 inch-pounds of torque, just about what is required to tighten a derailleur cable pinch bolt. Now consider hefting, with one hand, a case of twenty four 12-ounce beverage cans. Typically, that effort will be close to 20 pounds. That much effort on a wrench held six inches from the bolt is 120 inch-pounds, approximately the amount of torque required for hub cone locknuts and for many stem bolts. Cranks typically require about 300-400 inch-pounds, one of the highest torque values on a bicycle. That is at least 50 pounds of effort holding a wrench six inches from the crank bolt.

NOTE: For more on threaded fasteners and torque values, see Repair Help at www.parktool.com

If you are not using a torque wrench, it is still useful to use torque values as a guideline for perceived effort. To determine the effort, divide the inch-pound torque by the number of inches from the middle of your hand to the bolt or nut. For example, in the image below, a 300 inch-pound torque is desired to hold the wheel to the frame. The hand is holding a wrench 6 inches from the nut. Apply an effort of 60 pounds force (1-1_Figure 4).

1-1_Figure 4

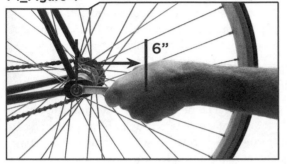

Apply force to wrench according to distance from hand to bolt

It is very useful to understand the concept of "mechanical advantage," especially when working on tight bolts and nuts. The wrench acts as a lever that pivots on the bolt or nut. In situations where two wrenches are used, position the wrenches to form a "V," with the bolt or nut at the point of the "V." This position allows more force to be applied effectively to the bolt head. Avoid positioning the wrench so the levers form an angle greater than 90 degrees When using one wrench, look for the second lever. This will sometimes be in the form of the opposite crank, as when working on pedals, or the frame tubing while working on the bottom bracket. (1-1_Figure 5 and 1-1_Figure 6).

1-1_Figure 5

Poor mechanical advantage

1-1_Figure 6

Good mechanical advantage

1-2
Lubrication, Thread Lockers, & Cleaners

Bicycles require various types of lubricants depending upon the part being lubricated and how it is used. Lubricants vary in how well they work, what they are composed of, and how they are sold.

The basic purpose of lubrication is to prevent friction, and in many cases, to prevent corrosion and rust. Motor engines use motor oil under pressure to insure that pistons and bearings run smoothly. The car engine has pumps to maintain oil pressure to keep friction between parts low, a luxury the self-propelled cyclist cannot afford. Lubrication on bicycles is based on a much simpler system called "boundary lubrication," which refers to a very thin film of lubricant that separates moving bearing surfaces. This boundary of just a few molecules of lubrication is all we have to prevent metal from being ripped off a hub bearing or chain rivet.

A good lubricant should stick to the part requiring lubrication. Unfortunately, that may mean dirt and grit will want to stick to the part as well. Water tends to wash off lubricants. Liquid lubricants, such as chain lubricants, may be resistant to washing off. However, this sticky quality may also cause dirt to stick. It is useful to have available several lubrication choices. A light liquid lubricant will penetrate easier into smaller areas, such as derailleur cable derailleur housing. Examples of a light lubricant are Park Tool CL-1 Synthetic Blend Chain Lube and Triflow®. Heavy lubricants stick better in very wet conditions, and are good for lubrication where grease is not useful. A chain used in the rain, or the internals of a freehub, would be good areas for a heavier lubricant. An example of a heavy lubricant would be Phil Wood® Tenacious Oil, or Finish Line® Cross-country.

Grease is simply oil suspended in a mixture of surfactant soap or other compounds. The grease keeps the lubricating oil in place on the component part, but it is the oil in the grease that provides the lubrication. When grease gets pushed out of the way of the bearings, there will be little or no lubrication left. Grease should be changed when it becomes contaminated with grit and dirt or when the oil in the grease dries out as it gets old and loses its lubricating properties. Water may also wash out grease, especially in the bottom bracket.

It can be difficult to know when the grease used in the component parts is contaminated. It will be necessary to simply disassemble a hub or part and inspect. By the time a bearing is making noise, the damage from poor lubrication is already done. As a rule of thumb, the grease should be replaced once a year. If the bike is used for racing and/or is ridden daily, replace grease 2-3 times per year.

Grease is commonly sold in tubes or in tubs. Use care to always replace the lid when using the tub so the grease does not become contaminated. Liquid lubricants come in spray aerosol and non-aerosol bottles. The non-aerosol bottles use a tube for dripping the lubricant, which allows the user to place it where it does the most good. Aerosols can easily over-lubricate parts by spraying too much lubrication. However, aerosols can be helpful when flushing away dirt. If the bike is ridden in heavy rain, taken through stream crossings, or is washed with soap and water, liquid lubricants should be applied to the pivot points. Do not drip or spray oil into greased bearings such as hubs, headsets, and bottom brackets.

Thread-lockers and retaining-compounds are special liquid adhesives for metal fasteners and fittings. These liquids are available at home improvement centers, hardware, and automotive parts stores. Thread-lockers are made by the Loctite® Corporation, the Wurth® Company, ND® Industries, and the Devcon® Company. Retailers commonly sell a type of thread-locker called "anaerobic." These liquids

cure independently of air, and will harden and expand when sealed in the threads of the part. This hardening and expansion is what gives the thread-lockers and compounds their special features. However, these products should not be used to replace proper torque and pre-load when the clamping load is important. Most thread-lockers are designed for use with metals. They are usually not intended for use with plastic, and may both harden and weaken the plastic.

Lighter duty thread-lockers are considered "service removable." This means the part can be unthreaded and removed with normal service procedures. An example of a service removable thread-locker from the Loctite® Corporation is #242. Stronger compounds require extra procedures to disassemble the part, such as heating with a heat gun.

Retaining-compounds are intended for press fit applications. On a bicycle, they may be used for poor cartridge bearing press fits and poor headset cups fits. The retaining compounds tend to have a higher viscosity than the thread-locking compounds. Many retaining compounds require special techniques for removal, such as excess force and or mild heat. An example of a retaining compound from the Loctite® Corporation is #RC-690.

Servicing bicycle components, such as the chain, will require cleaners and solvents. Never use highly flammable liquids, such as gasoline, kerosene, or diesel as a cleaning solvent. There are safer solvent choices on the market, including Park Tool CB-2 Chain and Parts Cleaning Fluid. Dispose of used and spent solvent by contacting your local hazardous waste disposal site, typically with a state or county agency.

For cleaning the paint on the frame use mild cleaners such as window cleaners or simply soap and water. Isopropyl rubbing alcohol is usually adequate for cleaning rim braking surfaces. It is important that cleaners for braking surfaces not leave an oily film.

1-3
Diagnosing Mechanical Problems

As you develop mechanical skills and become more experienced with the technical side of the bicycle, diagnosing particular problems will become easier.

To learn this skill, begin by paying attention to your bike while you ride, and become accustomed to how it sounds and feels when things are operating properly.

Diagnosing from the saddle, while riding, can be quite useful when repairing the problem later. For example, note if an unusual noise is repetitive, occurring with every pedal revolution. This would place the problem in the crankset area, like the pedal, bottom bracket or chainring. A noise every second or third revolution might be in the chain, such as a stiff link as it passes by the derailleur pulley wheels. Ask yourself if the noise occurs when pedaling only or when coasting. Make a mental note if the noise or problem occurs under load, such as on a hill, or when you hit a small bump. It can be very helpful to use another mechanically-minded friend when diagnosing problems. For example, a friend can stress the suspect part of the bike, such as the crank, while you listen and feel for creaking. Creaking can often be felt through the frame and parts as a resonance. It can also be useful to ride with a friend, first describing what you think you are hearing and experiencing before you both ride. Use extra care during these diagnosing/riding sessions so you don't run into each other or parked cars.

1-4
Tools and Tool Selection

Having the correct tool for the job makes the work easier. Bicycles require both general maintenance tools, common to any toolbox, and specialty tools unique to the bicycle industry. There are a wide variety of sources for tools, such as bicycle retailers, department stores, automotive stores, and general tool retailers. In some cities there are also public workshops that may rent special tools and workbench space by the hour.

It is possible to purchase tools only as they are required. This is economical in one sense, but when a part fails, the tools to repair the problem must be sought out, possibly creating a long delay in fixing the bike. Anticipating the use of tools and purchasing them ahead of time means initially spending money, but the tools are there when you need them. The priority in purchasing tools depends upon the type of maintenance desired, and the bike components involved.

Look for the "Tool Box" icon throughout the book, listing tools and supplies typically required for the described procedure. Some tools are common, such as screwdrivers. Other tools, such as crank pullers, are more specific to the bicycle industry. Because bikes are not all equipped the same, not every tool listed in the Tool Box is required on every bike. Keep in mind that older bikes may need special tools as well. Consult your local bicycle professional for recommendations on specific tools.

Tools differ between manufacturers in many ways including tool finish, fit in the hand, type of material, and tool fit to the part. The finish affects both the look of the tool and how it will resist corrosion. A hand tool should fit the hand comfortably and not be awkward to use. The type of material may affect the durability of the tool. Good quality steel will last longer than softer grades. Tools are typically made to a certain size. The size should fit the part correctly, and not be too large or too small. Keep in mind that bicycle component manufacturers sometimes limit what tool companies can do for tool design. For example, if a component part was poorly thought out and service only considered after the design was completed, a "correct" fitting tool may not be possible.

Box-end wrenches and open-end wrenches fit over the outside of a bolt head or nut. When choosing a wrench for a particular bolt, pick the smallest size that will fit over the head/nut. This also applies to spoke wrenches. Two different wrenches can appear to fit, but the smaller one will grab the part better.

Hex wrenches and screwdrivers (Phillips®, cross-tip, and straight blade) fit inside a screw head. The proper size here is the largest one that will fit inside. Although two different screwdriver tips may fit inside a screw head, always choose the larger one for more engagement to the head.

A complete tool table for a very complete home shop is listed in Appendix A. However, the table does not include some tools professionals might use, such as frame machining equipment.

It is important for all mechanics, casual home mechanics and professional mechanics, to correctly use tools at all times. Wrenches should be placed fully on the nut or bolt head before turning. Hex wrenches should be fully inserted into the socket fitting before turning. Hold wrenches for comfort and good mechanical advantage. When using a file or hacksaw, apply pressure on the forward cutting stroke, not on the backstroke. These basic habits may seem obvious and pedestrian, but they are what make good mechanics.

1-5 Repair Stands

The repair stand (work stand) is the basic piece of equipment for any shop or home. Getting the bike off the ground makes the repair quicker, easier and more fun. A work stand brings the work up to the mechanic, rather than force the mechanic to bend over to get to the work. Many stands come with a rotational feature that allows the bike to rotate up to the mechanic. Repair stands often have a height adjustment feature, which allows for raising and lowering the bicycle.

Some bike frames have oval, square, or other non-round shaped tubing, making it difficult to clamp onto the frame tubing. For certain frames, the bicycle manufacturer may recommend clamping only on the seat post, rather then the frame tubing. Most bikes can be clamped on the seat post. When in doubt, check with the manufacturer for acceptable areas to clamp.

There are several clamp and stand designs available. Models vary in adjustability, range of working height, and how they hold the bike (1-5_Figure 1 to 1-5_Figure 4). There are also repair stands available that do not clamp the bike on any tube (1-5_Figure 5).

1-5_Figure 1

Spring linkage clamp offers quick and easy use

1-5_Figure 2

The adjustable linkage of an over the center clamp offers adjustable pressure at any diameter setting

1-5_Figure 3

This screw-type clamp fits a wide range of tube sizes

1-5_Figure 4

Clamping jaws designed for use on any size or shape tubing

1-5_Figure 5

Popular with race teams, this stand holds the bike without clamping the frame tubes

1-6 Home Shop Set Up

Home mechanics may enjoy setting up a dedicated repair area, basically, their own "bike shop." The primary requirement for a shop is space for a workbench, a repair stand, the bike, and enough room to maneuver. A common size for commercial workbenches is 72 inches by 30 inches (182cm by 75cm). This is deep enough to hold a wheel. It is possible to use a bench shorter than the 72 inches, but avoid benches narrower than 30 inches deep. If you are building a custom workbench, it can be set for the height of the user. This may range from 32 inches to 40 inches high. For general technical work, the top of the workbench should be approximately 4 inches to 6 inches (100-150mm) below the height of the user's elbow. The bench top can be made of many different materials, but expect the top to take some punishment during work. It is very useful to bolt the bench to the floor and to a wall. This is especially important if a vise is to be mounted to the bench.

Tools may be mounted to a board on the wall. This allows the mechanic to quickly find the right tool. Pegboard provides a versatile system to hang and arrange tools. The higher quality pegboard measures ¼-inch thick. The pegboard should be at least as wide as the workbench. Hardware stores and home supply stores stock pegboard hooks. A mix of short and long hooks will be needed. However, the short hooks are better, as this avoids stacking too many tools on one hook. A tool magnet is also a very useful item for the work area. It can hold odd shaped steel tools, and even bolts that you don't want to lose during a repair.

If possible, select an area with good light. You may need to supplement the work area with extra lighting. Painting the pegboard surface white or off-white will reflect more light onto your work area.

A good repair stand is the most critical part of the repair shop. The repair stand should be positioned next to the work area. Keep the stand close to the workbench, to avoid taking even one step to the bike, but not so close you are crowded. Be sure to use the rotation and height adjustment features of the stand to move the work area of the bike closer to you, rather then bending over.

If possible, get a bench-mounted vise. A four-inch vise is typically adequate for bicycle repair. Mount the vise on a corner of the bench so the non-moving jaw is even with the bench edge.

When arranging tools on the wall, place the tools likely to be used in conjunction with the vise close to the vise. For example, place the axle vise, cone wrenches, hammer, and freewheel tools closer to the vise.

Another very useful piece of equipment is an air compressor. A floor pump can, of course, provide enough air pressure for tires. A small air compressor, however, is useful for drying parts after washing them with a solvent. A compressor is also very useful when inflating tubeless tires.

Tool arrangement preferences will vary from mechanic to mechanic. However, try to group specialty tools together. Brake tools should be with other brake tools. Non-specialty tools should be together, with hex wrenches grouped together and combination wrenches lined up in order (1-6_Figure 1). With time you will develop the system that is best for you.

1-6_Figure 1

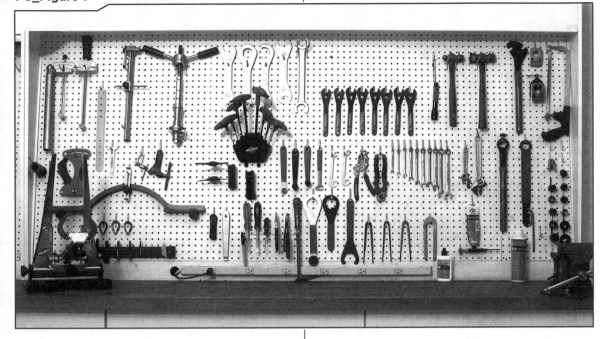

Work bench layout

Chapter 2

Tires and Tubes

The smooth ride of the bicycle comes in large part from the air in the tires. The common bicycle wheel uses a "wired on" or "clincher" wheel. The wheel rim is shaped to hold the beads or edges of the tires. Inside the tire body is an inner tube, or bladder, to hold the air, but the tire casing and body take the pressure and wear of riding. There are also "tubeless" systems available, similar to car tire systems. Professional level road racing will also use the sew-up or tubular tire system. Tubular tires are not discussed in this the book.

Servicing tires and tubes is a basic skill required for any cyclist. Sharp thorns, glass, nails, etc. can puncture tires and inner tubes and the tire itself will wear out with use and time.

2-1 Removing Wheels

TOOLS & SUPPLIES
• Wrench of correct size for wheels with axle nuts

The wheel must be removed to replace the tube and tire. If possible, begin by mounting the bike in a repair stand. If no stand is available, the bike should be laid on the non-drive side to avoid damage to the derailleur when the rear wheel is removed. Do not stand bike upright without the rear wheel in place, as this will damage the rear derailleur. Bikes with quick release wheels do not require tools for removal. Bikes with axle nuts will require the correct size combination wrench or adjustable wrench.

Wheels may be fitted to the bike with either a quick release hub or a solid axle. Quick release wheels use a hollow hub axle fitted with a shaft, a lever that operates a cam mechanism, and an adjusting nut. The cam puts tension on the shaft and pulls both the cam and the adjusting nut tight against the dropouts. This tension is what holds the wheel securely to the frame. The adjusting nut determines the amount of tension on the quick release lever and cam.

Non-quick release hubs use a solid axle, with nuts outside the dropouts. The axle nut may have a built in washer, or there may be a separate washer. If the washer has teeth or knurling, these face the dropout to help secure

the wheel. Lubricate the axle threads with the wheel off the bike. For wheel removal with axle nuts, loosen both nuts outside of dropouts.

The procedures for front wheel removal is as follows:

a. Release rim brake caliper quick-release, if any (2-1_Figure 1, 2-1_Figure 2, 2-1_Figure 3, 2-1_Figure 4)

2-1_Figure 1

Side pull or dual pivot rim brake caliper may have quick release lever at caliper arm

2-1_Figure 2

The quick release is located at the brake lever on some models

2-1_Figure 3

For linear pull calipers, squeeze lever arms together and disconnect cable from linkage

2-1_ Figure 4

For Cantilever calipers squeeze lever arms together and disconnect straddle wire cable

b. Release wheel quick-release by pulling quick release lever outward. If necessary, loosen quick release adjusting nut to clear any tabs at end of fork. (2-1_Figure 5)

2-1_Figure 5

Pull lever from closed to open position

c. Guide the wheel through the brake pads and out the fork ends.

The procedures for rear wheel removal is as follows:

a. Shift derailleur to outermost rear cog and innermost front chainring.

b. Release brake quick-release, if any (2-1_Figure 1, 2-1_Figure 2, 2-1_Figure 3, 2-1_Figure 4).

c. Release wheel quick-release by pulling on lever (2-1_Figure 5).

d. Pull back on rear derailleur to allow cogs to clear chain (2-1_Figure 6).

2-1_Figure 6

Pivot derailleur back to clear wheel and cogs

e. Lower wheel, guiding the wheel down through brake pads and forward to clear chain and derailleur.

2-2
Removing Tire
& Tube from Rim

The bead of the tire is fitted to the rim. Use tire levers to pry tire bead up and over rim sidewall. Tire levers come in different shapes and materials. A plastic lever (Park Tool TL-1 or TL-2) is typically adequate and will not leave blemishes on the rim. However, some tire and rim combinations are extremely tight and may require a steel lever, such as the Park Tool TL-5.

NOTE: Do not use a screwdriver, knife, or other sharp object, which might damage tire or tube.

The procedures for tire and tube removal is as follows:

a. Remove valve cap. Fully threaded valve shafts may also have a locking nut next to the rim. Loosen and remove locking nut before deflating.

b. Deflate tube completely. Even a small amount of air left in the tube can make it more difficult to get the tire off the rim. For best results, press downward on wheel while depressing the valve. For more information on releasing air from bicycle valves, see Outline Item 2-8 Inner Tube Valves.

c. Push tire bead toward rim center.

The tire bead will be pressed tight against rim. Pushing it inwards loosens the bead. Repeat on other bead. (2-2_Figure 1)

2-2_Figure 1

Push bead toward middle of rim

d. Engage one tire lever under bead of tire. Engage second lever 1-2" (2.5 cm) from first lever then push both levers toward spokes to lift bead off rim (2-2_Figure 2)

2-2_Figure 2

Engage levers under bead

e. Disengage one lever. Move it two inches (5cm) along the rim and re-engage lever under the bead. Push lever to lift next section of bead off rim.

f. Repeat engaging the lever until the bead loosens. Then slide the lever along the rim under the bead until the bead is completely removed from the rim.

g. Starting opposite the valve, pull inner tube from inside of tire. Lift valve from valve hole and remove tube from wheel.

h. Remove second bead from rim, which removes tire completely from the rim. To fully inspect the tube and tire, it is best to remove the tire completely. Pull inner tube from tire.

2-3 Inspecting the Inner Tube

When servicing a flat tire, always inspect the tire and tube carefully to locate the cause of failure. This will help prevent future flats.

TOOLS & SUPPLIES
- Air pump
- Marking pen

The procedures for inspecting the inner tube is as follows:

a. Re-inflate inner tube, if possible, twice its normal width. This extra tension makes small leaks easier to locate. (2-3_Figure 1 and 2-3_Figure 2).

2-3_Figure 1

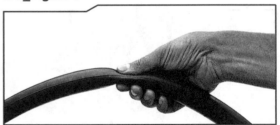

Inner tube before inflation

2-3_Figure 2

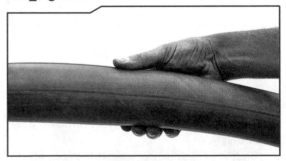

Inner tube after inflation for inspection

b. Inspect for air leaks. Move the tube past the sensitive skin of lips, holding it close. Small leaks can also sometimes be heard. Check around the entire tube. If this does not work, submerge tube in water and watch for bubbles at the hole.

c. If you plan to repair the inner tube, use a marking pen to make four marks, one to each side of hole (2-3_Figure 3). Do not mark directly on hole, as the marks may be sanded off, making hole location difficult to find.

2-3_Figure 3

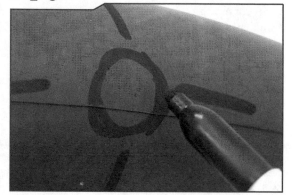

Mark inner tube after locating hole

d. Inspect remainder of inner tube for more holes.

It is important to inspect the inner tube and not simply install a new tube. The type of cut or hole in the tube will help determine the cause of the flat. Common cuts and their causes include:

- **Cut at valve**
  Misalignment of tube in rim or riding with low pressure. Be sure tube is mounted straight in rim and check tire pressure before every ride.
- **Leaky valve core**
  Loose core inside stem. Test with soapy water or saliva sealing the core. Inspect for bubbles appearing at the core. Tighten with a valve core tool.
- **Large shredded hole**
  Blowout. Usually not repairable. Check tire and rim for seating problems (2-3_Figure 4).

2-3_Figure 4

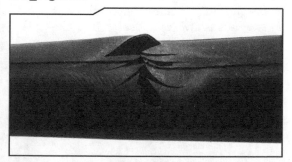

Shredded hole indicating blow out

- **Hole on the rim strip side of tube**
  Rim strip failure. Inspect inside of rim for protruding spokes and sharp points.
- **Long cut or rip**
  Tire blow out, tube is usually not repairable. Use care when seating tire during installation.
- **Single puncture or small hole**
  Thorn, wire, glass. These may be repairable. Check tire as well, the cause of the puncture may still be embedded in the tire.
- **Double slits**
  Rim pinch. Tube was pinched between rim and an object on the road or trail. Increase air pressure or use wider tires (2-3_Figure 5).

2-3_Figure 5

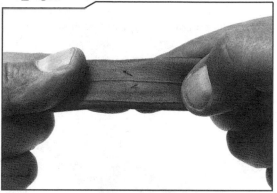

Two parallel pinch marks indicating tube was pinched between rim and tire

2-4 Inspecting the Tire

It is important to always inspect the tire as well as the inner tube. The cause of the flat, such as a nail or piece of glass, may still be embedded in the tire or tread. Inspect both the outside of the rubber tread and the inside of the casing. Check for "tire rot," a deterioration of the tire casing. Old and rotted tires are more susceptible to punctures and blow out from sidewall failure. (2-4_Figure 1).

2-4_Figure 1

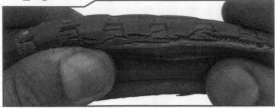

Rotted tire casing will not resist thorns or glass, and will eventually fail by blowout

The procedures for inspecting the tire is as follows:

a. Inspect outside of tread for protruding nails, pieces of glass, thorns, or other objects. Squeeze any cut to look inside for objects such as slivers of glass.

b. Visually inspect inside of tire casing for nails, glass or debris. Wipe inside of casing with a rag, and then carefully feel inside with fingers (2-4_Figure 2).

2-4_Figure 2

After visually inspecting the inside, carefully feel with the fingertips. Proceed slowly as there may be sharp objects

c. Inspect sidewall for rips, holes or damaged rubber and casing (2-4_Figure 3).

2-4_Figure 3

Damaged sidewalls will lead to failure under pressure

d. Inspect wire or fabric tire bead for damage.

2-5 Rim Strip

The wheel rim is made with holes between the rim sidewalls for spoke nipples. The rim strip covers the holes or nipples. It protects the inner tube from nipples and sharp edges in the base of the rim. The rim strip can be made of cloth, rubber, or polyurethane plastic. It should be wide enough to cover the bottom of the rim, but not so wide that it interferes with the seating of the tire bead. Inspect the rim strip whenever changing a tire or inner tube. Look for tears and rips, and make sure rim strip is centered over the nipple holes (2-5_Figure 1).

2-5_Figure 1

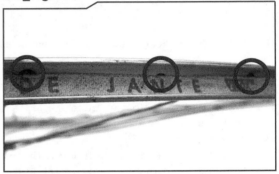

This rim strip is not properly centered over nipple holes.

High-pressure tires require a strong rim strip. Without a sturdy support, the inner tube will push down into the nipple holes, resulting in a blow out.

2-6 Repairing Inner Tubes

Replacing the punctured inner tube with a new tube is always the safest and most reliable procedure. However, it is possible in some cases to repair a small hole in an inner tube. If the hole is large, it may not be possible to repair. When in doubt replace the tube.

NOTE: Avoid the use of "packing tape" as rim tape. Fibers may separate from use, exposing tube to the nipples.

2-6.1 Pre-Glued Patch Repair

The Park Tool GP-2 Super Patch Kit uses pre-glued patches. The patch relies on the tube pressing against the tire for the hole to be sealed. If the inner tube is too small relative to the tire casing, the patch may become too stretched to hold effectively. Double check that the inner tube is an appropriate size for the tire.

TOOLS & SUPPLIES
- Patch kit (Park Tool GP-2)
- Alcohol or acetone
- Clean rag

The procedures for repairing inner tube with Park Tool GP-2 pre-glued super patch as follows:

a. Locate hole marked during inspection. (See Outline Item 2-3 Inspecting the Inner Tube) Using fine emery cloth or sandpaper, clean the tube by lightly abrading area around hole. Excessive sanding or heavy pressure can cause grooves in the rubber, which may lead to patch failure.

b. If possible, clean area with clean rag and alcohol. Allow it to dry completely.

c. Peel patch from patch backing. Handle patch as little as possible and by edges only (2-6.1_Figure 1).

2-6.1_Figure 1

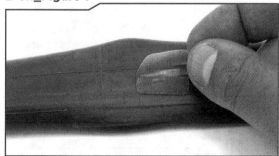

Center patch over hole and press evenly to bond patch to inner tube

d. Center patch to hole and lay patch on tube.

e. Apply pressure to patch to seal. Roll patch and tube between thumbs and forefingers.

f. Tube is ready to install. DO NOT test patch by inflating tube while outside of mounted tire. This may stretch the tube body and weaken the patch bond.

2-6.2 Repairing Inner Tubes with Self-Vulcanizing Patches

Self-vulcanizing patches require the application of a thin layer of self-vulcanizing fluid on the tube before the patch is applied. The patch reacts with the fluid to bond with the inner tube. However, inner tubes differ in their component chemical compounds and may have various success rates when patched.

TOOLS & SUPPLIES
- Patch Kit (Park Tool VP-1 Vulcanizing Patch Kit)
- Alcohol or acetone
- Clean rag

The procedures for repairing tube with self-vulcanizing patch is as follows:

a. Locate hole marked during inspection (Outline Item 2-3 Inspecting the Inner Tube).

b. Using fine emery cloth or sandpaper, lightly abrade area around hole. Abrade an area larger than patch size.

c. When possible, clean area with alcohol and allow it to dry completely.

d. Open self-vulcanizing fluid tube and puncture seal. Apply thin coat of self-vulcanizing fluid and spread evenly around hole area (2-6.2_Figure 2). Use a clean finger or back of patch to spread self-vulcanizing fluid evenly over an area that is larger than the size of the patch. Do not apply too much fluid. The layer should not appear "glopped" on.

2-6.2_Figure 2

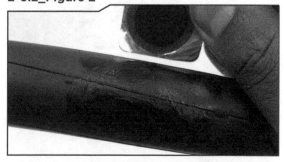

Spread a thin, wide layer of self vulcanizing fluid

e. Allow self-vulcanizing fluid to dry. This may take several minutes. Test by touching perimeter area of self-vulcanizing fluid only. Do not touch self-vulcanizing fluid where patch will contact.

f.   Peel patch from backing. Leave clear plastic cover on patch. Handle patch by its edges.

g.   Center patch to hole and lay on tube.

h.   Apply pressure to patch, especially at edges, to seal.

i.   If possible, maintain pressure for several minutes.

j.   Inspect edges of patch. Edges should lay flat and appear bonded to tube. (2-6.2_ Figure 3 and 2-6.2_Figure 4)

2-6.2_Figure 3

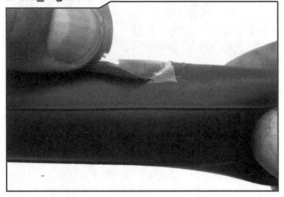

Edges did not seal well in this poorly bonded patch

2-6.2_Figure 4

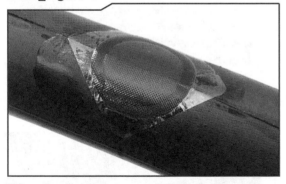

Edges lay flat in a successful patch

k.   Tube is ready to install. Do not remove plastic cover from patch, as this may pull on freshly bonded patch.

2-6.3 Liquid Inner Tube Sealant

Liquid sealants may be added to the inner tube. These products are available from various manufacturers and are intended to seal small holes in the tube. To add sealant to the inner

tube, install inner tube into wheel as normal. For Schrader valves, remove core using a valve core remover. Only some presta model tubes use a valve with a removable core. (Outline Item 2-8 Inner Tuber Valves) Place the valve at the 3:00 or 9:00 position, or so the valve is horizontal. Inject sealant according to the manufacturer's directions. Replace valve and inflate tire, again with valve placed horizontally. Spin wheel to spread sealant. When inflating or deflating the tire, the valve should be placed horizontally.

The sealant may make patching the inner tube difficult or impossible, as the sealant tends to prevent good patch bonding. Additionally, with time, the valve core may become plugged. Even a pump head may become plugged if contaminated with sealant. Always keep valve at horizontal position when inflating.

2-7
Temporary Repair of Tire with Tire Boot

If the tire has been ripped and the casing damaged, it may not hold an inner tube. It is possible, in some cases, to make a temporary repair with a Park Tool TB-1 Emergency Tire Boot. A booted tire should not be considered a permanent repair. The tire should be replaced as soon as possible.

Begin repair by locating rip in tire. Compare rip to size of tire boot. Tire boot must completely overlap rip to be effective. Clean inside of tire adjacent to rip. Cut patch to size. Align patch so edges do not extend beyond tire bead. Center patch to rip and press patch to inside of casing (2-7_Figure 1)

2-7_Figure 1

Park Tool TB-1 Emergency Tire Boot over cut in tire, and then replace tire as soon as possible

It is possible to affect a temporary boot using other material. If possible use a strong material that is resistant to tearing. Notebook paper or paper currency should not be considered acceptable boot material.

2-8 Inner Tube Valves

NOTE: Always replace tire when ride is finished.

There are two common types of valve stems on bicycles, Schrader ("American" type) and Presta ("French" type) (2-8_Figure 1). The Schrader or American-type valve is common on cars and motorcycles. It is also found on many bicycles. The valve stem is approximately 8mm (5/16") diameter and has an internal spring plunger (core) to assist in shutting the valve.

2-8_Figure 1

From left-to-right, a common Schrader valve, a presta valve, and a long stem presta

To deflate the Schrader valve tube, it is necessary to stick a small hex wrench or other object into the valve in order to press on the stem and release the air. Upon release of the stem, the valve spring shuts. Schrader compatible pump fittings press on the internal stem with a plunger, allowing the tube to be filled.

The Schrader valve core can be removed from the tube if necessary. This is rarely required, but a valve can become stuck and cause a slow leak. A loose core can also be the source of a slow leak. A valve core remover allows removal or tightening of the core (2-8_Figure 2).

2-8_Figure 2

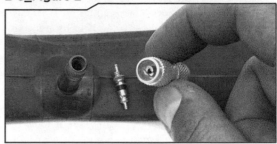

Valve core remover checks security of Schrader valves

The rim valve hole should match the valve of the tube. If a rim has been made with the smaller valve hole for presta, it can be drilled and enlarged to the 8mm size by using an 11/32-inch (8.5mm) hand drill. After drilling, use a small round file to remove any sharp edges. Rims that are less then 15mm outside width should not be drilled. It is also possible to use the smaller presta valve in a rim intended for the larger Schrader by using an adapter sleeve.

The presta or French-type valve is common on mid and higher priced road bikes and on higher priced MTB bikes. presta stems are 6mm (nominally 1/4") diameter, thinner than Schrader valves. Stem length will vary. Deep section rims require longer valve stems (approx. 60mm). At the top of the stem is a small valve locknut, which must be unthreaded before air can enter the tube (2-8_Figure 3). To deflate the inner tube, unthread the locknut and depress the valve stem. To inflate the tube, unthread the locknut and inflate using a presta compatible pump.

2-8_Figure 3

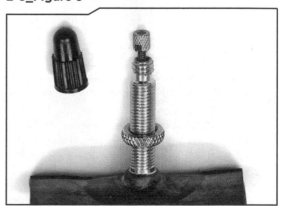

Component parts of the presta valve

Some brands of presta tubes use a valve shaft that is fully threaded. These come with an extra locking nut or ring. Loosen the ring by hand and remove it before installing the tube. Install and fully inflate the tube, then install the lockring and snug by hand. When deflating the tube, loosen and remove the nut first. When a tire is fully inflated and then deflated, the valve moves back into the tire casing. If the valve is locked to the rim by the nut, the valve may be ripped from the inner tube.

Presta compatible pump heads have no plunger and the rubber seal of the pump head is smaller than the pump head of a Schrader pump. To inflate a presta tube, unthread the valve stem locknut and tap lightly to release the seal. The seal tends to stick over time and tapping the stem breaks it free, making it easier to inflate. Press the presta compatible pump head onto the stem and inflate the tube. Some pump heads have a lever to help seal the valve.

There is no ride difference between the valves themselves. The Schrader valve, however, is wider and requires a larger rubber plate to bond it to the tube. Consequently, very narrow tubes use the presta valve. A presta-to-Schrader adapter is available, which allows Schrader pump heads to be used on presta valves (2-8_Figure 4).

2-8_Figure 4

A presta to Schrader valve adapter in place

Some models of presta valves use removable cores. If the valve has two wrench flats, use a small adjustable wrench to secure or remove the core.

2-9 Tire & Tube Sizing

Tires are made with steel wire or fabric cord, called the bead, molded into the edge of the tire. The bead forms a circle, and it is the diameter of this circle that determines the tire fit to the rim. The tire bead is made to fit into the rim bead seat, which is the area below the outer rim edge (2-9_Figure 1).

2-9_Figure 1

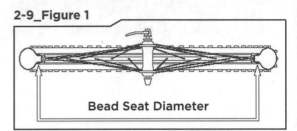

Bead Seat Diameter

Bead seat diameter of the rim and tire

Do not attempt to mix tires and wheels with different bead seat diameter standards. Although the bead seat diameter determines the tire and wheel fit, there is little consistency between manufacturers in how tires are labeled or identified. Different countries at times have used different nomenclature marking systems. This can cause confusion when selecting a tire for a wheel.

An antiquated, but still common method, uses inch designations, such as 27 inch or 26 inch. The inch size does not refer to the bead seat measurement directly. It is simply a reference code, and refers to the approximate outside diameter of an inflated tire. For example, there are several 26 inch tires that use different bead seat diameters. A 26" x 1⅜" tire, for example, will not interchange with the modern MTB 26" x 1.5" tire. There are three even more obscure tire standards that are called 26 inch diameter, but none are interchangeable.

Another common system is the older French system of sizing. The sizing numbers are reference numbers only, not actual measurements of anything. Road bicycles commonly use a 700c tire, which has a bead diameter of 622mm. The "700c" does not refer to bead diameter. The "c" is part of the code system. There are also 700a, and 700b tires and wheels, but none interchange with the more common 700c.

The ETRTO (European Tire and Rim

Technical Organization) system, which is the same as the ISO system (International Standards Organization) is now becoming more common. The ISO system uses two number designations for the tire and rim sizing. The larger number is always the bead seat diameter. Rims and tires with the same number are made to fit one another. For example, tires marked 622 will fit rims marked 622, because the bead seat diameter is 622 millimeters for both. Look for this sizing system on the tire. Rims may also have ISO sizing on the label (2-9_Figure 2).

2-9_Figure 2

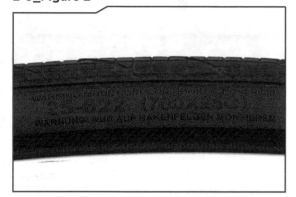

ISO (ETRTO) sizing on tire label along with French sizing system

The rim marking may also have a smaller number. This is the width in millimeters between rim sidewalls. Generally, a wider rim will accept a wider tire. A narrow tire on a relatively wide rim will mean the tire profile shape will be less rounded. A wide tire on a narrow rim will result in less support for the tire in cornering, causing the tire to laterally roll or twist. Additionally, rim caliper brakes will have very little room to clear the tire with this combination. As a loose rule, the ISO tire width should be between 1.5 to 2 times ISO rim widths. A rim width 25mm between the sidewalls should use an ISO tire width of about 37 to 50.

The inner tube should match the tire size diameter closely. Tires that are close in bead diameter may use the same inner tube. For example, an inner tube for an ISO 630 tire (27-inch) will also fit an ISO 622 (700c) tire. The inner tube must also match the tire width, but because inner tubes are flexible, one inner tube may fit a range of tire widths. If the inner tube is too narrow for the tire width, it will become

Table 2-9 Tire Sizing

COMMON SIZING NAME	ETRTO OR ISO BEAD SEAT DIAMETER	COMMON USES
29"	622	MTB using the 29" tires. Rim is same diameter as 622 below
27"	630	Older road bikes, and less expensive road bikes
700C	622	Road bikes, hybrid bikes
26" x 1 3/8"	597	Older Schwinn
26" x 1 3/8"	590	Department store three speeds, English 3-speeds
26" x 1 1/4" to 2.2" or bigger	559	MTB bikes
26" x 1 1/2" or 650c	571	Smaller road bikes or special tri-athlete bikes
24" x 1" to 1.75"	507	Juvenile MTB bikes
20" x 1" to 2.2"	406	Juvenile bikes, BMX, freestyle bikes, recumbents
16" x 1" to 2.2	305	Some recumbents and juvenile bikes

very thin when inflated inside the tire body. This will cause it to be more susceptible to punctures and failures. If the tube is too wide for the tire, it will be difficult or impossible for it to fit inside the tire casing. Part of the tube may stick out of the tire and then blow out when the tire is fully inflated. Here are some common sizes for the tire and wheel bead seating systems.

2-10
Installing Tire & Tube on Wheel

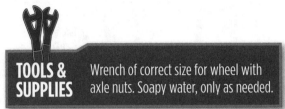

TOOLS & SUPPLIES Wrench of correct size for wheel with axle nuts. Soapy water, only as needed.

Tires are sized to match the rim. However, even within the same rim and tire sizing standard, certain tire/rim manufacturer combinations can be mounted with hands only while other combinations are difficult to mount. Never use a screwdriver or other sharp tool to mount the tire.

The procedures for tire installation is as follows:

a. Note directional arrows of tire manufacturer, if any. Directional arrows printed on the sidewalls indicate rotation of wheel. Not all tires have direction orientation.

b. Inflate tube enough for tube to hold its shape.

c. Install tube inside tire. Install with tube valve adjacent to air pressure recommendations written on tire sidewall (2-10_Figure 1).

2-10_Figure 1

Place tube into tire before mounting tire to rim

d. Lean rim vertically against your legs, with valve hole up.

e. Lower tire and valve into rim valve hole and align valve so it is pointing straight toward hub. A crooked valve can lead to a flat tire later (2-10_Figure 2).

2-10_Figure 2

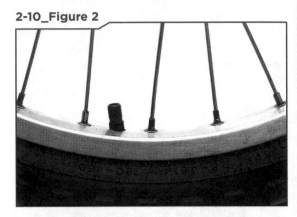

This valve will eventually be cut by the rim valve hole

f. Install one bead at a time. Begin with bead adjacent to your legs.

g. Work tire bead onto rim with hands. If tire bead will not seat using hands, use tire lever as a last resort. Use caution when using tire levers to avoid pinching inner tube. Use tire lever in same orientation as removal method.

h. Work tube over rim sidewall and into rim cavity.

i. Install second bead onto rim (2-10_Figure 3). Use care if using a tire lever. Use lever in same orientation as removal. Do not lift lever beyond 90-degrees from wheel plane (2-10_Figure 4).

2-10_Figure 3

Push bead onto rim

2-10_Figure 4

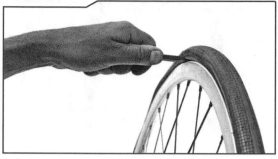

Use levers if necessary to lift bead over rim edge

j. Inspect both sides of tire for bead seating and for any sign of the inner tube sticking out. Re-install if necessary.

k. Inflate to low pressure and inspect bead again on both sides. Look for small molding line above bead. This line should run consistently above rim (2-10_Figure 5).

2-10_Figure 5

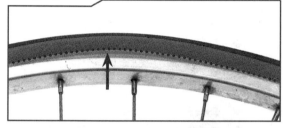

This bead seat line bulges upward from improper tire seating. The result may be a blow out

l. Inflate to full pressure and check with pressure gauge. It may be necessary to press downward above the valve in order to engage the pump head. For fully threaded valve shafts, re-install the locking nut, if any. Tighten finger tight only. Do not use wrench or pliers.

2-11 Installing Wheels on Bike

TOOLS & SUPPLIES
• Wrench of correct size for wheels with axle nut

The wheels must be properly mounted to the bicycle frame. Misalignment can result in problems with shifting, brake pad alignment, and bike handling. If the wheel is not securely mounted in the dropouts, it may come out when the bike is ridden, possibly causing injury to the rider.

The quick release is fitted with two conical shaped springs. The small end of the spring faces the axle, and the large end faces outward. These springs make the wheel easier to install. If one or both springs become twisted or damaged they may be removed. The springs serve no purpose once the wheel is tight on the bike (2-11_Figure 1).

2-11_Figure 1

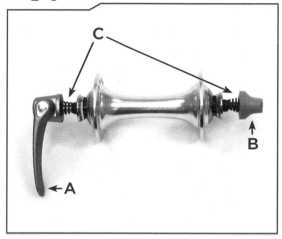

Common quick release hub with (A) Lever, (B) Adjusting nut, and (C) Springs

The quick release skewer uses a cam devise to hold the wheel securely to the frame dropouts. It is important that the skewer be tightened fully and consistently each use. This is also important for the pressure applied to the hub bearings. For most brands of skewers, hold lever parallel to the hub axle, which is half way through its swing from fully open to fully closed (2-11_Figure 2, 2-11_Figure 3, and 2-11_Figure 4). Tighten adjusting nut snug against dropout. Check results by moving lever. Lever should meet resistance to closing half way through the swing. Lubricate the cam mechanism if it appears sticky or dry.

2-11_Figure 2

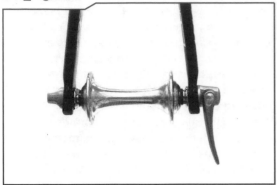

Lever in fully open position

2-11_Figure 3

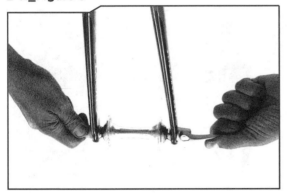

Adjust nut for resistance half way through swing

2-11_Figure 4

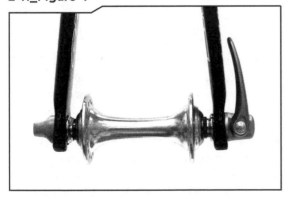

Close skewer lever parallel to center plane of bike

The cam mechanism is designed to be locked when the lever is parallel to the center plane of the bike. Inspect section of lever adjacent to cam. If the lever arm is not fully closed, the wheel is not properly secured (2-11_Figure 5). Double check skewer adjusting nut and pressure on lever.

2-11_Figure 5

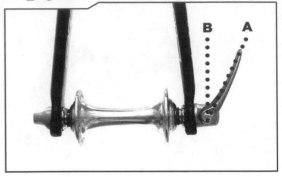

(A) Lever not fully closed,
(B) Lever fully closed

A common skewer design is called the "open cam" (2-11_Figure 6). The cam mechanism and press points are visible, and exposed to dirt and grime. Setting lever resistance at half way through swing may be too tight for some models. However, these skewers should still close with force. The open cam especially needs lubrication to work effectively. Consult specific manufacturer for recommended pressure of closing.

2-11_Figure 6

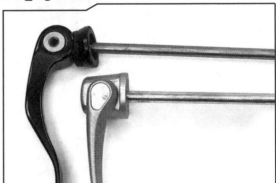

Open cam style seen on left, and closed cam seen on right

The procedures for installing front wheels is as follows:

a. Check that the quick release skewer lever is in open position.

b. Check that brake quick release mechanism is open.

c. Install front wheel between dropouts with skewer on left side as seen from rider's point of view.

d. Pull wheel fully up into dropouts.

Big Blue Book of Bicycle Repair

e. Close brake quick-release mechanism.

f. Determine final closing position of quick release lever. Move lever so it will end up just in front of fork (2-11_Figure 7 and 2-11_Figure 8). However, with some fork and dropout designs, it will be necessary to reposition the lever if it will not fully close.

2-11_Figure 7

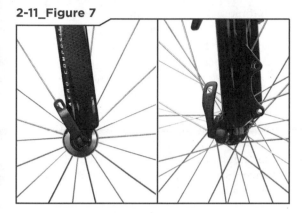

Place lever just in front of fork blade if possible

2-11_Figure 8

Skewer must be oriented to allow lever to fully close, even with wide fork ends

g. Adjust closing tension of quick release skewer and close skewer. Wheel should be centered between fork blades. If necessary, open skewer, move wheel either left or right until wheel appears centered, then close

skewer. The quick release skewer must be fully engaged on the dropout surfaces.

h. Inspect brake pad alignment and centering by closing and opening pads with brake lever. If brake pads are not centered to wheel, see (See Outline Item 8-4 Caliper Rim Brakes. If wheel fails to adequately center in frame, either the frame or wheel may be misaligned.

i. Spin wheel and check pad alignment to rim.

If it is difficult to manuveur the wheel into the dropouts, it can be an option to install the front wheel when the bike is standing on the ground. By placing the bike on the ground, the axle will seat fully up in the dropouts.

Installing Front Wheels with Disc Brakes

Bikes using disc brake calipers and rotors follow the basic process as described above. The rotor should be placed between the pads of the caliper as it is installed. Use care not to displace the brake pads. (2-11_Figure 9)

2-11_Figure 9

Guide rotor between brake pads

Solid Axle Types

For non-quick release wheels with axle nuts, washers go to outside of dropouts. Secure axle nuts fully and then double check alignment.

The procedures for intalling rear wheel is as follows:

a. Check that quick release skewer is in open position.

b. Check that brake quick release is in open position.

c. Pull rear derailleur back to open chain (2-11_Figure 10).

2-11_Figure 10

d. Place cogs between upper and lower sections of chain.

e. Guide wheel between brake pads and engage smallest cog on chain.

f. Guide axle up and into dropouts, pulling up and/or back depending upon dropout style. It may be necessary to flex dropouts open to get wheel in.

g. Orient skewer so lever will end up between the seat stay and chain stay, unless this prevents lever from fully closing (2-11_Figure 11).

2-11_Figure 11

h. Close skewer with same force described for front wheel.

i. Close brake quick release or attach MTB brake release wire.

j. View centering of wheel between chain stays and seat stays. Also sight rim centering to brake pads. Open skewer and adjust as necessary to center wheel in frame. If brake pads are not centered to wheel, see Chapter 6, Rim Brake Systems. If further attempts to align the wheel fail to adequately center it in frame, either the frame or wheel may be misaligned. Seek professional help in this case.

2-12 Tubeless Systems

The tubeless tire and wheel system acts in a similar manner to car or motorcycle systems. The rim interior is sealed airtight. A specially designed tire bead then seals the tire to the rim. A common cause of flat tires, especially for off-road riding, is a "rim pinch," where the inner tube is pinched when the tire strikes a rock or other object. Tubeless tire systems can be run at lower pressures because there is no inner tube to be pinched, making them more resistant to these types of flats. The tires, however, are still susceptible to punctures from nails, glass, etc.

TOOLS & SUPPLIES
- Tire lever (Park Tool TL-1 or TL-2)
- Air compressor (preferred) or floor pump
- Soapy water or tubeless tire bead lubricant

To remove tubeless tire, begin by fully deflating the tire. Push the tire bead all around one side to free it from the rim. It is usually possible to remove the tire with tire levers. If tire levers are used, use plastic levers. Pull the entire bead over the rim edge. Lift the second bead over the rim to fully remove tire.

The tubeless systems typically use a Presta valve. A special valve is secured into the rim and held in place by a nut (2-12_Figure 1). The valve is an air tight fit in the rim.

2-12_Figure 1

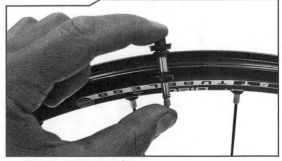

Tubeless valve system

To mount the tire, check that valve is fully seated inside of the rim. Clean the tire bead as needed. Treat the inside wall of the rim and the bead of the tire with soapy water, which will help seat and seal the tire. Ordinary dish soap is acceptable (2-12_Figure 2). Plain water may also be used. Insert one bead over the rim wall and into the center of the rim. Bead should be fully installed before inserting second bead over rim. Inflation is best done with a compressor. This allows the air pressure to quickly force the bead to the rim, creating a seal. If no compressor is available, quickly pump to form a seal. It can help to have a friend assist by holding the tire centered to the rim while it is pumped.

2-12_Figure 2

Use soapy water to help bead seat into rim

If it does not seem possible to seat the bead well enough to inflate the tire, it may help to use a long strap. Place the strap around the circumference of the tire. Tighten the strap to help hold bead to rim and inflate tire. (2-12_Figure 3)

2-12_Figure 3

Use a strap to apply even pressure on tubeless tires that are difficult to inflate

The beads will lock into place, often popping as they do. Inflate to full inflation and inspect bead for leaks. Use water at the bead and look for any bubbles. Deflate and re-seat as necessary.

The tubeless system is best patched by removing it from the rim. The inner surface of the tube is butyl rubber, similar to an inner tube. Locate the hole and clean an area inside the tire body. Use a vulcanizing patch with similar procedures as described for the inner tube repair. (See Outline Item 2-6.2). There are also "plug" systems to patch a tire without removal. The plug system relies on filling the hole with a rubber material. Irregular shaped holes can be difficult to repair using the plug system.

Liquid sealants for tubeless tires are available from various manufacturers and are intended to seal small holes in the tire. These are best applied to the tire before mounting.

The procedures for tubeless tire sealant installation is as follows:

a. Install one tire bead on the wheel.

b. Hang the wheel vertically, with valve at either the 3:00 or 9:00 position. If the bike is mounted in a repair stand, the handlebar ends can be used as a hanger.

c. Pour sealant into the tire at the 6:00 position. Consult sealant manufacturer's instructions for amount of sealant.

d. Carefully engage second bead, working from the bottom upward on both sides.

e. Inflate tire and seat bead.

f. Spin wheel to distribute fluid.

Chapter 3

HUB, REAR SPROCKETS

Hubs are centered in the wheels and allow the tires to rotate around the axle. The hub shell rotates with the tire and spokes, while the axle is fixed to the frame. On derailleur bicycles, multiple rear sprockets are affixed to the rear hub with a clutch mechanism that allows the rider to drive the wheel or to coast.

3-1 Rear Sprockets

The rear sprockets, also called cogs, mesh with the chain and drive the rear wheel and bike forward. The sprockets must be removed for replacement when worn. The sprockets must also be removed in order to service the axle bearings.

The clutch systems used on derailleur bikes allow the rider to coast. The sprockets will spin when the rider stops pedaling, but will lock and drive the wheel when the pedals are turned. The bearings fitted in the system allow the gears to turn freely. There is commonly play between the inner and outer parts of the bearing system. When the wheel is spun, as during coasting, the rear sprockets may appear to wobble side to side a small amount. This is common and is not usually a problem, because when the bike is pedaled, the inner and outer parts lock together as they drive, eliminating the wobble.

The rear sprockets are attached to the hub in one of two ways. Bikes may use a "freehub," which is mounted to the body of the hub (3-1_Figure 1). This cylindrical mechanism acts as a clutch that ratchets for coasting and locks for driving the bike when pedaling. The freehub body has a series of splines on the outer shell. "Cassette" sprockets, also called the "cassette stack," slide over these splines. A lockring threads into the freehub and holds the sprockets (3-1_Figure 2). When the sprockets are removed, the ratcheting freehub remains on the hub body. Most modern derailleur equipped bicycles use the freehub system.

3-1_Figure 1

Freehub body and hub with cassette sprockets

3-1_Figure 2

Lockring holds cassette sprockets secure to freehub body. (A) Lockring

Alternatively, the rear wheel may have a large thread machined onto the hub (3-1_Figure 3). Sprockets are fixed to a ratcheting mechanism called a freewheel, which threads onto the hub. The entire unit, sprockets and ratcheting mechanism, comes off when the freewheel is removed. It is common for freewheels to seize to the hub, so the threads of the freewheel should be thoroughly greased when installed (3-1_Figure 4).

3-1_Figure 3

Rear hub threaded for freewheel

3-1_Figure 4

Freewheel internal threading. Grease threads before installing

3-2
Cassette Sprocket Removal
& Installation

TOOLS & SUPPLIES

- Cassette lockring tool for brand/model of lockring
- Adjustable wrench (other option, Park Tool FRW-1)
- Hub skewer or axle nut from solid axle hub
- Chain whip (Park Tool HCW-16, SR-1 or SR-2)

With modern cassette sprocket systems, all sprockets are fitted with splines. Sprockets slide onto the freehub body and are held in place by a lockring. The lockring sits outward from the smallest sprocket. There is often the word "LOCK," and an arrow on the lockring indicating direction to turn for locking. Turn the lockring counter-clockwise to loosen. The teeth under the lockring help lock it in place. There may be a loud noise when the lockring breaks loose.

There are two non-interchangeable lockring tool standards. Cassette systems by Shimano®, SRAM®, Chris King®, Sun Race®, American Classic® and others use a lockring with 12 splines, approximately 23.5mm diameter (3-2_Figure 1a). Use the Park Tool FR-5 (3-2_Figure 1b). Another option is the Park Tool FR-5G, with built-in guide pin to keep the tool engaged in the lockring.

3-2_Figure 1a

Cassette lockring for Shimano® and others

3-2_Figure 1b

Park Tool FR-5

Campagnolo® cassettes use a lockring with 12 splines, approximately 22.8mm in diameter (3-2_Figure 2a). Use th Park Tool BBT-5 (3-2_Figure 2b).

3-2_Figure 2a

Campagnolo® cassette lockring

3-2_Figure 2b

Park Tool BBT-5®

The procedure for cassette sprocket removal is as follows:

a. Mount bike in repair stand and remove rear wheel.

b. Remove quick release skewer or axle nut of solid axle.

c. Inspect cassette and select correct type of cassette lockring remover.

d. Engage remover into splines of lockring.

e. Install quick release skewer (or axle nut) and install skewer nut on outside of remover (3-2_Figure 3).

3-2_Figure 3

Use skewer to hold tool firmly in place

f. Snug skewer nut against remover. Skewer acts as a holding device for remover.

g. Hold sprockets in clockwise direction with chain whip tool. Turn remover counter-clockwise, using a large adjustable wrench, the hex end of another Park Tool Sprocket Removing Chain Whip Tool SR-1, or the Park Tool Freewheel Wrench FRW-1. It will require force to remove the lockring. Expect to hear a loud clicking sound as the locking teeth of the lockring separate (3-2_Figure 4).

3-2_Figure 4

Loosen lockring while holding cassette sprockets

h. Turn remover only 1 full revolution counter-clockwise. Loosen and remove skewer before continuing to remove lockring.

i. Continue to hold sprockets and turn remover counter-clockwise until lockring is unthreaded from freehub body.

j. Remove lockring and sprockets. Note orientation of spacers behind sprockets. Spacers should be replaced in same order as removed.

For installing cassette sprockets and lockring, the sprocket removing chain whip tool is not required. The cassette ratcheting mechanism will hold the freehub body.

The procedure for cassette sprocket installation is as follows:

a. Inspect splines of freehub body. Look for a wide space between splines.

b. Inspect internal splines of sprockets. Look for a wide spline to mate with wide space in freehub body (3-2_Figure 5).

3-2_Figure 5

Align wide spline inside sprocket with wide space on freehub body

c. Align splines and engage all sprockets. Install spacers in same orientation as when removed.

d. Grease threads of lockring and thread lockring into freehub body.

e. Insert cassette lockring tool into splines of lockring. Install quick release skewer and thread skewer nut on outside of lockring tool.

f. Snug skewer nut against remover. Skewer acts as a holding device for remover.

g. Turn cassette lockring tool clockwise until lockring is fully tight (3-2_Figure 6).

3-2_Figure 6

Tighten lockring

3-3
Freewheel Sprocket Removal & Installation

TOOLS & SUPPLIES

• Freewheel remover
• Large adjustable wrench (other options: Park Tool SR-1, FRW-1, or bench vise)
• Grease (Park Tool PPL-1) or anti-seize

These types of sprocket systems will have either recessed notches or splines in the freewheel body. These are usually recessed inside the smallest sprocket.

To remove freewheel sprockets begin by determining type or brand of freewheel and the removal tool required. The removal tool must fit the part correctly or both may become damaged. To determine the type or brand of freewheel, remove the wheel from the bike and look at the flat surfaces of the freewheel near the axle for a brand name. See Table 3-3 Freewheel Removal Tools for the matching freewheel tool. Be aware

that there are some brands that use fittings that are now obsolete.

The procedure for freewheel removal is as follows:

a. Mount bike in repair stand and remove rear wheel from bike.

b. Remove quick release skewer or drive side axle nut.

c. Inspect freewheel center and select correct type of remover.

d. Engage remover into splines notches of freewheel.

e. Install quick release skewer. The skewer nut should be on the outside of the remover.

f. Snug skewer nut or axle nut against the remover. Nut acts as a holding device for remover.

3-3_Figure 1

Turn tool counter-clockwise to remove freewheel from hub

g. Turn remover counter-clockwise using a large adjustable wrench (3-3_Figure 1). Park Tool removers will also fit the hex end of the Park Tool Sprocket Chain Whip Tool SR-1, or the Park Tool FRW-1 Freewheel Removal Wrench. It will typically require some force to turn the freewheel. Another option is to mount remover flats in the jaws of a vise, and turn the rim counter-clockwise.

h. Turn the remover only 1 full revolution counter-clockwise. Loosen and remove skewer or axle nut before continuing to remove freewheel.

i. Turn remover counter-clockwise until freewheel is unthreaded from hub. Lift freewheel from hub.

Table 3-3 Freewheel Removal Tools

FREEWHEEL BRAND	FREEWHEEL FITTING	APPROPRIATE TOOL	TOOL & DESCRIPTION
Shimano®, Sun Race®, and Sachs®			Park Tool FR-1 12 splines 23mm approx. diameter
Suntour® two notched			Park Tool FR-2 2 notches 25mm across
Suntour® four notched			Park Tool FR-3 4 notches 24mm across
Atom®, Regina®, some "Schwinn® approved"			Park Tool FR-4 20 splines 21.6mm approx. diameter
Single speed			Park Tool FR-6 4 notches 40mm across
Falcon®			Park Tool FR-7 12 splines 23mm approx. diameter (slightly larger than FR-1)
Compact single speed (30mm thread, "flip-flop hub")			Park Tool FR-8 4 notches 32mm across

The procedure for freewheel installation is as follows:

a. Grease heavily inside mounting threads of freewheel.

b. Lay wheel on bench, and hold flat. Hold freewheel sprockets parallel to wheel and lower freewheel onto threads.

c. Axle should be centered in hole of freewheel. If axle appears off center, freewheel is cross-threaded on hub threads (3-3_Figure 2). Remove and re-align.

3-3_Figure 2

If axle appears off center, freewheel is cross-threaded

d. Begin threading freewheel clockwise by hand until freewheel feels fully threaded.

e. Use chain whip tool to fully seat freewheel against hub, or ride bike to seat freewheel.

f. If a new freewheel is installed or if new wheel is installed, check both derailleur limit screw settings and indexing. See Outline Item 7-4 Rear Derailleur.

3-4
Rear Sprocket Inspection & Cleaning

Rear sprockets will eventually wear out. The teeth are cut to fit a chain with a one-half inch pitch. Riding the chain places load on one side of the teeth, and material is eventually ground away, changing the shape and widening the space between the teeth. Inspect the sprockets from behind where the chain would engage. Look at various sprockets and notice any that are shiny and smooth compared to the rest (3-4_Figure 1 and 3-4_Figure 2).

3-4_Figure 1

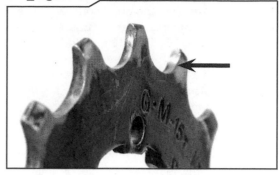

Look for smooth and shiny surface of worn sprocket.

3-4_Figure 2

This sprocket shows signs of original stamping marks, called "breakage." It has had very little use.

The chain will be unable to hold itself to a worn sprocket, especially when it is pedaled hard. The roller of the chain will ride up the tooth and then skip over the sprocket (3-4_Figure 3).

3-4_Figure 3

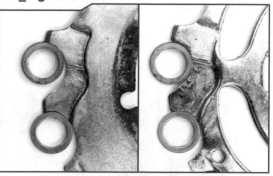

On the left are chain rollers sitting in a worn sprocket, showing poor engagement. On the right are chain rollers showing better engagement on a new sprocket.

Cyclists tend to use two or three rear sprockets more than the other sprockets. These favorite sprockets will wear out first. Commonly, these tend to be the 15 to 18 tooth sprockets. Individual sprocket replacements are not commonly available. The entire sprocket set is typically replaced as a unit.

The rear sprockets and front chainrings require cleaning if the entire drive train is to be maintained. Use care not to get solvent into the bearings of the freewheel/freehub or the bearings of the bottom bracket. Freehub mechanisms and freewheel bodies use ball bearings running on bearing surfaces and small springs and pawls. These parts are not "overhauled" by disassembly. The unit may be removed from the hub, flushed and scrubbed clean in solvent. The solvent must then be blown out with compressed air or allowed to evaporate. Lubrication is then dripped into the mechanism. Grease is not recommended for freehubs or freewheel internals because it may cause the small springs and pawls to stick. If the freewheel/freehub spins rough after cleaning, it is worn out and should be replaced. There are no internal parts available for freehubs or freewheels from manufacturers.

Rear sprockets can be cleaned while still mounted to the wheel. Begin by scraping between sprockets with the comb part of the Park Tool GearClean® Brush (3-4_Figure 4), or a thin screwdriver, to remove dirt and debris. Hold wheel so sprockets are tilting downward, then use a dry stiff bristle brush between sprockets. Dip brush in solvent, and scrub sprockets, again holding sprockets facing downward. This helps to keep solvent out of bearings. Use rag to wipe solvent off sprockets, rim and tire. Grab two corners of rag and pull taut. Use this section to "floss" between sprockets.

3-4_Figure 4

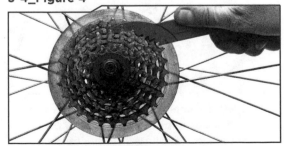

Clean the debris between sprockets

3-5
Adjustable Hub Bearing Service

TOOLS & SUPPLIES

- Cone wrenches (Park Tool SCW-13 through 20 or DCW-1 through 4)
- Adjustable wrench or wrench fitting locknuts
- Axle vise (Park Tool AV-1 or AV-4)
- Bench vise
- Rags
- Solvent (Park Tool CB-2)
- Grease (Park Tool PPL-1)
- Pencil Magnet
- Spacers or washers, approximately 7/16" or 11mm inside diameter
- Ballpoint pen

Hubs are centered in the wheels and allow the tires to rotate around the axle. The hub shell rotates with the tire and spokes while the axle is fixed to the frame. The hub bearing system uses round ball bearings trapped between two bearing surfaces. The bearing surfaces and balls are greased to minimize wear. These systems are shielded from dirt by covers and seals. Excessive exposure to the elements will increase wear on the bearing surfaces and shorten bearing life.

Bearing surfaces are made from hardened steel and are cut by grinding. Even the highest quality bearing surfaces will have slight grinding marks. Better quality bearing surfaces are ground smoother and will have less friction and resistance to turning. However, all bearings will have some friction as they rotate. This is normal and does not affect the ride. Generally, the lighter load a bearing is expected to experience, the "smoother" the feel. Bearings which experience more stress and pressure will seem to have more drag, even when the adjustment is correct. For example, a bearing for a rear derailleur pulley, which is designed for lower loads will seem to have less spinning resistance compared to a bottom bracket bearing, which experiences more load.

Adjustable type hubs use a cone shaped race threaded onto an axle. The hub shell holds a cup shaped race. Ball bearings are trapped between the cone and cup. Rear hubs must allow for the sprockets and tend to be more complex than front hubs. The modern freehub or cassette hub uses a separate freehub mechanism that may be removed in a separate operation. The procedures below are written primarily for Shimano® hubs, but are also applicable to other adjustable type hubs.

Hub cones have narrow wrench flats that require a special thin wrench called a cone wrench. The common cone wrench size for front hubs is 13mm and for rear hubs is 15mm. If the locknut is a simple hex nut, use a combination wrench or even an adjustable wrench. Hex locknuts are commonly 17mm or 16mm. Some locknuts will accept only a cone wrench.

Freehub bodies on rear hubs are lubricated internally with a light lubricant. Soaking the freehub body with solvent will remove lubrication. Avoid getting solvent into the mechanism during the hub disassembly and cleaning. Wipe freehub clean of old grease. Freehub can be removed in a separate operation for cleaning. See Outline Item 3-8 Freehub Removal & Installation.

3-5.1 Disassembly

On any disassembly, it is a good idea to take notes on parts orientation. Note especially any differences between left and right side parts, for example, if an axle appears asymmetrical. The parts arrangement of a Shimano® hub is seen below (3-5.1_Figure 1).

3-5.1_Figure 1

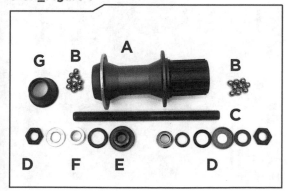

Parts of a Shimano® rear hub
(A) Hub shell, (B) Ball bearing, (C) Axle, (D) Locknuts, (E) Cone, (F) Washers, (G) Rubber seal

The procedure for adjustable hub disassembly is as follows:

a. For rear hubs, begin by removing rear sprockets (Outline Item 3-2 or 3-3).

b. For front or rear hubs, remove the quick release skewer. For solid axle type hubs, remove axle nuts. If the hub has a disc brake rotor, it should be removed to avoid contamination by grease.

c. Inspect axle ends. Measure and note the amount of axle protruding past locknut. For quick release hubs, counting the number of threads is an adequate measurement (3-5.1_Figure 2).

3-5.1_Figure 2

Count or measure the amount of axle protrusion past locknut face

d. Mount in axle vise, if one is available. Axle vise should be clamped in a bench vise. Mount right side of hub down with left side facing upward. Begin dismantling from the left side.

e. Remove rubber covers or seals, if any.

f. Hold cone using cone wrench and loosen locknut counter-clockwise.

g. Remove locknut and washers. Place parts on a string, piece of wire or zip tie in the same orientation as they came off hub. This makes re-installation easier (3-5.1_Figure 3).

3-5.1_Figure 3

Hold parts in order with tie

h.   Remove cone by turning counter-clockwise and place on tie.

i.   Place hand below right side of hub and lift wheel slowly. Be prepared to catch bearings that fall from hub. Place wheel on bench.

j.   If inspecting for bent axle, remove right side locknut and cones. Note that left side and right side cones, washers and locknuts may be different. Do not confuse left and right side parts. Use tie method to keep track of parts. Also note axle thread may be asymmetrical. The side with more axle spacers gets more axle thread

k.   Count the number of bearings on each side, and then use pencil magnet to remove bearings from hub shell. Measure ball bearing size. For most adjustable hub models, including Shimano®, the rear hub has 9 ball bearings per side of ¼ inch diameter. Front hubs commonly have 10 balls per side of ³⁄₁₆ inch diameter.

l.   Leave dust cap in place. Dust caps may be fragile and removal may result in damage. Use a small brush or a rag used over a small screwdriver to clean inside and under dust caps.

m.   Clean all parts. Parts must be dry for assembly. Wipe freehub mechanism using damp rag. Do not soak freehub in solvent unless it is to be removed.

3-5.2 Parts Inspection

View hub cups and cones for pitting or damage. Use a ballpoint pen to trace the bearing path. Roughness and wear will be felt as the small ball of the pen passes over pits. Inspect ball bearings for brightness. If balls are dull looking, they should be replaced. If the cup is damaged, it typically cannot be replaced. The hub must be replaced. If inspecting axle, roll axle on flat surface. Watch for gap appearing as axle rolls. Bent axles cannot be straightened and should be replaced.

3-5.3 Assembly

Refer to any notes from the disassembly procedure. For example, axle thread length may vary between left and right side. Do not take apart cone, spacer and locknut tie until ready to install.

The procedure for adjustable hub assembly is as follows:

a.   Grease axle threads.

b.   Grease heavily inside hub shell cups. Place ball bearings in both cups and cover with more grease. Make sure balls are seated flat in cup. The balls should be covered in grease. For most adjustable hub models, including Shimano®, the rear hub has 9 ball bearings per side of ¼ inch diameter. Front hubs commonly have 10 balls per side of ³⁄₁₆ inch diameter.

c.   If all parts were removed from axle, install right side parts. Use care to install in the same orientation as they came off. Note rear axle threads may be asymmetrical. Refer to earlier notes.

d.   Return axle protrusion, past locknut face, to the original measurement, as noted in disassembly. Tighten right side locknut fully against cone.

e.   Install axle through right side of hub.

f.   Install left side axle parts using care to install in the same orientation as they came off. Do not set axle protrusion on this side and do not tighten locknut at this time.

g.   For quick release type hubs, snug the cone down until it contacts the ball bearings, then turn back counter-clockwise one quarter turn (90 degrees). This will purposely make the bearing adjustment too loose. Hold cone with cone wrench and tighten locknut fully. Proceed to Outline Item 3-5.4 Adjustment.

NOTE NOTE NOTE NOTE **NOTE:** For quick release wheels, it is critical that the axle end sit inboard or recessed inside the dropout. This allows the quick release skewer to secure onto the frame or fork end. If the axle end protrudes even a very small amount, the wheel may not properly secure and the wheel may come out during use. It may be necessary to grind off the axle ends in some cases until it is safely recessed (3-5.3_Figure 1).

3-5.3_Figure 1

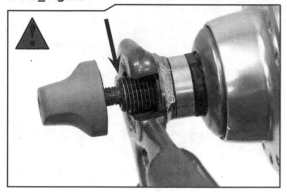

Axle protrudes past dropout. Wheel will not secure.

3-5.4_Figure 1

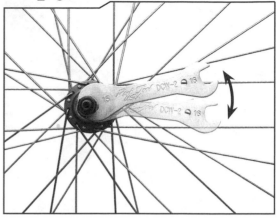

When adjusting bearings, make small incremental movements

3-5.4 Hub Adjustment

Adjustable bearing systems are sometimes referred to as "cup and cone" systems. One convex bearing race (cone) and one concave bearing race (cup) oppose one another, with the ball bearings trapped between them. The races can be moved relative to one another. If the adjustment is too tight there will be too much pressure on the bearing surfaces and the system will quickly wear out. If the adjustment is too loose there will be movement or "play" between the parts. This causes a knocking in the bearing surfaces and again they will wear out prematurely. Generally, the bearings should be adjusted as loose as possible but without play or knocking in the system.

For adjustable bearing systems, the bearing surfaces move on threaded parts. It is normal for threaded parts to have play between the internal and external threads. A hub cone will wiggle on the axle thread until the cone locknut is tightened down against the cone. When checking bearing adjustments, the locknut must be tight against the cone.

The goal for adjustable bearings is to have the bearings rotate as freely as possible, but not have any knocking or play. When beginning a bearing adjustment, start with it loose and then proceed to tighten the adjustment in small increments until the play disappears. This insures the adjustment is as loose as possible but is without play. In most cases, try to make small changes, in increments of $1/32$ of a complete rotation (3-5.4_Figure 1).

Quick release hubs have hollow axles that allow for the quick release skewer shaft. These axles flex slightly when the quick release is closed and pressure is applied to the dropouts. Hub bearing adjustments must account for this extra compression. For adjustable type hubs, when not clamped tight in the frame, there should be a slight amount of play in the axle. This play should disappear when the hub and wheel are clamped in the frame.

To test if a quick release hub has an acceptable adjustment, grab the wheel while it is still in the frame and pull it side to side laterally. Rotate wheel and test again, feeling for a knocking sensation (3-5.4_Figure 2). If no play is felt, remove the wheel. Grab the axle (not the skewer) and rock it up and down to check for play. If the axle has play when the wheel is outside the bike, but no play inside the bike, the hub is properly adjusted. If there is no play in the axle when the wheel is outside the bike, the adjustment is too tight, even if the axle seems to turn smoothly when out of the bike. Over tight bearing adjustments will lead to premature bearing surface wear. A rear hub bearing that is too tight can also result in freehub drag.

3-5.4_Figure 2

Grab wheel and pull side to side laterally to check for knocking or play

The following procedure simulates the on-the-bike compression while still allowing access to a cone and locknut for adjustment. This procedure requires the use of a spacer or washers to simulate the dropout thickness. For example, a 10mm box end wrench (forged type) can be used as the spacer. The wrench offers a lever to hold while adjusting the opposite cone. Do not use larger wrenches, because the wrench surface must support the skewer housing. The adjustment is made on the side of the axle opposite the wrench/spacers. On a rear wheel, the wrench/spacer will go on the sprocket side (right side) of the hub. On a front wheel, the wrench/spacer can go on either the left or right side.

The procedure for hub adjusting is as follows:

a. Remove wheel from bike.
b. Remove quick release skewer and springs. Remove any rubber boot covering cones and locknuts on side being adjusted.
c. Insert skewer through wrench/spacers and then through axle. Skewer should pass through right side of either the front or rear hub (3-5.4_Figure 3). Install quick release adjusting nut on left side. The quick release nut must press only on the axle end, not on the axle locknut (3-5.4_Figure 4).

3-5.4_Figure 3

Secure spacers or wrench to act as dropout on fixed side

3-5.4_Figure 4

Quick release nut must press only on axle end, not on adjusting side locknut

d. Use the same pressure to close quick release lever as you would use when normally clamping wheel in bike. If in doubt see Outline Item 2-11, Installing Wheels on Bike.
e. Place the wheel on your lap. Use cone wrench to hold the "adjusting side" cone. Note position and angle of "fixed wrench" on right side relative to cone wrench on "adjusting side." Use a second wrench to loosen locknut counter-clockwise (3-5.4_Figure 5).

3-5.4_Figure 5

Loosen locknut and make adjustment to cone

f. Loosen cone counter-clockwise about ⅛ to ¼ turn. The purpose is to first create play, then remove it incrementally.

g. Hold cone from moving with cone wrench and tighten locknut. Locknut must be fully tight before play can be checked. Do not check for bearing play until locknut is fully secure. Locknut pushes on cone and will affect bearing adjustment.

h. Test for play by grabbing lever (wrench) and pulling side to side laterally (3-5.4_ Figure 6).

3-5.4_Figure 6

Test adjustment for lateral play

i. When play is felt, adjustment is too loose. To tighten adjustment:

  1. Use a cone wrench and hold "adjusting" side cone from moving. Note position and angle of adjustable side wrench relative to "fixed" side wrench.

  2. Loosen locknut, using care not to allow cone wrench to turn.

  3. Recall angle of cone wrench and tighten adjustment by turning cone clockwise ¹⁄₃₂ of a turn.

  4. Hold cone from moving with cone wrench and tighten locknut.

j. Test again for play. Rotate axle and check for play at various points of rotation.

k. If play is still present, repeat step "i" until play just disappears. Remember to make small adjustments clockwise one at a time. Check for play after each adjustment. It may take several small adjustments before play is gone.

l. Once play has disappeared, test that final adjustment is not overly tight. Open skewer lever and check for axle play by pulling axle laterally.

m. If no play is felt when skewer is released, hub adjustment is too tight. Tighten skewer as before. Loosen locknut and loosen adjustment only slightly. Check for play while axle is still clamped. If no play is detectable, test again as in "l".

n. Adjustment is finished when there is no play felt when skewer is closed, but some play is felt when axle is not secured by quick release

o. Remove skewer and any extra adjustment spacers (wrench). Re-install rubber covers over axle ends. Remount sprockets, if removed. Install skewer springs and install skewer to normal position.

p. Install wheel on bike. Use same skewer clamping pressure when mounting the wheel as was used when making adjustments.

If an adjustment cannot be found to allow smooth rotation of the axle, the bearing surfaces may be worn out. If play does not disappear until bearing adjustment is very tight, a locknut may not be tight against cone, which will allow movement. It can also occur that the bearing cups inside hub shell have come loose. It may be possible to get a retaining compound or a thin thread-locker behind the cup to re-secure it. However, replacement is the best option.

3-5.5 Hub Adjustment-Solid Axle

Non-quick release hub systems use axle nuts and washers on the outside of the dropouts to hold the wheel in place (3-5.5_Figure 1). Adjustment of solid axle hub bearings is similar to the hollow axle quick release type, but there is no need to allow for axle flex. Remove the wheel from the bike. The adjustment for solid axle hubs does not change when mounted in the bike. It can be useful to mount a "fixed wrench" to act as a lever on the right side when adjusting. This allows you to tighten or loosen relative to the fixed cone. If no play is present, create play by loosening bearing adjustment. Proceed to adjust tighter in small increments until play is gone. The goal is to find the loosest adjustment that has no play.

3-5.5_Figure 1

Solid or non-quick release axle on derailleur type bike

3-6
Cartridge Bearing Hub Service

TOOLS & SUPPLIES

- Cone Wrenches (Park Tool SCW-13 through 20 or DCW-1 through 4)
- Hammer
- Drift Punch
- Hub presses and drivers from hub manufacturers

The cartridge type hub uses an industrial or rolling element bearing. These tend to be non-serviceable bearing units that are simply used until they wear out. Ball bearings are trapped between inner and outer rotating races (3-6_Figure 1). There should be no play between the inner and outer races of the cartridge. With use, play will develop between these two races and the entire cartridge unit will require replacement. Proprietary tools may be required for some cartridge bearing hubs.

3-6_Figure 1
Cut away of cartridge bearing showing inner races and ball bearings

Cartridge hubs are not serviceable in the sense that they are overhauled and adjusted. The bearings use rubber covers but the bearing is not fully "sealed," and

is susceptible to dirt and water. The bearing is removed as a unit and a new one pressed in. Some hub models require specialty tools and service of these hubs is best left to professional mechanics.

Cartridge hub designs typically press the outer race of the cartridge bearing into the hub shell. Removal of the bearing from the hub shell may involve impact or pressing of the bearings. It is likely that the impact will damage the bearing. If a bearing is being removed, it is assumed it will be replaced.

The hub axle may be threaded or non-threaded. The axle holds the inner race of the cartridge bearing secure. Threaded axles typically use a "sleeve nut" system. The nut will be tightened until it touches the bearing, then backed away ¼ turn. A locknut then secures the sleeve nut. This prevents the sleeve nut from pressing on the inner bearing race. The inner and outer cartridge races align vertically for smooth operation. If the inner race is pushed inward, the bearing tends to wear out quickly (3-6_Figure 2).

3-6_Figure 2

Threaded sleeve nut holding axle to cartridge bearing

Bearings of the threaded axle system are commonly removed by impact. A punch is placed through the hub and the bearing is struck first on one side, and then the other. This tapping "walks" the bearing out of the hub shell (3-6_Figure 3).

3-6_Figure 3

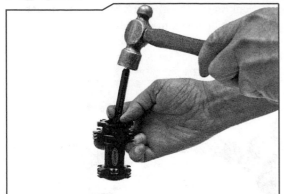

Removing pressed races

Non-threaded axles are typically made with a collar (3-6_Figure 4). These axles use end-caps, either threaded or push-on fit. Look for wrench flats either on the cap or inside the axle. After end-caps are removed, the axle is struck with a mallet, and acts as the punch to drive out the bearing.

3-6_Figure 4

Non-threaded axle with a cartridge bearing

The installation of cartridge bearings typically involves an interference fit, with the bearing being slightly larger than the hub shell. Hub manufacturers provide pressing and impact tools. It is possible to use steel sockets that match the diameter of the bearing race at the interference fit (3-6_Figure 5). For example, if the interference fit is on the outer race of the bearing, the diameter of the driving tool must match the diameter of the outer race of the bearing.

3-6_Figure 5

Driving in a cartridge bearing with a socket

3-7 Campagnolo® Hub Service

TOOLS & SUPPLIES
- 5mm hex wrench (Park Tool- various models)
- 2.5mm hex wrench, but screwdriver on some models
- Solvent (Park Tool CB-2)
- Grease (Park Tool PPL-1)
- Small adjustable wrench

There are several generations and designs of the Campagnolo® hub. Certain generations used a traditional cup and cone design with a threaded axle, similar to Shimano® hubs. Campagnolo Record®, Centaur® and Chorus® since 2001 share the same basic design and service procedures described below (3-7_Figure 1). The cones are not threaded internally, but slide on a threadless axle. While Campagnolo® lists the hub shell cups as replaceable, this should be done by a Campagnolo® service center.

3-7_Figure 1

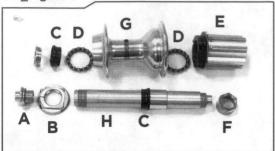

(A) Axle end Cap, (B) Left side lockring, (C) Cone, (D) Ball Bearings, (E) Freehub, (F) Right side axle nut, (G) Hub Body, (H) Axle

The cone and bearing adjustment are locked in place by a compression ring and a lockring with a pinch bolt. The front hub is a simple version of the rear, with bearing adjustments made from the lockring side.

The rear hub uses ball bearings for the axle rotation, and cartridge bearings inside the freehub body. The freehub bearings can be greased by removing a setscrew in the freehub body. Leave axle inside of freehub and use a small tip on a grease-gun to add grease as necessary. Leave the freehub together with the axle for axle bearing overhaul.

3-7.1 Disassembly

The procedure for Campagnolo® hub disassembly is as follows:

a. There are 5mm socket fittings on each side of the axle. Insert 5mm hex wrenches into each side of the axle (3-7.1_Figure 1). Loosen and remove the left side axle end cap counter clockwise. Note any washers under the end cap.

3-7.1_Figure 1

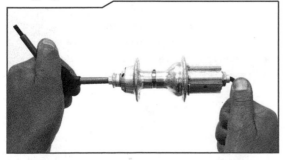

Remove left side axle end cap using two 5mm hex wrenches

b. Loosen the binder bolt on the left side lockring. Use either a 2.5mm hex wrench, #2 Phillips, or small straight blade screwdriver, as appropriate (3-7.1_Figure 2).

3-7.1_Figure 2

Loosen the lockring binder

c. Unthread and remove lockring counter-clockwise. It may be finger tight at this time, but use an adjustable wrench if necessary. (3-7.1_Figure 3)

3-7.1_Figure 3

Remove locking counter-clockwise

d. The axle and freehub may now be pulled to right and removed. Use care not to drop or misplace freehub pawls or springs. Cone on freehub side slides off axle to the left.

e. Retainers in the bearing cup hold the axle ball bearings. To remove bearings, use a thin tipped screwdriver and gently pry upward on the seal (3-7.1_Figure 4). Note orientation of seal and bearing retainer for assembly.

3-7.1_Figure 4

Carefully pry up the bearing covers

f. If desired, remove freehub from axle. Right side axle nut is left-hand threaded. Hold axle using a 5mm hex wrench and loosen right side axle nut turning clockwise. Freehub will now slide off axle (3-7.1_Figure 5).

3-7.1_Figure 5

Remove right side axle end cap

g. Clean axle parts and hub with a solvent. However, do not soak freehub. Clean pawls and spring with solvent, but use care not to contaminate freehub bearings.

3-7.2 Parts Inspection

View cups and cones for pitting or damage. Use a ballpoint pen to trace the bearing path. Roughness and wear will be felt as the small ball of the pen passes over pits. To check for a bent axle, roll axle on flat surface. Watch for gap appearing as axle rolls. Bent axles cannot be straightened and should be replaced.

3-7.3 Assembly

The procedure for Campagnolo® hub assembly & adjustment is as follows:

a. Grease the entire length of the axle and the threads at the ends of the axle.

b. Slide freehub body over right side of axle.

c. Install and secure right side axle nut. Turn nut counter-clockwise to secure while holding axle with a 5mm hex wrench.

d. Pack grease into bearing retainers and into bearing cups of hub body.

e. Place both bearing retainers into cups, with bearings facing cone. Cover bearings with seal and press seal into place by hand.

f. Install right side cone onto axle.

g. Grease pawls and right side hub ratchet gear.

h. Place axle through right side of hub body.

i. Engage pawls of freehub body into hub ratchet gear (3-7.3_Figure 1). Rotate freehub counter-clockwise to assist engagement of pawls into the gear of the hub body. It may be necessary to use a thin tipped screwdriver and gently push each pawl inward while pressure is applied to freehub.

3-7.3_Figure 1

Install freehub body and rotate to engage pawls into ratchet gear

j. Place left side cone on axle.

k. Slide compression ring onto axle and engage into cone.

l. Thread left side locking collar onto axle until it contacts compression ring and cone. Turn back approximately ⅛ turn counter-clockwise and snug binder bolt.

m. Hold axle from right side with 5mm hex wrench inserted into axle. Install washer onto axle end cap and thread onto axle. Secure end cap using a second 5mm hex wrench.

3-7.4 Adjustment

The procedure to adjust the Campagnolo®
Record hub is as follows:

a. Install cassette sprockets and quick release.

b. Install wheel into bike and close skewer
    with normal pressure.

c. Adjust bearings using lockring. Grab wheel and
    pull side to side. If play is present, loosen binder
    in locking collar and turn collar clockwise ¹⁄₃₂ to
    ¹⁄₁₆ of a turn (3-7.4_Figure 1). Snug lockring collar
    binder and check play again.

d. Repeat as necessary to remove play.

3-7.4_Figure 1

Loosen lockring binder before making bearing
adjustment

3-8
Freehub Removal & Installation

TOOLS & SUPPLIES
- 10, 11, or 12mm hex wrench, depending upon brand
- Seal pick
- Solvent (Park Tool CB-2)

The ratcheting mechanism of the freehub may
eventually wear out. There are no serviceable
parts inside most freehubs. The freehub may
be removed on many models for cleaning or
replacement. Dust caps in the freehub may
be damaged easily if removed. It is possible
to work around the dust cap. The procedures
below are for Shimano® and similar freehubs.

   **The procedure for freehub removal and
installation is as follows:**

a. Remove cassette (Outline Item 3-2 Cassette
    Sprocket Removal & Installation).

b. Remove axle (Outline Item 3-5.1 Disassembly.

c. Inspect inside freehub body for bolt fitting.

If no fitting is apparent on right side,
inspect through left side.

d. Insert hex wrench and turn counter-
    clockwise. Shimano® typically uses 10mm,
    other brands may use 11mm or 12mm hex
    wrenches (3-8_Figure 1).

3-8_Figure 1

Loosen and remove freehub bolt

e. Remove freehub. Inspect for any washers
    or spacers behind freehub and remove.

f. Use a seal pick to remove dust seal behind
    freehub body, if present (3-8_Figure 2).

3-8_Figure 2

Remove seal (if present) behind freehub body

g. Flush freehub with solvent. Scrub bearing
    cup clean.

h. Blow dry freehub. If no compressor is
    available, allow freehub to dry until no
    solvent is left inside.

i. Drip lubricant inside the freehub body from
    the backside and front side. Install dust seal.

j. Grease freehub installation bolt.

k. Install washers or spacers as necessary.

l. Install freehub onto hub body.

m. Install and secure freehub bolt.

n. Assemble axle assembly into hub and
    adjust. (Outline Item 3-5.3 Assemby and
    3-5.4 Adjustment)

Chapter 4
Wheel Truing

The wheels drive the bike forward when we pedal, allowing us to roll down the road or trail. Having wheels that spin straight and round adds to the bike's performance. Some adjustment to the wheel run-out, or trueness, is possible by making adjustments to spoke tension. Wheels using non-serviceable blades or a large carbon disc, rather than spokes, have no truing adjustment or repair options.

Wheels also help slow the bike. Rim caliper brakes such as linear pull, cantilever, side pull, and dual pivot brakes, use the rim sidewall as the braking surface. There may be problems when riding or braking if the wheel wobbles side to side, or is "out of true." Brake pad adjustment will be difficult with an out-of-true wheel.

Bicycle wheels are composed of a hoop (rim) that is suspended by spokes around the hub. Each spoke is under tension and pulls on a limited section of rim. Spokes coming from the right side hub flange pull the rim to the right. Spokes coming from the left side hub flange pull the rim to the left. Spokes are oriented at the rim in a left-right-left-right pattern to counter the pull from each flange. Having spokes tight with relatively even tension makes the wheel spin straight. Changes to spoke tension will change the amount of pull on the rim where the spoke attaches and affect its position, or true. This process of changing spoke tension is called "truing." Professional mechanics will use tools such as truing stands, centering gauges (dishing tools), spoke wrenches, spoke tension meters, and his/her experience to adjust spoke tension and produce a durable and strong wheel (4_Figure 1).

Truing will be occasionally required to keep the rim running straight. Spoke tension is adjusted by tightening or loosening a threaded nut, called the nipple, at the end of the spoke. Although a common phrase among mechanics is to "tighten the spokes," it is the nipples that are turned, not the spokes. The nipples are turned with a spoke wrench (4_Figure 2).

4_Figure 2

Spoke wrenches for various sized spoke nipples

When truing, it is especially important to use the correct fitting wrench. Spoke nipples are typically made of brass or aluminum, both relatively soft materials. Nipples are typically square and come in different sizes. A wrench that is even slightly too large easily damages the nipple by rounding the corners (4_Figure 3). Use a caliper to measure across the nipple flat and purchase the correct sized wrench. There is no correlation between spoke diameter and nipple size. See Table 4 Spoke Wrench Fit. If you own spoke wrenches of different sizes, use the smallest that will fit, even if it seems slow putting the wrench on the nipple (4_Figure 4).

4_Figure 1

Equipment used by professional mechanics

4_Figure 3

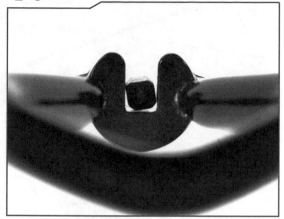

If spoke wrench is large for the nipple, damage may occur

4_Figure 4

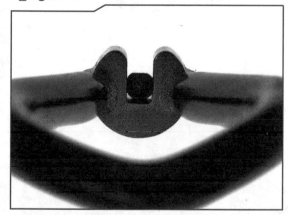

A proper fitting wrench will help insure properly tightened spokes

Table 4 Spoke Wrench Fit

Size of Nipple Across Flats	Park Tool Spoke Wrench Model & Color Of Handle
3.22mm (0.127")	SW-0, black
3.3mm (0.130")	SW-1, green
3.45mm (0.136")	SW-2, red
3.96mm (0.156")	SW-3 (blue handle)

There are some styles of nipples made with a special pattern or size (4_Figure 5). Wrenches for these nipples are usually only available from the manufacturer of the nipple.

4_Figure 5

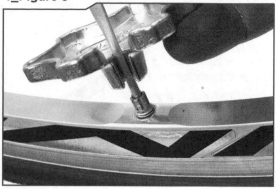

Some nipples are a proprietary design and require a special wrench

There are four basic aspects of wheel truing: lateral true, radial true, rim centering over the hub (dish), and spoke tension. A properly trued wheel will have all four aspects adjusted for best performance.

LATERAL TRUE: Also called "rim run-out," this is the side-to-side wobble of the rim as the wheel spins (4_Figure 6). This aspect is the most critical to rim brake caliper settings. Too much run-out will make it difficult to set the brake pads without the pads rubbing the rim. Extreme run-out problems will result in the tire hitting the frame or fork.

4_Figure 6

Lateral true of the wheel

RADIAL TRUE: This is the amount of up and down run-out or wobble (4_Figure 7). If the wheel becomes out-of-round, it moves or hops up and down with each revolution. In severe cases this will affect brake pad placement and can be felt by the rider as a bump every wheel revolution.

4_Figure 7

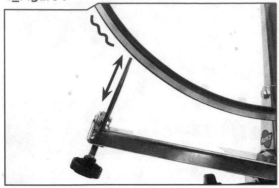

Radial movement of the rim inward or outward from the hub

RIM CENTERING OR DISH: This is the rim being centered in the middle of the front fork or rear frame. If the rim is offset in the frame to either side it may be difficult to adjust the brakes. Severe cases of poor centering can also cause handling problems because the front and rear wheel will not track in a straight line (4_Figure 8).

4_Figure 8

This rear wheel is off centered to the right side of the frame

TENSION: This is simply the tightness of the spokes. Spokes are tensioned just like other fasteners. Spoke tension is best measured using a tool called a spoke tension meter (tensiometer) such as the Park Tool TM-1, which flexes the spoke using a calibrated spring. With experience, spoke tension can be roughly estimated by squeezing pairs of spokes and feeling the deflection (4_Figure 9).

4_Figure 9

Spoke tension measurement with a tension meter

4-1 Truing Procedures

TOOLS & SUPPLIES

- Spoke wrenches (Park Tool SW-0 through 3 or SW-7)
- Lubricant (Park Tool CL-1)
- Dishing Tool (Park Tool WAG-3 or WAG-4)
- Spoke tension meter (Park Tool TM-1)
- Truing Stand (Park Tool TS-2, TS-8) or substitute bike frame and zip-ties
- Isopropyl alcohol or window cleaner

It is useful to use a steady pointer as a reference when sighting rim movement and deviations, such as found on a wheel truing stand. Park Tool truing stands allow easier and faster work when truing. The truing stand uses a caliper indicator as a reference to gauge the rim run out. If no truing stand is available, it is possible to use anything that will hold the wheel as steady as a truing stand, even the bicycle frame itself. Use the brake pads or a zip-tie to create an indicator as a reference gauge. Secure and snug a zip-tie at braking surface height on each side of the seat stay or fork blade. Cut zip-tie to a length able to touch the rim (4-1_Figure 1).

4-1_Figure 1

Use zip-ties for reference indicator if truing stand is not available

When truing, it is critical to get the spoke wrench fully engaged on the nipple before turning. A wrench that is partially engaged may damage the nipple and make truing difficult. When truing a wheel, the wrench and nipples may end up being viewed upside down. This happens if the wrench and nipple are viewed below the axle center. The wrench will appear to the mechanic as turning to the left when tightening the nipple. Do not allow this to confuse you. Keep in mind that the nipple is rotating around the fixed spoke. If in doubt, imagine a screwdriver at the nipple end, and turn it clockwise or counter-clockwise as required (4-1_Figure 2).

4-1_Figure 2

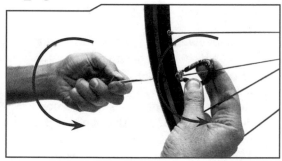

Visualize turning the wrench as if a screwdriver is turning the nipple

There are some models of wheels where the nipple is located at the hub flange. These wheels true the same as conventional wheels. Tightening a spoke will draw the rim toward the hub flange side where it connects. The threading of the spokes and nipples is still a right-hand thread, and nipples tighten clockwise as seen from the orientation of the nipple.

NOTE NOTE NOTE: If the wheel has bladed spokes, it is often necessary to hold the spoke near the nipple with an adjustable wrench or other tool in order to keep the spoke blade from twisting. Keep blade parallel to bike mid plane.

The image below is a "mechanic's eye" view of the rim (4-1_Figure 3). The spoke nipples labeled A, C, and E, are on the left side of the rim and come from the left side hub flange. Spoke nipples B, D, and F are on the right and come from the right side hub flange. Left side spokes pull the rim toward the left. Their pulling is offset by the pull of spokes on the right. Each nipple affects a relatively wide area of the rim. For example, spoke C pulls mainly at the nipple hole of the rim, but this spoke also affects the rim up to and even past A and F. Turning nipple C to increase spoke tension will move that section of rim to the left. Turning nipple D to increase tension will move that section of rim to the right. Loosening nipple C will also move the rim to the right, because of the constant pull of D and B.

4-1_Figure 3

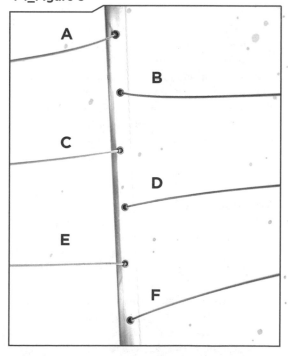

Spoke tension will determine wheel trueness

Before making any adjustments to spoke tension, use a light lubricant and lubricate the threads of the spokes and where the nipple exits the rim (4-1_Figure 4). This will allow the effort of turning the nipple to tension the spoke.

4-1_Figure 4

Use a drop of lubrication on the spoke threads and where the nipple exits the rim

4-1.1 Lateral Truing

Lateral, or side-to-side truing, is the most common truing procedure. The lateral run out shows up relatively easily when viewed at rim caliper brake pads. Tightening or loosening spokes at a section of rim can change lateral movements of the rim. However, inexperienced mechanics should generally tighten nipples when correcting deviations. Tightening the spoke tension will typically produce more rim movement while making these corrections.

Wheel rims do not need to spin perfectly straight, with zero run out, in order to be completely serviceable. Most wheels will be adequately true if they wobble laterally less then $\frac{1}{16}$" (1.0mm), and the rim does not strike the brake pads.

The procedure for lateral wheel truing is as follows:

a. If a truing stand is available, remove wheel from bike. Alternatively, mount wheel in bike and attach zip-ties on each side of the rim at the seat stays or fork blades. If the wheel requires extensive truing, remove the tire.

b. Place wheel in truing stand. Move indicators close to rim.

c. Spin wheel and inspect for left-right deviations.

d. Adjust indicator of truing stand (or zip-tie end) so that it lightly touches the rim in one area. Work off of either left or right side.

e. Stop wheel where rim and one indicator are closest or touch. This area is the largest lateral deviation of the rim-run out, and should be corrected first.

f. Rotate rim back and forth past indicator and find center of rim deviation. It is easier to see the run out as it moves toward an indicator, rubbing it, rather than as a deviation that moves away from an indicator (4-1.1_Figure 1).

4-1.1_Figure 1

Isolate rim lateral deviation

g. If rim deviation moves toward the left side, find the right flange nipple at the rim closest to center of deviation. If rim deviation moves toward the right side, find the left flange nipple closest to center of deviation. Tightening this spoke will move rim deviation in this section of rim.

h. Tighten appropriate spoke nipple $\frac{1}{4}$ to $\frac{1}{2}$ turn. A $\frac{1}{4}$ turn is a 90-degree turn of the nipple, while a $\frac{1}{2}$ turn is a 180-degree turn. Spin the wheel and check deviation again. It is often necessary to repeat the process at one area. Do not tighten more than $\frac{1}{2}$ turn at a time. It is better to proceed in small increments and to check progress between each tightening by spinning the wheel.

i. Locate another side-to-side deviation using indicator. Repeat process of finding center of deviation and correcting deviation by finding and turning nipple from spoke of opposite flange.

j. After making three corrections on one side of the rim, switch to other side indicator or zip-tie. This will help maintain previous wheel centering.

k. Continue making corrections. To check tolerance, use indicator so it just barely rubs the rim in one area. Spin wheel slowly from this point and inspect for the largest gap between indicator and rim. This area is then the worst left to right lateral deviation. If this gap appears less then the 1mm (approximately the thickness of a dime), wheel is adequately trued laterally. In some cases it will be necessary to continue truing for tighter tolerances.

l. If only lateral true is being adjusted, clean rim braking surface with a solvent such as rubbing alcohol or window cleaner. If used, cut zip ties from frame. Remount tire if removed and re-install wheel into bike.

4-1.2 Radial Truing

The wheel rim may appear to move in and out toward the center as it rotates around the hub. This can also be viewed as an up-and-down movement. This radial aspect of the wheel can be affected by spoke tension. Sections of rim moving away from the hub are called "high spots." Sections of rim moving toward the hub are called "low spots." Sections of rim can be moved toward the hub by tightening spokes from both flanges at high spots. Loosing spokes from both flanges will tend to move a section of rim slightly outward at low spots. In correcting radial run out, it is necessary to correct both high spots and low spots. It is typically best to work using pairs of spokes, one from the left side and one from the right side. By working with adjacent left-right spokes there is less of a tendency for the wheel to become laterally out of true. It is necessary, however, to always double check the lateral true after making radial corrections.

The procedure for radial wheel truing is as follows:

a. Remove tire from wheel.

b. Mount wheel in a truing stand or mount wheel in bike frame and attach zip-tie indicator to frame. Attach tie close to outer edge of rim.

c. Bring indicator (zip-tie) close to outside edge of rim.

d. Spin rim and bring indictor (zip-tie) slowly closer to rim until there is a very light rub. This point is the largest high spot, or radial deviation away from the hub.

e. Stop rim at light rub. Move rim back and forth through rub and locate center of deviation. This section of rim needs to move closer to hub (4-1.2 Figure 1).

4-1.2_Figure 1

Isolate the radial run out and select a left-right pair of spokes to correct problem

f. Tighten the two spokes in the middle of the deviation. Tighten one left side and one right side spoke, each the same amount, beginning with ½ turn.

g. Move the rim back and forth through the selected area. Repeat tightening if necessary.

h. Spin the wheel and move the calipers (zip-tie) slightly closer to the rim to find next deviation. Correct rub by tightening a left-right pair at the center of the rub.

i. After making three radial corrections, stop and double check lateral true. Correct lateral true as needed before proceeding with further radial corrections.

j. After making several radial corrections to high spots, the rim may show only areas moving toward the hub, or low spots. It will be necessary to loosen the low spot areas. Spin the rim and move caliper (zip-tie) to create a light continuous scrape. The areas not scraping are low spots and need to move away from the hub to be corrected. Isolate the center of the worst low spot.

k. Loosen two spokes on either side of the center of the low spot. Spokes should be adjacent left side and right side pairs.

l. Repeat procedure on other low spots. Occasionally check and correct lateral true.

m. Check for acceptable radial tolerance. Adjust indicator so it just barely rubs the rim in one area. Spin wheel slowly from this point and inspect for the largest gap between indicator and rim. This area is the largest radial deviation. Wheel is adequately trued for round when the deviation from the highest to lowest is less then 1mm (1/16 inch).

n. Check and correct lateral true as needed.

o. If no other truing is to be done, clean rim braking surface with a solvent such as rubbing alcohol or window cleaner. Cut zip ties from frame. Reinstall tire and re-install wheel to bike.

If the wheel rim has been damaged and deformed from impact, such as during riding or even during shipping, it may not be possible to correct the rim to a tight tolerance. If the rim shows an inward movement in one section toward the hub, and the spokes in that area are already loose, the rim has been bent. This type of damage is not repairable. Replacement of rim or wheel is recommended. Contact a professional mechanic.

4-1.3 Wheel Centering (Dishing)

The rim should be centered in the frame, either between the front fork blades or the rear stays. Use a ruler and measure from the left and right stay or fork blade to the rim. If the distances are equal and the rim looks centered, it is centered. If there is a greater distance from one stay or blade compared to the other, the wheel is off-center, or "miss-dished."

The rim can be moved over to the frame center by adjusting spoke tension. Again, spokes from the left flange pull the rim toward the left while spokes from the right flange pull the rim toward the right. Tightening all left side spokes evenly will move the rim to the left. Tighten all right side spokes evenly moves the rim right. Alternatively, loosen all left side spokes to move the rim right. Loosen all right side spokes to move the rim left.

The most accurate method to check rim centering over a hub is with a centering gauge called a dishing tool, such as the Park Tool

WAG-4 Wheel Alignment Gauge, or WAG-3 Portable Wheel Dishing Gauge. The Park Tool WAG-4 comes with two sliding blocks on the feet. These blocks allow the tool to measure off the wheel rim even when a tire is still mounted.

The procedure for checking wheel centering with a dishing tool is as follows:

a. Note which side of the wheel is being checked. This example will assume the right side is being checked first and will act as a reference for the left side.

b. Lower the sliding gauge until the end rests on the face of the right side locknut (4-1.3_Figure 1). Do not rest gauge on end of axle. The wheel will reference the locknut face when mounting in the frame.

4-1.3_Figure 1

Dishing gauge set to reference right side of wheel

c. Turn wheel over to check opposite side. Place feet of dishing tool on rim. Note indicator relative to locknut face. There are three possible results.

Situation A: Both feet of dishing tool rest on the rim and the indicator pointer lightly contacts left locknut face, or is within 1mm of the face. This rim is adequately centered to the locknuts. No correction of centering is required (4-1.3 Figure 2).

4-1.3_Figure 2

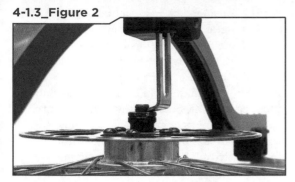

Three-point contact of tool feet and indicator showing a correctly dished wheel

Situation B: Both feet of the dishing tool rest on the rim, and there is a significant gap between the indicator and locknut face (4-1.3 Figure 3). This situation shows rim is off center toward left side. If the gap is greater than 1mm, the wheel should be re-centered. This example rim should be moved to right. However, a rim is off-centered in the bike only half the distance from indicator to locknut. For example, if indicator is 3mm from locknut, wheel is off centered to mid plane of the bike by 1.5mm.

4-1.3_Figure 3

Dishing gauge indicator showing rim is off center

In Situation B, it is better to view the error (if any) at the rim rather than at the hub. If after checking the wheel you find Situation B described above, it is best to reset the indicator using the left side as a reference, and re-check the opposite side. You will find there is now a gap between rim and dishing tool foot when the indicator rests on the locknut face. This method makes it more obvious that the rim should be moved toward the leg of the tool. If you see the error or gap at the hub, the rim is actually pulled toward the opposite side to close the gap of the locknut face to indicator.

Situation C: Three-point contact of both feet and indicator at locknut is impossible. If indicator rests on locknut face, only one foot will contact rim, with other foot higher than rim (4-1.3 Figure 4). If both feet are on rim, indicator will be below level of locknut face. This situation indicates the rim is off center toward right side. The rim should be moved to the left.

4-1.3_Figure 4

Dishing gauge indicating wheel is off center

d. Correct centering error by tightening spokes from the flange on the same side as the gap between the rim and the foot of the dishing gauge. Tighten each spoke on one side only ¼ turn.

e. Double check and correct lateral true as necessary. The dishing tool assumes the rim is laterally true.

f. Use dishing tool and check wheel again, starting with step "a" above. Keep in mind that the original reference side has changed the position of the rim to the locknut face. Repeat corrections if necessary. If the rim to dishing tool gap is less then 1mm, wheel is adequately centered.

g. If no other truing is to be done, clean rim braking surface with a solvent such as rubbing alcohol or window cleaner.

When making corrections to dish, keep in mind that it will also make changes to overall tension. Corrections by tightening one side will increase overall tension of both sides, while corrections by loosening will decrease overall tension of both sides.

4-1.4 Spoke Tension

Spokes are long thin bolts with nipples as the nuts, making the system similar to other fasteners. Like any threaded fastener, there is an acceptable range of tightness, called tension. Spoke tension is the amount of force pulling on the spoke.

As the wheels rotate while you ride, the spokes that are on the bottom, next to the ground, will momentarily become lower in tension, then regain tension as they rotate past this low point. This change of tension each revolution is called a "stress cycle." Wheels with a relatively low overall spoke tension actually see a greater swing in tension as compared to wheels with greater overall tension. Stress cycles, this tightening and then loosening of tension, fatigue the metal and lead to spoke breakage. Wheels with low overall spoke tension will continue to loosen even more as the bike is ridden. This results in shortened spoke life and a wheel that requires continuous re-truing.

While low overall spoke tension can result in problems, too much tension can also result in issues. Spokes with too much tension can deform or crack the rim near the nipple holes. Too much tension can also lead to failure of the hub flange. Spoke nipple wrench flats can become deformed and rounded by forcing the nipple to turn when the spoke tension is too high. However, the spoke itself can typically take more stress then rim, nipple or hub flange.

When adding or subtracting tension, work slowly and in relatively small increments. For example, to add tension to a wheel, begin with a spoke next to the tire valve hole and add only ¼ turn to each spoke. After adding this tension, double check the lateral trueness. It is common to make corrections to the other aspects of truing after adding overall tension. If more tension is desired, add another ¼ turn to each spoke and again check the other aspects of truing. Repeat the process until the desired tension is achieved.

It is common for the spokes to become twisted along their long axis as the nipples are turned. The is called "spoke wind-up." The safest method to relieve this torsional stress on the spoke is to simply ride the bike. You may hear an initial popping or pining sound while the spokes untwist. In some case, it may be necessary to re-true the wheel laterally.

Spoke tension is best measured with a spoke tension meter (also called a tensiometer), such as the Park Tool TM-1 Tension Meter. It is possible to some degree to "feel" the tension by squeezing crossing or parallel spokes. The squeezing technique can be quite deceiving and inconsistent, because the stiffness of the rim and thickness of spokes vary widely. A tension meter allows the user to determine both relative spoke tension between spokes and the tension force of each spoke measured in kilograms force, abbreviated here as "kgf." The TM-1 is calibrated to read tension for sixteen different types of spokes, including bladed, titanium and aluminum (4-1.4 Figure 1).

4-1.4_Figure 1

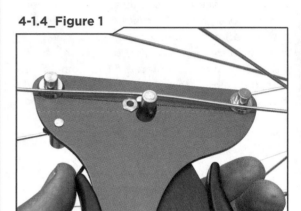

Park Tool TM-1Tension Meter flexing spoke to determine tension

Rim manufacturers have set tension recommendations from as low as 60 kgf to as high as 200 kgf. However, 100 kgf is a common tension recommendation. It is the rim, not the spoke type or diameter, that determines the limits of tension. Generally, the heavier and stronger the rim, the more tension it can handle. A light rim may weigh from 280 grams to 350 grams. A relatively heavy rim may weigh 450 grams or more. Additionally, rim eyelets may help distribute the load on the rim wall. A lack of eyelets on a light rim implies that less spoke tension should be used. Because there is a wide range of tension possibilities, it is always best to consult the rim manufacturer for the most up-to-date specifications.

Manufacturers typically give specifications for the wheel with no tire pressure. Tire pressure will have the effect of lowering the tension slightly. Generally, do not try to account for this drop by adding more tension than recommended by the manufacturer. Manufacturers list tension for the tight side of the wheel. For rear wheels, this will be the sprocket side, or right side. For front wheels with a disc, the tighter side is the disc side. If the flanges are equally spaced from the hub center, then either side can be measured. This is the case for most front wheels made without a rotor mount.

The procedure for measuring tension with Park Tool TM-1 Tension Meter is as follows:

a. Measure the diameter of the spoke using the included spoke diameter gauge. The smallest slot the spoke fits into determines the diameter. A measuring caliper can also be used to measure the spoke diameter. The diameter at the middle section of spoke will determine the appropriate spoke-type column on the Conversion Table.

b. Squeeze the TM-1 at the handle grips. Place the spoke between the two fixed posts and the moveable post. With butted spokes, position the posts so they rest on the narrowest portion of spoke. With aero/bladed spokes, position the posts so they rest against the wide, flat side of the spoke.

c. Gently release the handle. Releasing the tension rapidly will cause erratic reading results.

d. With the TM-1 engaged on the spoke, the pointer will be pointing to a number on the tool's graduated scale. This number is a deflection reading that is used in conjunction with the TM-1's conversion table to determine the actual tension of the spoke.

e. For the most accurate measurement, measure all spokes on one side and take the average reading. However, measuring approximately ¼ of the wheel will give you a good idea of the overall tension. If you have a 32 spoke wheel, measure eight spokes and take the average.

f. Using the conversion table, find the column corresponding to the material and diameter of the spoke being measured. Follow the column down to the row corresponding to the spoke's deflection reading (as determined in step "d"). The number at this intersection is the actual tension of the spoke in kilograms force (kgf).

The spoke tension will vary slightly from spoke to spoke with even a well trued wheel. However, a wheel that has the same relative tension for all the spokes on a flange will tend to stay true longer. The use of a spoke tension meter will help get the spokes closer to the same relative tension. Generally, attempt to get the spokes within 20 percent of one another. On wheels with dish (rear wheel or front disc wheels), the left and right side tensions will not be equal. This is normal and will not be a problem for the wheel. Using a tensiometer will also help get the overall tension acceptably high.

NOTE: For more detail on spoke tension, see Repair Help at www.parktool.com

4-2
Replacing Broken or Damaged Spokes

A broken spoke will cause the wheel to come out of true. It may be possible to correct lateral true enough to keep riding until the spoke can be replaced. However, low spoke-count wheels (28 spokes or less) may develop substantial lateral run-out from a single broken spoke. It may not be possible to correct the run out enough to safely finish a ride.

To repair a wheel with a broken spoke, begin by removing the tire. On rear wheels, also remove the rear sprockets. (Outline Item 3-2 Cassette Cog Removal Installation or 3-3 Freewheel Removal and Installation) Remove the old spoke from the wheel and hub. The new spoke should be the correct length. If possible, measure the old spoke, or remove a second spoke for measurement. Feed the new spoke through the hub in the same orientation as the original spoke, with spoke head facing inward or outward in the flange. It may be necessary to flex and bend the spoke, but avoid kinking it (4-2_Figure 1). Inspect another spoke of the same flange and same orientation, and follow the same pattern.

4-2_Figure 1

Bend spoke to lace into wheel

Replace the nipple as well as the spoke. If possible, use a spoke tension meter to measure spokes on the same side as the broken spoke, and average the readings. Tighten the new spoke until it reaches the average. True the wheel with the procedures described above.

4-3 Wheel Wear, Damage & Repair

Rims may become damaged from impacts, such as hitting a rock, pothole or street curb. Impacts to the side of the rim from falling down or crashing can also cause damage. Limited repair by truing is sometimes possible to crashed wheels. Begin by checking relative tension in the damaged area. For example, if a wheel deviates in one section to the right, check left and right side spoke tension in that area. If this wheel deviates to the right, but the right side spokes in that area appear relatively loose and the spokes on the left side in that area appear tight, the rim metal is bent. Normally, to correct a wobble to the right, it would be necessary to tighten left side spokes, but we have seen that the left side is already tight. The second option of loosening right side spokes is not effective because the right side spokes at that section are already loose. This indicates the rim has been deformed beyond the point where spoke tension can repair it (4-3_Figure 1).

4-3_Figure 1

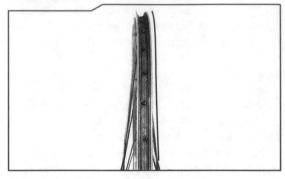

Wheel rim deformed beyond repair

Adjusting spoke tension on a wheel with a badly bent rim is unlikely to help, except possibly to get the rider home from a ride. Attempting to re-bend the rim back in the problem area is a desperate repair measure, and is unlikely to help return the wheel to a useable condition. Wheel rims can be replaced and a new rim laced around the old hub. See a professional mechanic for this service, or purchase a new wheel.

For bicycles with rim caliper brakes, the rim acts as the braking surface. The brake pads will in effect grind the rim walls thinning the metal. The pressurized tire is held in place by the rim sidewall, which is now weakened. Thin sidewalls may break or fail during a ride, causing a tire blowout. Inspect visually and feel the rim-braking surface for a dished, concave surface. If the rim appears worn, remove the tire and place a straight edge along the rim surface. Inspect for a gap between the straight edge and the rim. If the gap is larger then 0.2 mm (approximately the thickness of a business card), the rim should be replaced (4-3 Figure 2).

4-3_Figure 2

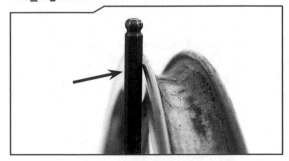

Rim showing unacceptable wear on braking surface

Chapter 5

Pedals, Cranks &
Bottom Brackets

The parts of the bicycle that transform your muscular energy into the mechanical energy pushing you forward are called the "drive train." Along with the chain and rear sprockets, the drive includes the shoes, pedals, crankset, and bottom bracket.

5-1 Pedals and Riding Shoes

Pedals are attached to the end of each crank. Occasionally check security of all threaded fasteners on the pedal body. It is necessary to remove the pedals for replacement or to service the pedal bearings.

Some types of pedals may be used with any shoe, while other models require special cleated shoes. Cleated pedals will have hardware that allows the cleat on the shoe to engage with pedal.

Pedal spindles turn on bearings inside the pedal body. Some brands are serviceable and can be overhauled. However, bearing service will not be covered here because service varies significantly between brands and models, and pedal bearings are typically not serviced.

NOTE: For more detail on pedal bearing service see Repair Help at www.parktool.com.

The common pedal thread for aluminum cranks is $9/16$-inch x 20 tpi. The pedal thread of the steel one-piece crank is $\frac{1}{2}$ inch x 20-tpi. Pedal threads tend to be made of bearing hard steel and are relatively difficult to damage. However, minor pedal thread damage may be repaired with a thread file.

Shoes, especially cleated riding shoes, should be considered bicycle equipment, just like pedals or cranks. Even the fit of the shoe will affect the rider's performance on the bike. The cleat of a riding shoe should be securely fastened to the shoe (5-1_Figure 1). Use a mild thread-locker or grease on the cleat screws. The cleats will wear down and will eventually require replacement.

5-1_Figure 1

Check cleat security to shoe

5-1.1 Pedal Removal

TOOLS & SUPPLIES
- Pedal Wrench (Park Tool HCW-16, PW-3, PW-4, RW-1, RW-2)
- 8mm hex wrench for some pedals (Park Tool HR-8, PH-8)
- Repair stand (optional)
- Grease (Park Tool PPL-1) or anti-seize

Pedals need to be removed to service the bearings or to pack a bike for shipment. Most pedals have wrench flats on the pedal axles adjacent to the crank. It is important to use a pedal wrench, not a cone wrench, for the narrow wrench flats of the pedal. This is because the tightening torque of a pedal is much greater than a cone wrench is designed to deliver. Some pedals use a hex socket at the end of the spindle behind the cranks rather than pedal wrench flats.

The right side (drive side) pedal has a right-hand thread. It will remove counter-clockwise, and install clockwise. The left side (non-drive side) pedal has a left-hand thread. It will removes clockwise, and install counter-clockwise. Pedals are commonly marked with an "R" on the right side pedal, and an "L" on the left side pedal.

The procedure for pedal removal is as follows:
a. Mount bike in repair stand and shift chain to largest chainring. This helps protect against cuts from chainring teeth.
b. Rotate bike until right pedal is easily accessed. Reach over or through frame as necessary.

c. Place pedal wrench securely onto wrench flats. Remember to never use a cone wrench to remove or install a pedal.

d. Position wrench until crank and wrench form an angle of 90 degrees or less. Correct mechanical advantage is critical on pedals, which are often overly tight. If possible, grab opposite crank for second lever. See Outline Item 1-1 Threaded Fastener Tension and Torque.

e. Loosening both the right and left side pedal can be seen as pedaling forward while the wrench engages the pedal flats. Turn pedal wrench counter-clockwise to remove right pedal or turn crank so it is pedaling forward (5-1.1_Figure 1). Remove pedal completely from crank arm. Use care not to abrade skin on crank or chainring.

5-1.1_Figure 1

Pedal in a forward direction to remove pedals from cranks

f. Rotate bike as necessary until left pedal is easily accessed.

g. Place pedal wrench onto left pedal, and grab right crank for second lever. Position wrench and crank for good mechanical advantage.

h. Turn pedal wrench clockwise to remove left pedal or turn crank so the pedal is pedaling forward. Remove left pedal completely from crank.

5-1.2 Pedal Installation

Pedal threads are made of hardened steel and can damage the aluminum thread of the crank if the threads are misaligned. Start threading with only your fingers to avoid forcing the pedal into the crank threads. Using a pedal

wrench to start the thread will not allow the feel necessary to detect cross threading of the pedal. Pedals are secured to a relatively high torque range, approximately 300 inch pounds. A common pedal wrench may be held 8 inches from the pedal, so it would require an effort of approximately 35 pounds.

The procedure for installing pedals is as follows:

a. Identify right and left pedals. Look for "L" or "R" marking on pedal axle or wrench flats. If no "L" or "R" marking is seen, use pedal thread direction to identify pedals. Left threaded pedals (threads sloping upward to the left) go to left crank. Right threaded pedals (threads sloping upward to the right) go to right crank. Refer to Outline item 1-1 Thread Fastener Tension and Torque to determine thread direction.

b. Grease threads of both pedals.

c. Start threading right side pedal into right crank using only your fingers to avoid cross threading.

d. Position wrench on flats. Hold wrench with one hand while holding pedal with other. Pedal the bike backward to install.

e. Using opposite arm as second lever, fully tighten pedal.

f. Repeat for left pedal, but thread pedal counter-clockwise to install. (Pedal the bike backward while holding wrench to thread in pedals).

g. Fully secure left pedal.

5-1.3 Damage to Crank Pedal Threads

If the crank threads are damaged, the pedal may difficult to install. To repair thread, use an appropriate sized tap, either $9/16$ inch x 20 tpi, or $1/2$ inch x 20 tpi and chase the threads of the crank.

 Do not attempt to have the larger $9/16$ inch threads cut into cranks made for the smaller $1/2$ inch threads

If a pedal has come loose and fallen out, the outer thread of the crank hole may be mangled and damaged. Use a pedal tap to align thread. A tap will not restore metal that has been removed or torn away.

If the pedal threads in the crank are damaged

beyond a tap repair, they may be repairable using a thread insert system. An oversized tap is used to cut new larger threads. A threaded coil or insert is threaded into the arm. The new threads are the correct inside diameter for the pedal. This repair is best left to professional mechanics.

5-2 Cranks

The cranks, also called crank arms, are levers that connect the pedals to the bottom bracket spindle. The cranks are sometime removed in order to replace chainrings, or to better clean the rings and arms. The most common design is called the "three piece" crank (5-2_Figure 1). Two cranks are bolted to a bottom bracket spindle. These are removed from the spindle to service the bottom bracket bearings. External bearing crankset systems such as Shimano® Hollow Tech II and other similar systems permanently fix the spindle to one crank (5-2_Figure 2). They are, in effect, a "two piece" crankset.

5-2_Figure 1

Three-piece crankset, consisting of two arms and one spindle

5-2_Figure 2

External bearing system crank with spindle permanently attached to one arm

Another type of crank system is the "one piece" or Ashtabula crank (5-2_Figure 3). One piece of steel is bent in an "S" shape, and the crank acts as both arms and spindle for the bearings. This system requires a larger unthreaded bottom bracket. The pedal threads are $9/16$ inch by 20 tpi. The one-piece system was popular in the USA prior to 1980. Service of the one-piece crank is not covered in this book.

5-2_Figure 3

The one-piece crankset

NOTE: For service of the one-piece crank, see Repair Help at www.parktool.com

5-2.1 Crank Removal-Square Hole
The square-spindle arms have a square hole to accept a square ended spindle. The square spindle presses tightly into the arm with pressure from a crank bolt. Most square spindles can be seen where the arm meets the spindle. However, it may be necessary to remove the crank bolt and inspect inside for a square hole (5-2.1_Figure 1).

TOOLS & SUPPLIES
- Crank bolt wrench (Park Tool HR-8, PH-8, PH-10, CCW-14R)
- Crank puller (Park Tool CWP-6, CCP-2)
- Adjustable wrench

5-2.1_Figure 1

A square crank hole with square spindle inside

Some cranks may use a "one-key" release system, where the crank puller is effectively built into the crank (5-2.1_Figure 2). A crank arm cap acts as a retaining ring and threaded into the crank. This crank arm cap takes the place of the dust cap and surrounds the crank bolt head. To remove this crank, leave the cap in place. Turn the crank bolt counter-clockwise. The bolt backs against the crank arm cap, pulling the arm from the spindle. It is important to keep the crank arm cap tight. If the crank arm cap uses pin holes, secure with a pin spanner such as the Park Tool SPA-2 (5-2.1_Figure 3).

5-2.1_Figure 2

One-key release system with crank arm cap and crank bolt

5-2.1_Figure 3

Check security of one-key release system crank arm cap

For cranks without the one-key system, a crank puller is required. A crank puller extracts the arm from the press fit after the crank bolt is removed. The puller uses a threaded stud to push against the spindle end. This stud threads into a "nut," which is then threaded into the 22mm thread fitting of the crank. The spindle and arm are pushed apart when the stud presses against the spindle.

The procedure for square spindle crank removal is as follows:

a. Shift chain to largest chainring to protect hands against chainring teeth.

b. Look for bolt or nut on crank. If no bolt is visible, remove dust caps. Some caps pry out, while others unthread.

c. Turn bolt or nut counter-clockwise and remove bolt or nut. Inspect inside arms for washers and remove if present.

d. Before installing crank puller into crank, turn puller nut away from internal driver as much as possible. If puller nut unthreads from internal driver, thread it back on only 3-4 turns.

e. Thread nut of puller into arm, taking care not to cross thread. Tighten puller nut into crank using wrench (5-2.1_Figure 4). Failure to tighten nut may result in crank thread failure during removal.

5-2.1_Figure 4

Tighten puller nut securely into arm before extracting crank

f.   Thread internal driver into puller nut. Using handle or adjustable wrench, tighten driver (5-2.1_Figure 5). When resistance is felt, continue threading stud into nut until crank is removed.

5-2.1_Figure 5

Tighten internal driver of puller to extract arm

g.   Pull arm from spindle and unthread both parts of tool from arm. Use care not to skin knuckles when removing tool.

h.   Repeat process on other crank.

5-2.2   Crank Installation-Square Hole

Square type cranks are made with a square tapered hole, and are pressed tightly to a tapered square spindle. The crank bolt or nut acts as the pressing tool and forces the arm up the slope of the spindle. The bolt or nut must be tight enough to keep the arm from loosening, but not so tight that the arm becomes split and damaged. Aluminum cranks typically do not

require lubrication of this press fit. Aluminum by its nature is covered with a thin layer of oxidation, which acts as self-lubrication. When possible, use a torque wrench to secure the bolt. The crank bolt may need 300 to 450 inch pounds, depending upon brand. Adequate torque is typically enough to keep arms from creaking. If a crank creaks even at full torque, remove and grease the pressed surfaces.

TOOLS & SUPPLIES

- Crank bolt wrench (Park Tool HR-8, PH-8, PH-10, CCW-14R)
- Torque wrench (Park Tool TW-2) with correct bit (optional)
- Grease (Park Tool PPL-1) or anti seize

The procedure for square spindle crank installation is as follows:

a.   Grease under head and threads of bolts/nuts.

b.   Install right crank onto right side of spindle.

c.   Install bolt/nut and tighten. Refer to Appendix C for recommended torque.

d.   Grease threads of dust cap (if any) and install snug.

e.   Install left crank onto left side of spindle with arm pointing opposite direction of right side arm.

f.   Install bolt/nut and tighten (5-2.2_Figure 1).

5-2.2_Figure 1

Torque wrench use will help assure full pre-load on bolt

g.   Grease threads of dust cap (if any) and install.

5-2.3 Crank Removal-Splined Hole

TOOLS & SUPPLIES

- Crank bolt wrench (Park Tool HR-8, PH-8, PH-10, CCW-14R)
- Crank puller for non one-key release cranks (Park Tool CWP-6, CCP-4)
- Adjustable wrench

The splined type cranks have round holes fitted with splines (5-2.3_Figure 1). The spline pattern of the spindle matches the pattern in the arm. The cranks are held tight to the spindle by the tension from the crank bolt. Splined spindles can usually be seen where the arm meets the spindle. However, it may be necessary to remove the crank bolt and inspect inside for a round, splined shaped hole.

5-2.3_Figure 1

Spline type arm of the ISIS Drive® system

There is more than one spline standard. Shimano® uses two different styles of Octalink® bottom bracket spindle fittings. Both have an 8-spline fitting. The original is called Octalink® V1, and was used on models BB-7700, 6500, 5500, M950 and M952. The Octalink® V2 fits the BB-ES70/71, BB-ES50/51 (5-2.3_Figure 2). The V2 system uses a thicker and longer spline (approximately 9mm), while the V1 spline is relatively narrower and shorter (approximately 5mm). The V1 and V2 Octalink® standards do not interchange for spindles or cranks.

5-2.3_Figure 2

Shimano® Octalink V1 spindle is seen on the left. The Octalink V2 spindle is on the right. Do not mix standards.

There is only one ISIS Drive® standard for the crank and spindle fitting. The standard uses a 21mm diameter spindle with 10-splines. The ISIS Drive® is a standard, not a particular brand. The ISIS Drive® and Shimano® Octalink systems are not interchangeable for either bottom bracket or cranks.

Some cranks may use a "one-key" release system, where the crank puller is effectively built into the crank (5-2.3_Figure 3). A crank arm cap acts as retaining ring and is threaded into the crank. The crank arm cap takes the place of the dust cap and surrounds the crank bolt head. To remove this crank, leave the crank arm cap in place. Turn the crank bolt counterclockwise. The bolt backs against the crank arm cap, pulling the arm from the spindle. It is important to keep the crank arm cap tight. If the crank arm cap uses pinholes, secure with a pin spanner such as the Park Tool SPA-2 (5-2.3_Figure 4).

5-2.3_Figure 3

One-key release system crank arm cap and crank bolt

5-2.3_Figure 4

Check security of one-key release system crank arm cap

If there is no one-key release system, a special crank puller will be required (5-2.3_Figure 5). The spline system spindles use a larger bolt compared to the square spindles. This means the square crank pullers simply have nothing to push against and will not work on the spline systems. Spline type cranks may use the Park Tool CWP-6 or CCP-4 Crank Puller when no one-key system is in place. The CWP-6 Crank Puller includes changeable tips to work on the Octalink®, ISIS Drive®, and square spindle cranks.

5-2.3_Figure 5

Spline type arm without one-key release system may use the CWP-6 Crank Puller

The procedure for splined crank removal is as follows:

a. Shift chain to largest chainring.
b. Remove crank bolt and any washers inside the crank.

c. Unthread nut from handle stud of CWP-6 or CCP-4 until it contacts the flat, rotating tip.
d. Turn nut and handle together into crank and tighten with wrench until snug. If nut is not completely threaded into crank, the threads of the arm or nut may be damaged during removal.
e. Turn stud clockwise into nut. When resistance is felt, continue threading stud into nut until crank is removed.
f. Remove tool from crank and repeat process on other side.

5-2.4 Crank Installation—Splined Hole

TOOLS & SUPPLIES
• Crank bolt wrench (Park Tool HR-8, PH-8, PH-10, CCW-14R)
• Torque wrench (Park Tool TW-2) with correct bit (optional)
• Grease (Park Tool PPL-1) or anti-seize

One-key release systems require extra care when installing the arm to the spindle. The one-key release systems make it difficult to see how the arm is fitting to the splines on the spindle. Crank splines and spindle splines must align and match as the crank is pressed into place. A forced mismatch can damage the crank. Splined cranks without the one key system allow easy viewing of the spline fit. One key and non-one key systems are installed the same way. If there is concern about mating the spindle to the arm, remove the one-key system, install the arm, and re-install the one-key system.

The procedure for splined crank installation is as follows:

a. Grease threads inside bottom bracket spindle and grease outer splines of bottom bracket spindle.
b. Rotate splined spindle until one narrow spline aligns to the 12:00 position or top dead center.
c. Position right crank on spindle until arm points straight down to the 6:00 position (5-2.4_Figure 1). Carefully thread bolt into spindle. View opposite side of spindle and check that a narrow spline is aligned to top dead center. Threading should continue

without resistance until crank visually covers spindle splines as seen from the bottom bracket side.

d. Tighten bolt fully. See Appendix C for torque.

e. Align left arm so it points directly opposite the right arm. Thread bolt into spindle and tighten bolt fully.

5-2.4_Figure 1

With right crank at 6 o'clock position, spline is at top dead center

5-3
Bottom Bracket Bearings & Spindle

Bearings on a bicycle allow parts to rotate or move relative to one another. The cranks are attached to a spindle or axle, which is supported by the bottom bracket bearings. These bearings see quite a bit of load and wear from riding. Bottom bracket bearings are housed in the bottom bracket shell, and are usually the lowest point of the bicycle. Any water that gets inside the frame tends to drain to the bottom bracket shell.

The bearing systems on bikes typically use ball bearings. Round ball bearings are trapped between two bearing surfaces. The bearing surfaces and balls are greased to minimize wear. These systems are shielded from dirt by covers and seals. Excessive exposure to the elements will increase wear on the bearing surfaces and shorten bearing life.

Bearing surfaces are made from hardened steel. The surfaces are cut typically by grinding. Even the highest quality bearing surfaces will have slight microscopic grinding marks. Better quality bearing surfaces are ground smoother and will have less friction and resistance to turning. Ball bearings roll on curved bearing surfaces. Bearings will have some friction as they rotate. This is normal and does not affect the ride. Generally, the lighter load a bearing is expected to experience, the "smoother" the feel. Bearings experiencing more stress and load will seem to have more drag. For example, a bearing for a rear derailleur pulley, which is designed for lower loads will seem to have less spinning resistance compared to a bottom bracket bearing, which experiences more load.

The two basic ball bearing systems are the cartridge bearing systems, and the adjustable bearing systems. Neither system is inherently better for use on a bicycle. The adjustable type systems can be overhauled, re-greased, and then adjusted. The cartridge type systems rely on replacement of the cartridge bearing rather than cleaning and greasing.

Cartridge bearings use an industrial or rolling element bearing. Ball bearings are trapped between inner and outer rotating races (5-3_Figure 1). There should be no play between the inner and outer races of the cartridge. With use, play will develop between these two races and the entire cartridge unit will require replacement.

5-3_Figure 1
Typical cartridge bearing shown with outer race cut away. Ball bearings ride on inner and outer curved races

A bottom bracket spindle must be compatible with the crank. The square-spindles and square cranks are generally not interchangeable between brands. Consult the manufacturer. Additionally, there are different spindle lengths available. Spindle length is measured end to end. The longer the right side of the bottom bracket spindle, the further the chainrings will sit from the frame. There are limits to where the cranks can be placed, as described in Outline Item 8-5, Chainline.

Round spindle standards include the Shimano® Octalink V1 and Octalink V2 systems, ISIS Drive®, and the external bearing systems. The various external bearing crankset systems vary on interchangeability between manufacturers. For further discussion of the Shimano® Octalink and ISIS Drive® crank fit, see Outline Item 5-2.3 Crank Removal-Splined Hole.

The common threading for bottom brackets is the ISO standard (International Thread Standard). This is also called the BSC (British Standard Cycle), or "English" threading, which is a thread size of 1.37 inches x 24 tpi. The left side (non-drive side) thread is a right-hand direction thread, which removes counter-clockwise and tightens clockwise. The right side (drive side) thread is a left-hand direction thread. It removes clockwise and tightens counterclockwise.

There are some exceptions to the ISO bottom bracket threading. Bikes made in Italy may have both drive and non-drive right hand thread, and both remove counter-clockwise. The thread sizing is 36mm x 24 tpi. This bottom bracket is too large to fit into an ISO sized frame. The ISO bottom bracket will simply slide into the larger "Italian" threading, with no thread engagement. The Italian thread is often designated with "36 x 24" markings on the flange of the bottom bracket bearing. Additionally, French made bikes prior to 1985 may have a 35mm x 1mm threading with left and right cups being right hand thread.

The bottom bracket must also be compatible with the shell width. There are now several possible standards. Shell width is measured from face to face of the shell in millimeters. Some bottom bracket models will work on more than one shell width. In Table 5-5 below, only the 68mm and the 73mm are currently common widths.

Table 5-3 Bottom Bracket Shell Widths

Shell Width- Face To Face In Millimeters	Typical Uses
68mm	Many road and MTB bikes, both cross country and downhill.
70mm	Road bikes with the 36mm x 24tpi "Italian" threading.
73mm	Many MTB bikes, both cross country and downhill.
83mm	Downhill and freeride bikes.
100mm	Downhill and freeride bikes.

If a bottom bracket bearing seems to install with excessive force, the shell threads may require tapping (5-3_Figure 2). A professional mechanic will be able to diagnose and repair this problem.

5-3_Figure 2

Tapping the internal threads of a bottom bracket

Another machining issue is called "facing" (5-3_Figure 3). The left and right shell faces should be machined, or faced, so they are parallel to one another. The shell can become deformed during welding, or even from simply from being made less then precise. If the shell faces are deformed, left and right side bearings may not be properly aligned to one another.

5-3_Figure 3

Facing the shell surface

As a rule, if the bearings use the shell face as a reference for the bearing race alignment, facing is important. If the bearings do not use the shell face for bearing race alignment, facing is not needed. There are cartridge type bottom bracket bearings where the bottom bracket housing contains a non-removable and non-adjustable spindle. The bearing adjustment is made at the factory and does not rely on the shell faces for bearing surface referencing. Unless the shell faces are extremely deformed, facing will not be required.

5-4
Bottom Bracket Tool Selection

Bottom brackets are designed with tool fittings to allow installation and removal. Do not attempt to "fake" the tool by unusual service techniques, such as with a punch and hammer. Table 5-4 below outlines the common bottom bracket fittings and the Park Tool choice. The list of brands and models is not exhaustive, as new models are brought to market often. Inspect the lockring or cups of the bottom bracket and check the table on page 70.

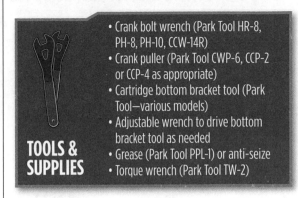

- Crank bolt wrench (Park Tool HR-8, PH-8, PH-10, CCW-14R)
- Crank puller (Park Tool CWP-6, CCP-2 or CCP-4 as appropriate)
- Cartridge bottom bracket tool (Park Tool—various models)
- Adjustable wrench to drive bottom bracket tool as needed
- Grease (Park Tool PPL-1) or anti-seize
- Torque wrench (Park Tool TW-2)

TOOLS & SUPPLIES

5-5 Cartridge Bottom Brackets

Cartridge bottom brackets use common industrial bearing designs, similar to bearings found in pumps, electrical motors, etc. These bearings are intended to be disposable. Generally, the bearings are used until they wear out, then they are replaced.

For most brands of bottom brackets, the entire bottom bracket unit is replaced, including the spindle. To determine if the bottom bracket is worn out or has developed play, drop the chain off the chainrings to the inside. Grab both cranks firmly at the ends but do not hold the pedals. Push laterally with one hand and pull laterally with the other hand, forcing the arms side to side. If a knocking is felt, remove cranks and double check tightness of bearing locking cups or rings, and check play again. If the cups are adequately tight and knocking continues, the bearings are worn and the bottom bracket should be replaced. Next, spin the cranks while holding the frame (5-5_Figure 1). Worn bearings will grind and this can be felt through the frame as a vibration. If in doubt, compare the feeling of an old bottom bracket to that of one of a new bike.

5-5_Figure 1

Spin cranks to feel for grinding of a worn bottom bracket bearing

Table 5-4 Bottom Bracket Tool Selection

BRAND / MODEL EXAMPLES	BOTTOM BRACKET FITTING	APPROPRIATE PARK TOOL PRODUCT	TOOL & NUMBER OF SPLINES OR NOTCHES IN BOTTOM BRACKET FITTING
Many Shimano® cartridge types, also Race Face®, FSA®			Park Tool BBT-2 20 splines
Bontrager®, Truvativ®			Park Tool BBT-8 8 notches
External bearing systems for Shimano® Hollowtech II, Race Face®, FSA®, Truvativ®			Park Tool BBT-9 16 splines
Campagnolo® Veloce, Mirage, Xenon			Park Tool BBT-4 6 notches
Campagnolo® Record, Chorus, Centaur			Park Tool BBT-5 12 splines
Adjustable type Shimano® Dura-Ace bottom brackets (BB-7700)			Park Tool BBT-7 6 notches
Lockring of various brands of adjustable bottom brackets			Park Tool HCW-5 3 or 6 notches (lockring on cup)
Adjustable bottom bracket, right side cup. Two wrench flats			Park Tool HCW-4 2 flats at 36mm
Various adjustable bottom bracket left side cups			Park Tool SPA-1 2, 4, 6 or 8 holes of 3mm diameter

Some cartridge bottom bracket cup fittings may be very shallow. It is important that the tool be held securely to the cup. If the axle is hollow, the tool may be held in place using a rear hub quick release skewer. If no holding system can be arranged, press the tool tightly to the ring or cup while turning.

Spindle length determines chainring position or chain line. Chain line affects shifting performance. Chainrings must not be too far outward or inward for good shifting performance. For more discussion on chainline see Outline Item 7-5 Chainline.

The procedure for cartridge bottom bracket removal is as follows:

a. Remove both cranks. See Outline Item 5-2 Cranks.

b. Insert bottom bracket cartridge tool fully into or onto fittings of non-drive cup (left side). Hold tool firmly in place while turning counter-clockwise to remove for ISO/BSC threaded bikes.

c. Insert tool fully into or onto fitting of drive side (right side) cup. Remove by turning clockwise for ISO/BSC threaded bikes.

5-5.1 Cartridge Bottom Bracket Removal

It is common for cartridge bottom brackets to be marked "Left" and "Right". These markings refer to side of bike, not thread direction (5-5.1_Figure 1). The drive side of the bike is the "right" side, and the non-drive side is the "left" side. For the common ISO/BCS threading, the "right" side will have left hand threading, and the "left" side will have right hand threading.

5-5.1_Figure 1

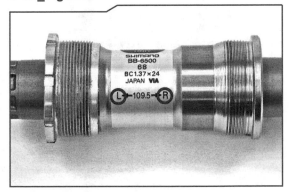

Bottom bracket marking indicating side of bike

Thread preparation is critical for the bottom bracket (5-5.1_Figure 2). There are two issues in preparation. First, the threads need lubrication to pull up fully tight. Second, the threads should be protected from corrosion. Grease will help for both issues, but anti-seize compounds are far more durable and are better at preventing corrosion. Anti-seize is especially recommended for titanium frames.

5-5.1_Figure 2

Greasing the threads of the bottom bracket

Another option is to use a service removable thread-locker. Place a bead of the thread locker around the first three or four threads on both lockrings. The thread-lock will form a seal against water. Use of a thread locker is especially recommended for the Italian threaded bottom brackets, which tend to loosen during use.

Plastic lockrings or cups need only grease on the threads. Do not use thread-lockers on plastic as they may cause the plastic to become brittle.

When threading a bottom bracket into the frame, begin turning by hand to feel and avoid cross threading. Look at opposite side of the bottom bracket shell, and keep the spindle centered in the shell. If spindle appears off center in the shell, it may be cross-threaded (5-5.1_Figure 3).

5-5.1_Figure 3

If spindle appears off center in the shell, bottom bracket may be cross-threaded

The procedure for cartridge bottom bracket installation is as follows:

a. Prepare the threads of the bottom bracket with grease, anti-seize or thread locker.

b. Look on body of cartridge for "L" and "R" marking. The "L" goes to the left side of bike, and the "R" goes to the right (drive train) side. For most bikes, right side ("R") has a left-hand thread. Thread the drive train side by turning counter-clockwise. If bottom bracket has a plastic threaded side and a metal threaded side, install the metal threaded side first.

c. Once threads are correctly aligned, thread body fully into bottom bracket shell using bottom bracket tool.

d. Install locking cup or ring into other side of shell and tighten both sides to manufacturer's torque (5-5.1_Figure 4). See Appendix C for Torque specifications.

5-5.1_Figure 4

Use a torque wrench to secure and lock bottom bracket in place

5-6 Adjustable Bottom Brackets

TOOLS & SUPPLIES
- Lockring spanner (Park Tool HCW-5. For Dura-Ace® 7700 use BBT-7)
- Left side cup spanner (Park Tool SPA-1. For Dura-Ace® 7700 use BBT-2)
- Right side cup spanner (Park Tool HCW-4. For Dura-Ace® 7700 use BBT-7)
- Grease (Park Tool PPL-1)
- Solvent (Park Tool CB-2)
- Masking tape and marker

Adjustable bottom brackets include some square spindle bottom brackets, and the Shimano® Dura-Ace 7700 bottom bracket. These bottom brackets may be dismantled and cleaned (5-6_Figure 1). Adjustable type bearing systems are sometimes referred to as "cup and cone" systems. A convex and a concave bearing race oppose one another, trapping the ball bearings trapped between them. If the adjustment is too tight there will be too much pressure on the bearing surfaces and the system will "bind" and quickly wear out. If the adjustment is too loose there will be movement or "play" between the parts. This causes a knocking in the bearing surfaces and the surfaces will wear out prematurely.

5-6_Figure 1

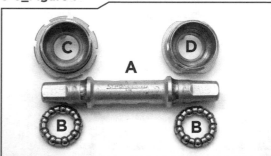

"Cup and cone" design of adjustable bottom bracket. (A) Spindle, (B) Bearings, (C) Left side cup and lockring, (D) Right side cup

For adjustable bearing systems, the bearing surfaces move on threaded parts. It is normal for threaded parts to have play between the internal and external threads. For example, a bearing cup will wiggle in the shell thread until the lockring is tightened down against the frame. Play in the thread is removed when a locking nut or ring is tightened. When checking bearing adjustments, the lockring must be tight. Play felt after the ring is tight will come from the bearing adjustment, not from thread movement.

The goal for adjustable type bearings is to have the bearings rotate as freely as possible, but not have any knocking or play. When beginning a bearing adjustment, start with it loose and then proceed to tighten the adjustment in small increments until the play disappears. This insures the adjustment is as loose as possible but is without play. In most cases, try to make small changes, in increments of $1/32$ of a complete rotation.

5-6.1
Adjustable Bottom Bracket Removal

When dismantling components, it is a good idea to take written notes of the parts orientation. For a bottom bracket spindle, one side of the spindle may be longer than the other side. Note which side was longer or shorter, and re-assemble in the same orientation.

If the bottom bracket is being overhauled, it is optional to remove the fixed side (right side) cup. Removal makes inspection and cleaning easier. The cup may remain in the frame. It will simply slow the service.

The procedure for adjustable bottom bracket disassembly is as follows:

a.   Remove cranks. See Outline Item 5-2 Cranks
b.   Using a lockring spanner, loosen and remove left side lockring.
c.   Use a pin spanner or appropriate tool and remove adjustable cup (left side) (5-6.1_Figure 1).

5-6.1_Figure 1

Remove adjustable cup (left side), lockring & bearings

d.   Remove bearings and spindle. Note and record if right side or left side of spindle seems longer.
e.   Remove dust sleeve inside bottom bracket shell, if present.
f.   Remove bearings from right side cup (inside shell).
g.   Fixed cups (right side) are commonly left hand threaded. Use a fixed cup spanner and remove clockwise, if desired.
h.   Clean all parts in solvent and dry.

> **NOTE NOTE NOTE:** The Shimano® Dura-Ace 7700 bottom bracket uses small roller bearings in the cups as well as small round ball bearings against the spindle. Both types of bearings are in plastic cages. Leave bearings in cages and clean with solvent.

After cleaning and drying all parts, inspect for wear and damage. View cups and spindle races for pitting and damage. There will likely be a smooth line worn on both cup and spindle. There should not be holes or gouges in either. Use a ballpoint pen to trace the bearing path (5-6.1_Figure 2). Roughness and wear will be felt as the ball of the pen passes over worn areas. This roughness will get worse with use. It does not "smooth out" or "break-in" with time.

5-6.1_Figure 2

Trace bearing surface to feel for roughness

If the ball bearings have a shiny silver color and are smooth, they can be re-used. If the bearings appear discolored, they should be replaced. The ball bearings are generally the last part of the system to wear out. If the bearings are worn, it is likely that the cups and races are also worn.

5-6.2
Adjustable Bottom Bracket Installation

Thread preparation is critical in bottom brackets. Use either grease or anti-seize for cups. Fixed cups (right-side) may also use mild thread-lockers rather than lubrication. The common bearing size for square spindle adjustable bottom brackets is ¼ inch.

The procedure for adjustable bottom bracket installation is as follows:

a. Prepare threads using grease or anti-seize compound. Right side (drive side) cup may use a thread locker as an option.

b. If removed, install fixed cup (right side). Even if fixed cup was not removed, check for cup tightness. For ISO/English threading, turn counter-clockwise. Secure to a minimum of 360 inch/pound.

c. Heavily grease bearing cages. Press grease into cage and between bearings.

d. Refer to notes from disassembly and place bearing retainer on fixed cup side (right side) of spindle. Place open side of cage against cone-shape of spindle. Install spindle through shell and into fixed cup.

e. Install dust sleeve, if any.

f. Grease second bearing cage and install into adjustable cup (left side). Place open side of cage toward cone-shape of spindle.

g. Thread adjustable cup (left side) into place.

h. Install but do not tighten lockring onto adjustable cup.

5-6.3
Adjustable Bottom Bracket Adjustment

Rotating bearings should be adjusted as loose a possible, but without play or knocking. To insure you are making adjustments in small increments, use a piece of tape as a reference. Use about two inches of masking tape and make pen marks on one edge every ⅛" (3mm). Stick the tape on the left side of the bottom bracket shell so the marks face outward. These will be reference marks when adjusting the bearings and represent the small increments used when turning the adjustable cup (5-6.3_Figure 1).

5-6.3_Figure 1

Use a sticker for reference marks when adjusting bearings

If bottom bracket bearing surfaces are worn out, it will not be possible to have a smooth adjustment when play disappears. Worn bottom bracket parts will need to be replaced.

The adjustment procedure below assumes the fixed cup (right side) is fully secure. If the bottom bracket was not disassembled, it is still important to test that it is secure. Remove cranks and loosen left side cup by turning counter-clockwise ½ turn. Hold spanner firmly to right side cup and check its security by tightening counter-clockwise. If cup seems tight, it is tight.

The procedure for adjusting bottom bracket bearings is as follows:

a. Re-install right crank only and tighten fully. Arm will be used as a lever to check for play in adjustment.

b. Gently tighten adjustable cup (left side) clockwise, just to the point you can feel it bump into the ball bearings.

c. Use marker and make a line on the cup face. Have a look at the reference tape and note which mark aligns with cup reference mark. It is also possible to use a mark already on the cup, such as the first letter of the manufacturer if the cup is stamped.

d. Hold the adjustable cup firmly with the correct spanner. Using the lockring spanner, tighten the lockring fully. Locking typically requires 300-360 pounds/inch.

e. Check for knocking in the spindle. Grab end of right crank arm and push left to right.

Repeat this as you rotate the crank all the way around.

f. If there is no play, adjustment may be too tight. Loosen lockring and loosen cup slightly to create play. Secure lockring and check for play.

g. If there is knocking (play), make note of which reference tape mark aligns with the cup mark. Loosen the lockring counter-clockwise. Move the adjustable cup clockwise one mark at the reference tape. Secure the lockring and check for play.

h. Repeat tightening one mark at a time until play disappears, checking for play with the right crank in different positions of rotation. When play is not felt at any rotation, adjustment is finished.

i. Use solvent to remove pen mark from cup or frame.

j. Install left side crank.

5-7
External Bearing Crankset Systems

TOOLS & SUPPLIES
- Bottom bracket tool (Park Tool BBT-9)
- Grease (Park Tool PPL-1) or anti-seize
- Hex wrenches (Park Tool-various models)
- Soft mallet (optional)

External bearing crankset systems integrate the bearings, cranks and spindle (5-7_Figure 1). Examples are Shimano® Hollowtech II, FSA® MegaExo, Race Face X-type, and Truvativ® Giga X Pipe. These systems tend to be proprietary and do not necessarily share interchangeable component parts.

5-7_Figure 1

External bearing crank set system from Race Face®

The bearings sit outside the face of the bottom bracket shell (5-7_Figure 2). These systems use non-serviceable cartridge bearings, and the entire bearing assembly is replaced when it wears out.

5-7_Figure 2

Externally mounted bottom bracket bearings

The spindle of the external bearing system crank is a permanent part of either the left or right crank, depending upon manufacturer. The other arm slides onto splines of the spindle, and is then secured. Crank installation and removal procedures vary between manufacturers.

5-7.1
Bearing Installation

The bearings of all external bearing crank systems press against the shell face. It is important that the shell surfaces are machined square to the threads and one another. Misaligned shell faces can cause the bearing cups to rock out of alignment as they seat and secure to the frame. A misaligned shell face may show up when a crank spindle appears to not be centering in one bearing after being installed through the opposite bearing. Another indication of poor shell face alignment is if the bearings do not seem to spin evenly, or if the bearings wear out prematurely.

The bearings of Shimano®, Race Face®, and FSA® use a similar design and installation procedure. The cups are designed to be spaced 75.5mm apart. Three spacers of 2.5mm are supplied to achieve this width. Front derailleurs with a built-in mounting bracket ("E-type"), are counted toward the width total. Any chain guide mount is also counted toward the width total. Spacer arrangement will vary between 68 and 73mm shell widths.

Table 5-7.1 External Bearing Crankset System Spacer Arrangement

Bottom Bracket Shell Width	Left Side Of Bike	Front Derailleur Or Chain-guide	Right Side Of Bike
68mm	One 2.5mm spacer	Clamp-on front derailleur Two 2.5mm spacers	Two 2.5mm spacers
68mm	One 2.5mm spacer	E-type front derailleur	One 2.5mm spacer plus E-type bracket
73mm	No spacers	Clamp-on front derailleur	One 2.5mm spacer
73mm	No spacers	E-type front derailleur	E-type bracket

The Truvativ® Giga X Pipe Stylo uses spacers under the bearings. For the single speed or triple crankset, use one spacer per side with a 68mm shell, and no spacers for the 73mm shell.

The external bearing system design for double chainring cranksets (road) from Shimano®, FSA®, and Truvativ® are made for 68mm bottom bracket shells. No extra spacers are required or used for these systems. Bearings simply install into the shell.

The bearing cups from Shimano®, FSA®, Truvativ® and Race Face® all use the Park Tool BBT-9 Bottom Bracket Tool. The cups have 16 notches that are engaged by the tool.

The procedure for external bearing installation is as follows:

a. Prepare threads of shell with grease, anti-seize, or a mild thread locker.

b. Install correct number of spacers as described above on cup marked with "R" (drive side). Install dust seal on cup. Thread the drive side cup counter-clockwise into right side of bike. Tighten fully,

approximately 305 to 435 inch pounds. Using the BBT-9, apply approximately 45 to 60 pounds of effort on the handle (5-7.1_Figure 1).

5-7.1_Figure 1

Tighten bearings using Park Tool BBT-9 Bottom Bracket Tool

c. Install correct spacers as needed on cup marked "L" (non-drive side). Thread cup clockwise into left side (non-drive) of bike and tighten fully as before. Cups are ready for crank installation.

There is no bearing adjustment during bearing installation. Cranks are pushed slightly against the bearing for a light pre-load as part of crank installation for all models.

5-7.2
Crank Installation and Removal of Shimano® and FSA®

The Shimano® Hollowtech II and FSA® MegaExo both use a left crank with a compression slot that is secured by two pinch bolts. These systems do not use a conventional crank puller. A threaded cap is used to bring the arm against the bearings. The cap acts as a bearing adjustment only and does not hold the arm in place.

The procedure for Shimano® Hollowtech II and FSA® MegaExo crank installation is as follows:

a. Grease spindle surface and install drive side crank and spindle from the right side through both bearings (5-7.2_Figure 1).

5-7.2_Figure 1

Install crank with spindle through both bearings

b. Place drive side crank in the 6:00 position. Hold left side arm in 12:00 position and press arm onto spindle using hand pressure.

c. Grease threads of crank cap and secure gently. Cap pushes arm to bearing. Recommended torque is only a very light 4 inch pounds. Arm should not push into bearing with force, as over tightening will cause bearings to drag and wear. FSA® MegaExo cranksets use an 8mm hex wrench for cap. Shimano Hollowtech II uses Park Tool BBT-9 or equivalent tool.

d. Grease threads of arm pinch bolts and secure. Switch between bolts repeatedly to insure both are fully tight.

The procedure for Shimano® Hollowtech II and FSA MegaExo removal is as follows:

a. Loosen fully any pinch bolts on left side crank (5-7.2_Figure 2).

5-7.2_Figure 2

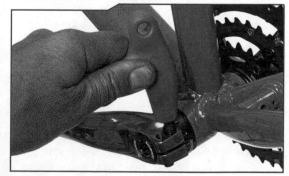

Loosen pinch bolts

b. Remove the left side crank cap counter-clockwise. Shimano® cranks use the star fitting on the Park Tool BBT-9, or equivalent tool. Cap is fitted with an eight-point socket fitting (5-7.2_Figure 3). FSA® crank caps use an 8mm hex wrench.

5-7.2_Figure 3

BBT-9 tool is used to remove crank cap

c. Pull arm off spindle by hand. In some cases it may require light tapping with a soft mallet to remove arm if spindle/arm interface is dirty or sticky.

d. Pull on drive side arm to the right. This removes spindle from bearings and the bike. It may be necessary to use a mallet to gently tap the spindle.

5-7.3
Installation and Removal of Race Face® X-type Cranks

The spindle of the Race Face® X-type crankset is fitted permanently to the left arm. There is no crank end cap for bearing adjustment. Instead, the crank uses elastomer spacers that will preload the bearings when the arm is tightened.

The alignment of the front rings to the rear sprockets, called chainline, is manipulated with two spindle spacers, each 1mm thick. Using one spacer on the left and right side of the spindle will place the middle ring of the crankset 49mm from the center plane of the bike. Using only one spacer against the left arm will move the ring inward one millimeter for a chainline of 48mm (5-7.3_Figure 1). Using two spaces on the right side will result in a 50mm chainline.

5-7.3_Figure 1

Moveable chainline spacer installed next to left crank

The procedure for Race Face® X-type crank installation is as follows:

a. Grease spindle surface.
b. Install left crank with spindle through left side of bike after installing appropriate chainline washers. The fit of the spindle may be snug and some mild force may be necessary. Use a soft mallet with care. Guide the spindle through the right cup and install any needed chainline washers. Grease internal threads of spindle and grease spindle splines. Spline system of right arm is unique to the X-type and will not interchange with other ISIS Drive® types.
c. Align right arm 180-degrees from left arm and begin to turn bolt clockwise using an 8mm hex wrench. Secure bolt to a torque of 360 to 600 inch-pounds. Bolt will come to a "hard stop" as the arm fully presses to spindle.

The Race Face® X-type right side crank has a special one-key release system. The retaining cap uses a left-hand thread and is secured to the arm with a 10mm hex wrench. It is not necessary to remove the one-key system in order to remove the arm.

The procedure for Race Face® X-type crank removal is as follows:

a. Loosen right side crank bolt with 8mm hex wrench. The one-key release system will remove arm from spindle.

b. Remove any spacers from spindle.
c. Pull left crank with spindle toward left. Use a soft mallet only if necessary to remove crank and spindle from bike.

5-7.4
Installation and Removal of Truvativ® Giga X Pipe Crankset

The spindle of the Truvativ® Giga X Pipe is permanently fixed to the drive side (right side) arm. The drive side cup has a rubber lip that compresses as the arms are pressed. As the left arm is tightened onto the spindle, it compresses into the lip to apply pressure to the bearings.

The procedure for Truvativ® Giga X Pipe crank installation is as follows:

a. Grease the splines and surface of the spindle.
b. Insert right side crank and spindle through the right side cup.
c. Install left arm and tighten to a torque of 420 to 480 inch-pounds (5-7.4_Figure 1).

5-7.4_Figure 1

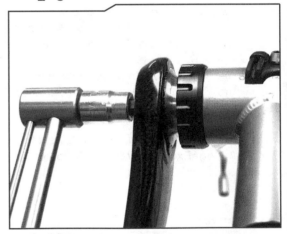

Truvativ® Giga X Pipe arm pulled to bearings

The procedure for Truvativ® Giga X Pipe crank removal is as follows:

a. Loosen the crank bolt on the left arm. The one-key release system pulls the arm from the spindle.
b. Pull the right arm and spindle from the bearing cups. If necessary, use a soft mallet with care to remove the crank and spindle from the bike.

5-8 Chainrings

Chainrings are toothed sprockets attached to the cranks. Cranks may be designed to accept one, two or three chainrings. Some models of cranks are designed so the rings are replaceable. The old ring is unbolted and removed. A new ring may be installed as it wears out, or if the rider desires a different gear ratio. There are models of cranks that use chainrings permanently mounted to the arm and the entire crankset must be replaced if the rings wear out or are damaged.

The part of the crank that attaches to the chainrings is called the "spider." The spider may have three, four, five, or six mounting arms. The chainring mounting holes must match the spider mounting holes in order to fit. As the chainrings turn, the mounting bolts trace a circle. This circle is called the "bolt circle diameter," abbreviated as BCD. New chainrings must match both the number of mounting holes and the bolt circle diameter (5-8_Figure 1).

5-8_Figure 1

Bolt circle diameter of a five-arm crankset

If there are four or six spiders on the crank, measure the bolt circle diameter directly using opposite chainring bolts. It is easier to measure edge-to-edge on the bolt, rather than center-to-center.

It is difficult to directly measure the BCD of five-arm spiders. Measure one "cord," which is one side of the five-sided pentagon created by the bolts (5-8_Figure 2). Measure from bolt to adjacent bolt. Multiply this figure by 1.70, the mathematical constant for pentagons to get the diameter, which is the BCD.

5-8_Figure 2

Measure pentagon cord by measuring bolt-to-bolt

Table 5-8 below lists the bolt-to-bolt (cord) measurements for the common BCD five bolt chainrings, as well as the common BCD's for the four arm cranks.

Table 5-8 Bolt Circle Diameter

Bolt Circle Diameter (BCD)	Cord Measurement (Five Spider Arms Only)
Four Arm Spider Cranks	
58	N/A
64	N/A
104	N/A
112	N/A
146	N/A
Five Arm Spider Cranks	
56	32.9
58	34.1
74	43.5
94	55.3
110	64.6
118	69.4
130	76.4
135	79.4

5-8.1 Chainring Replacement

TOOLS & SUPPLIES

- 5mm hex wrench (Park Tool-various models)
- T40 Torx wrench for some models of chainring bolts (Park Tool TWS-1)
- Chainring nut wrench (Park Tool CNW-1)
- Lubricant (Park Tool CL-1) or mild thread locker

Replaceable chainrings are held to the crank by special fine thread fasteners called chainring bolts. The bolt commonly uses a 5mm hex wrench. The nut is made with only a slot to hold. Use a chainring nut wrench, such as the Park Tool CNW-1, to hold the chainring nut while the bolt is turned. Chainring bolt threads should be lubricated or treated with a mild thread locker before installing and tightening.

Before removing the old chainrings, pay special attention to how they are oriented on the cranks, as there is a left and right side of the ring. Additionally, some chainrings may have specially shaped teeth and shifting ramps to help in shifting. These features require correct alignment on the crank for them to work. Inspect chainrings before removal and make a note on special ramps or markings (5-8.1_Figure 1).

5-8.1_Figure 1

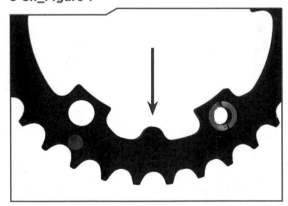

Inspect for any special marking to indicate chainring orientation relative to crank

5-8.2 Chainring Wear & Damage

The chain meshes with the chainring as it turns. The leading or forward part of the chainring tooth takes the load as the bike is ridden. With use, the tooth wears down, and eventually develops a hooked shape. The chainring teeth may also wear thin. Shifting performance will suffer and the chain may skip on the chainring when pressure is applied to the pedals. Compare old suspect rings to new ones of the same type (5-8.2_Figure 1).

5-8.2_Figure 1

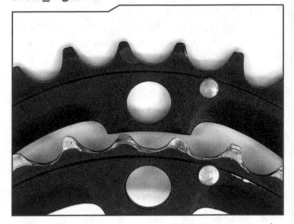

Worn middle chainring compared to new ring of same type

If a tooth is bent it may cause shifting problems. It may be possible to pry it back in line. Use a small adjustable wrench, and close the jaws on the bent tooth. Bend the tooth back slowly, checking often so as not to over correct. Severely bent teeth may break off, but even if the tooth breaks, the ring may still be usable. Ride the bike after the repair and shift back and forth testing the result. If shifting is adequate, the ring is usable.

A bent tooth on the largest ring can be directly grabbed for alignment. Bent teeth on the middle or smallest rings are difficult to access with a tool. The bent tooth will typically have been bent inward, toward the bottom bracket. It must be bent back to the outside (away from the bottom bracket). The outer ring usually prevents any tool from working on the tooth. It is possible to remove the ring with the bent tooth for alignment.

Begin by spinning the rings without the chain in place. Inspect which tooth appears bent, and mark the tooth on the ring. Remove the ring from the spider. Find the bent tooth. Use a small adjustable wrench to straighten the tooth. Do not grab on the ring itself, just the

tooth. Hold the ring firmly below the wrench and bend the tooth slightly back. Compare bent tooth to the other teeth (5-8.2_Figure 2).
It may be necessary to remount the ring and try shifting, then remove and repeat the repair.

5-8.2_Figure 2

Sight along the chainring to find any bent teeth

The ring may also become bent from impacts, from a chain getting jammed between the frame and the ring, or even from very stressful riding loads. Some emergency repair by re-bending is possible, but the ring will never be "perfect". Four-spider rings are especially susceptible to bending under hard use. It is best to replace bent rings rather then repair them.

Chapter 6
Chains

The chain connects the front chainrings to the rear sprockets. Chains are made of repeating pairs of outer plates and inner plates, held together by rivets (6_Figure 1). A roller separates the pair of inner plates. The rivet is pressed tightly through the outer plates and pivots freely on the inner plates and roller.

6_Figure 1

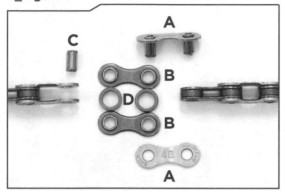

Component parts of the bicycle chain
(A) Side plates, (B) Inner plates, (C) Rivet,
(D) Rollers

Drive train manufacturers design the derailleur, rear sprockets, shifters and chain to work together as a system. Chains vary in side plate design and width. These differences will cause variations in shifting performance between brands and models. Chains should be selected to be compatible with the particular shifting system of the bicycle. Contact chain manufacturers for details on compatibility.

Chain width varies with the number of rear sprockets. Bicycles with ten rear sprockets use chains less then 7mm wide as measured across the rivet. 6, 7 and 8-speed systems use a slightly wider chain. A narrower chain can generally be used on sprockets designed for wider chains. However, a wider chain cannot be used on sprocket sets designed for narrow chains.

Chains pass through the frame to form a closed loop. They are joined together by the rivet pressing through the inner plates and into the outer plates. Chains may use a special rivet system or a "master link" to close the loop. Master links are specially made outer plates that mate together, holding the chain closed.

6-1 Chain Sizing

A chain that is too long or too short may cause shifting and riding problems. A chain that is too long will sag between derailleur and chainrings when the bike is in the smallest rear sprocket and smallest front chainring (6-1_Figure 1). The chain may have low tension in this position, but it should not sag.

6-1_Figure 1

Chain sag in the smallest front to smallest rear sprocket position

Another symptom of a chain that is too long is if the chain contacts itself as it passes by the upper derailleur pulley when the bike is in the smallest rear sprocket and smallest front chainring (6-1_Figure 2).

6-1_Figure 2

Chain contact indicating chain is too long

To determine if a chain is too short, shift to the largest chainring and second largest rear sprocket. Chain tension will be tighter in this position. Inspect chain for a double bend ("S"-bend) as it passes through the pulley wheels

(6-1_Figure 3). Shift slowly and carefully to largest rear sprocket. If chain appears to jam, it is too short. If chain does shift, but loses the double bend at the pulley wheels, it is too short (6-1_Figure 4). In extreme cases, trying to shift to the large rear sprocket and largest front chainring combination may damage the derailleur and or the derailleur hanger.

6-1_Figure 3

Double bends at pulley wheels indicate adequate chain length

6-1_Figure 4

Double bends are lost with chain too short

The rear derailleur cage takes up chain slack as the chain is moved between the various front and rear gear combinations. Some bicycles are fitted with sprocket combinations and derailleur models that do not allow the derailleur to take up the chain slack in every gear combination. The sprocket selections exceed the capacity of the derailleur.

If the derailleur capacity does not match or exceed the sprocket range on the bike, the chain length will appear either too long in the smallest sprocket to smallest chainring combination, or too short in the largest sprocket to largest

chainring combination. When using a derailleur that does not meet the gearing capacity, it will be necessary to avoid certain gear combinations that cause problems in pedaling or shifting. This is the case when a "short cage" derailleur is used on a bike with a wide gear range. For more discussion of derailleur capacity, see Outline Item 7-4.1 Derailleur Capacity & Maximum Sproket Size.

 Do not attempt to lengthen an old chain by adding new links. A new chain should be installed. Mixing newer and older chain pieces may result in chain failure.

The procedure for sizing a chain on a derailleur bike is as follows:

a. Remove the old chain. See Outline Item 6-2 Chain Cutting.

b. Using shift levers, position the front derailleur over the largest chainring and the rear derailleur on the smallest sprocket.

c. Thread the new chain through the front derailleur, but do not thread the chain through the rear derailleur. Simply wrap the chain around the largest front chainring and around the largest rear sprocket.

d. Pull the chain tight, and note the closest rivet where the two ends could be joined (6-1_Figure 5). Keep in mind a chain can only be joined by mating inner and outer plates.

6-1_Figure 5

Wrap chain around largest front and rear sprockets

e. From the closest rivet where it could be joined, count over an additional inner and outer plate. This is adding one-inch to the length. Cut the chain at this point (6-1_Figure 6). Cut the end having inner plates.

6-1_Figure 6

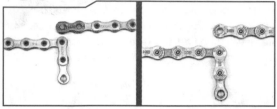

The left example has one-inch added including master link. The right example uses no master link and also has one-inch added

NOTE: If the bike will have the rear sprockets changed to various sizes, install the larger sprockets and size the chain to this sprocket set.

6-2 Chain Cutting

TOOLS & SUPPLIES
- Chain Tool (Park Tool CT-3, CT-5, or CT-6)
- Chain Lubricant (Park Tool CL-1)

Because bicycles vary in the distance from rear to front gears and in size differences between the front and rear sprockets, new chains are packaged longer than needed for most bicycles. New chains have to be "cut" (a link separated or removed) to fit each bike. Sometimes chains are removed for cleaning. To remove a chain, a link also must be separated, or cut. To install or remove a chain, a chain tool is usually required, unless the chain uses a removable master link. See Outline Item 6-2.3 Chain with Master Links.

Chain tools are made up of a driving pin and a cradle to hold the chain-roller (6-2_Figure 1). Some models have two cradles. The primary cradle supports the chain for pressing the chain rivet in and out. The tight link cradle is only for fixing a tight link.

6-2_Figure 1

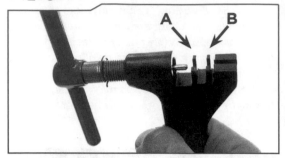

Chain tool with tight link cradle (A) and primary cradle (B)

6-2.1 Shimano® Chain Service With Replacement Rivet

Shimano® chains use a special replacement rivet when the chain is installed new or when a chain is removed and re-installed. This replacement rivet has special flaring that is guided in by a long tapered pilot (6.2.1_Figure 1). The pilot is snapped off before riding. Only Shimano® brand chains should use the Shimano® replacement rivet. The 7 and 8 speed chains use a black replacement rivet. The narrower 9-speed chain uses a silver colored replacement rivet. The Shimano® CN-7800 chain for 10-speeds uses a silver colored rivet with an extra-machined line for identification on the pilot. The Shimano® CN-7801 chain for 10-speeds uses a replacement rivet with three machined identification lines. The 10-speed chain rivets are not interchangeable.

6-2.1_Figure 1

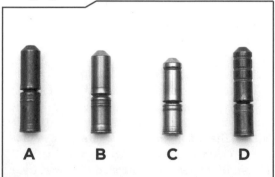

Special replacement rivets from Shimano®
(A) Rivet for 7 or 8 speed chains
(B) Rivet for 9 speed chains
(C) Rivet for CN-7800 10-speed chains
(D) Rivet for CN-7801 10-speed chains

**The procedure for removing the Shimano®
chain is as follows:**

a. Select a chain rivet that has peening marks. If
a rivet looks different from adjacent rivets, do
not select that rivet. Do not select a previously
installed replacement rivet, or a rivet
immediately adjacent to a replaceable rivet.

b. Place the roller of the chain fully in the
primary cradle of the chain tool.

c. Turn the chain tool pin until it contacts the
chain rivet and stop.

d. Note position on tool handle (6-2.1_Figure
2). For most non Park Tool brand chain
tools, turn handle 5 complete turns. Use
care not to drive out the chain rivet. For
Park Tool CT-3 Chain Tool, turn handle until
it is stopped by the C-clip. For Park Tool
CT-5 Chain Tool, turn handle until body
stops screw.

6-2.1_Figure 2

Note position of handle

e. Back out chain tool pin and lift chain out
of cradle.

f. Grab chain on either side of protruding
rivet. Flex chain toward the protruding
chain rivet then pull on chain to separate
(6-2.1_Figure 3).

6-2.1_Figure 3

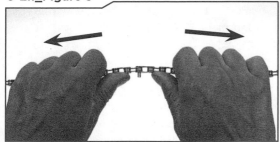

Flex chain and pull to separate

g. Remove chain from bicycle by pulling on
the rivet end.

The design of the Shimano® chain requires
that the replacement rivet leads the chain plate
as it engages the sprockets (6-2.1_Figure 4).
When installing the Shimano® chain, use the
left rivet of an outer plate when viewing the
chain between the lower derailleur pulley and
lower section of front chain wheel.

6-2.1_Figure 4

Replacement rivet correctly pressed into
leading side of outer plates

**The procedure for installing the Shimano®
chain is as follows:**

a. If reinstalling a chain on the bike, install
with protruding chain rivet facing away
from mechanic.

b. Lubricate replacement rivet.

c. Open outer plates slightly and insert inner
plates between outer plates.

d. Install correct Shimano® replacement
rivet into chain outer plate, with tapered
end first. Replacement rivet will protrude
toward mechanic and will be driven
toward bike.

e. Unthread chain tool pin into tool body to
make room for replacement chain rivet in
cradle of tool.

f. Place chain roller with rivet into primary
cradle of chain tool.

g. Drive replacement rivet into chain (6-2.1_
Figure 5). Replacement rivet will drive out
original rivet. Continue to drive chain tool
pin until it is almost adjacent to outer
side plate.

6-2.1_Figure 5

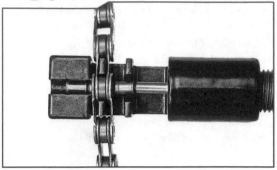

Drive new rivet into chain to remove original chain rivet

h. Remove the chain from the tool and inspect the rivet. Non-tapered end of replacement rivet should protrude same as any neighboring rivet. Press further if necessary.
i. Break off pilot of replacement rivet. Use groove of CT-3 or CT-5 Chain Tool body and twist pilot sideways (6-2.1_Figure 6). Pliers can also be used to break pilot. Inspect rivet again and press further if necessary. Rivet should be centered between outer plates.

6-2.1_Figure 6

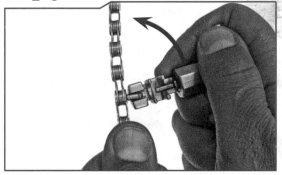

Break off pilot after replacement rivet is pressed

j. Inspect for tight links and repair as necessary. See Outline Item 6-3 Tight Link Repair.

After installing a replacement chain rivet, the rivet is left in the chain and never again removed to separate the chain. Re-using the same rivet hole wears plate holes and may weaken the chain. Use other original rivets for future chain cutting.

6-2.2 Campagnolo® 10-speed Chain

Since 2004, Campagnolo® 10-speed chains have used a special system called the HD-Link for joining chains. A new chain will be joined with only one special rivet. However, if a chain is removed from a bike, it must be joined with the HD-Link, which consists of a short section of links and two special piloted rivets. The HD-Link is 7 links of the chain. There are outer plates at each end (6-2.2_Figure 1). These ends must attach to the inner plate section of the chain. It is necessary to shorten the chain an amount equal to the short section that is installed with the HD-Link.

6-2.2_Figure 1

Campagnolo® HD-link and the two piloted rivets

The procedure for installing the Campagnolo® chain is as follows:

a. Remove old chain. Cut at section of chain opposite any special rivets.
b. If re-installing the chain, remove 7 links. Each end of the chain must have inner plates for the HD-link.
c. Lubricate pilot and rivet.
d. The rivet uses a removable pilot. Engage rivet into pilot and engage both in the chain plate facing inward, which is the plate facing the spokes. The pilot is then pushing outward, away from the spokes. The chain tool handle should be toward the mid plane of the bike, and the tool pin should drive the chain rivet away from the mid plane (6-2.2_Figure 2).

6-2.2_Figure 2

Push the Campagnolo® replacement rivet from inside the bike outward

e. When driving the rivet, it is especially important to press downward with the thumb on top of the chain to keep it fully engaged in the tool (6-2.2_Figure 3).

6-2.2_Figure 3

Hold chain roller firmly against chain tool cradle

f. After the rivet is fully pressed, remove the pilot by pulling outward. Inspect rivet for centering between outer plates.
g. Repeat process for second rivet and pilot.

6-2.3 Chain With "Master-link"

Several chain manufacturers offer a "master-link" to join the chain. Be sure to read the manufacturer's specific directions. Typically, the bicycle chain ends must have inner plates on each end before jointing. In other words, neither chain end has an outer plate with a rivet. The master link comes in two pieces. Install one piece through the inside face of the chain and install second piece through the outside of the other chain end (6-2.3_Figure 1). Engage the two pieces so link rivet mates to link plate hole. Pull chain to lock the link. To fully lock

chain, move link to top section between rear sprockets and front chainrings and press on pedals. Inspect link to insure that it is fully engaged.

6-2.3_Figure 1

Common derailleur chain master link

Some brands of master links are re-useable, while others are disposable and should be replaced after each removal. Use a chain tool on the rivet of a non-removable master link and push it through the outer plate. This will destroy the link. Install a new master link when installing the chain.

For re-useable master links, drop the chain off the front rings to relax tension. Squeeze the outer plates together. Push one plate forward and one plate backward. This will disengage the two outer plates. Pull plates sideways and remove the master link pieces from the chain (6-2.3_Figure 2).

6-2.3_Figure 2

Push plates of removable master links to disengage

6-2.4 Chain With Reusable Rivet

There are some brands and models of chains that are serviced by pressing out a rivet partially, then re-pressing the same rivet to re-install. Generally, these tend to be on the wider chains for 5, 6 or 7 cog rear sprocket sets. Check the manufacturer's literature when in doubt.

The procedure for removing chain with re-useable rivets is as follows:

a. Inspect chain for "master link." If master link is found, see Outline Item 6-2 Chain with Master link.

b. If no master link is present, place a roller of the chain fully in the primary cradle of the chain tool.

c. Drive chain tool pin until it contacts chain rivet.

d. For most non Park Tool brand chain tools, turn handle 5 complete turns. Use care not to drive out chain rivet. For Park Tool CT-3 Chain Tool, drive handle until it is stopped by C-clip. For Park Tool CT-5 Chain Tool, drive handle until body stops screw.

e. Back out chain tool pin and lift chain out of cradle.

f. Grab chain on either side of protruding rivet. Flex chain toward the protruding chain rivet and pull on chain to separate.

g. Remove from bicycle by pulling on rivet end of chain.

The procedure for installing chains with re-useable rivets is as follows:

a. Re-install chain on bike, with protruding rivet facing toward mechanic.

b. Open empty outer plates slightly and insert inner plates. Push inner plates until hole aligns with chain rivet.

c. Back the chain tool pin into tool body to make room for chain rivet.

d. Place roller into primary cradle with chain rivet facing chain tool pin.

e. Drive chain rivet back into chain, taking care to center rivet exactly between both outer plates. If more chain rivet appears on one side of outer plate than other, push rivet until it is evenly spaced (6-2.4_Figure 1).

6-2.4_Figure 1

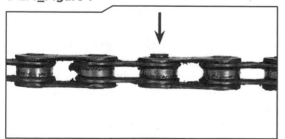

A rivet not centered between the plates

f. Inspect for tight links and repair as necessary. See Outline Item 6-4 Tight Link Repair.

6-3
New Chain Installation on Derailleur Bikes

It is necessary to weave the correctly sized or cut chain through the front derailleur, rear derailleur and frame before it is joined. It may be useful to have another derailleur bike on hand as an example of chain routing when attempting this procedure. The process described here will insure that the left outer plate on the lower section of chain will receive the Shimano® replacement rivet, if a replacement rivet is used.

The procedure for installing a sized chain on the bike is as follows:

a. Shift derailleurs to smallest front and rear sprockets.

b. Beginning at crankset, feed end of chain with inner plates between the cages of the front derailleur and back to the top of the rear sprockets (6-3_Figure 1).

6-3_Figure 1

Feed chain from front to back

c. Guide chain over the top and then behind smallest rear sprocket.

d. Pass chain in front of top derailleur pulley, and then in a straight line to the backside of the lower pulley. Be sure chain stays inside built-in guides on the cage (6-3_Figure 2).

6-3_Figure 2

Route chain through rear derailleur

e. Pull chain end toward chainrings

f. Join chain according to type or model of chain described in Outline Item 6-2 Chain Cutting. If tension makes joining chain difficult, drop chain off chainring and onto bottom bracket.

g. Test chain for tight link and repair as necessary. See Outline Item 6-4 Tight Link Repair.

6-4 Tight Link Repair

A tight link occurs when a chain does not pass smoothly through the bends of the rear derailleur. This may be from a lack of lubrication at the offending link or the result of chain installation. If the two outer chain plates are pushed tightly against the inner chain plates, the link will tend to hop and skip at the derailleur. If the pressure on the inner plates can be removed, the tight link can be fixed.

Some chain tools have a tight link repair system built into the tool. Some very narrow chains may not fit the tight link cradle. Repair these narrow chains by flexing by hand, as described below.

To locate a tight link, put the chain in the smallest rear sprocket in back and on the middle ring of a triple crankset or the smallest ring of a double crankset. This relieves tension on the chain and allows problem links to show up. Back pedal slowly and watch chain as it passes through the two pulley wheels of the rear derailleur. Look for a popping or jumping of the chain or movement in the derailleur arm. Keep backpedaling slowly. Tight links should show up as they pass by the bends of the lower pulley wheel (6-4_Figure 1).

6-4_Figure 1

Watch for jumping or hopping of chain while backpedaling

Isolate the tight link and move it to lower section of chain between chainring and rear sprockets. Engage tight rivet in tight link cradle. Turn handle until chain tool pin just touches rivet of tight link and note position of handle (6-4_Figure 2). Turn handle only ⅛ turn clockwise. Remove chain tool and feel tight link. Repeat as necessary, pushing rivet from other side of chain. Inspect chain rivet. Rivet must be centered in chain plates.

6-4_Figure 2

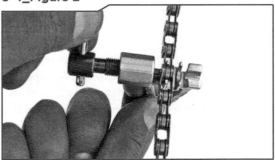

Press as little as necessary to spread outer plates of tight link

It is also possible to repair tight links without the tight link cradle system. This method requires physically stressing and flexing the chain laterally. Use care not to bend and deform the plates by using too much force. To avoid damaging your chain, practice on a section of scrap chain. Your hands are likely to get dirty from grabbing the chain. If this is a problem use a rag over the chain.

Locate the tight link as described above. Grab either side of chain with your hands, and place both thumbs at the tight rivet. Pull outward with your hands, while pressing inward with your thumbs to flex the tight link (6-4_Figure 3). Reverse pressure to flex chain the opposite direction, pressing inward with your hands and pressing outward with the index fingers centered on tight rivet. Test link to see if it moves freely and repeat if necessary.

6-4_Figure 3

Grab chain and flex laterally at tight link

6-5 Chain Wear and Damage

TOOLS & SUPPLIES
- Chain wear indicator (Park Tool CC-2 or CC-3)

The chain is a critical part of bicycle performance and safety. The common cause of chain failure is the result of a rivet being pulled from an outer plate. This is typically the result of a poorly installed chain. Inspect chains often. Sight the chain from above and look at each rivet for centering in the side plates. If a rivet sticks out of one plate more than the other links, the suspect link may fail. Use the chain tool to correct this problem. Also inspect the side plates for spreading. If a chain becomes jammed during an over shift, it may stress the plates, pulling them apart.

6-5_Figure 1

Damaged side plate. Repair of plate is not possible.

6-5_Figure 2

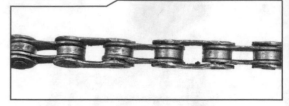

Twist in chain requires replacement

6-5_Figure 3

Rollers are showing signs of wear

As the chain is used, wear develops at the rivet and inner plates where it pivots. This wear or "play" is at each link. The cumulative effect of wear in many links is that the chain appears to "stretch." However, chain plates do not literally stretch and get longer, the wear is in the joint and rivet. Reversing the chain or flipping the chain around will not add to chain life, as the rivets will still have the same amount of wear.

Bicycle sprocket teeth are cut to fit chains with one-half inch between each rivet. However, even brand new bicycle chains are not exactly one-half inch between rivets, as a small amount of play must be included for new chains to bend. As the chain is ridden and it wears, play at each link gets greater and the distance between each rivet increases. Eventually, the chain rollers will no longer sit fully down in the sprocket teeth. The rollers will begin to ride up the side of the sprocket teeth. The chain will then skip over the teeth, especially when extra force is applied to the pedals. Although chain manufacturers vary, most recommend chain replacement when the chain reaches 1% wear from the nominal ½ inch pitch. This wear can be measured with chain measuring tools such as the Park Tool CC-2 or CC-3 Chain Wear Indicators (6-5_Figure 4).

6-5_Figure 4

The Park Tool CC-3 Chain Checker wear indicators shows when to replace the chain

As the bike is ridden, the entire drive train will wear. Generally it is most economical to replace the cheapest item first, in order to extend the overall life of the drive train. The cheapest component of the chainrings, chain, and rear sprockets is the chain, and it also takes the most wear. If a new chain skips over worn rear sprockets or front sprockets, they must also be replaced.

6-6 Chain Cleaning

TOOLS & SUPPLIES
- Brush (Park Tool GSC-1)
- Chain Cleaner (Park Tool CM-5)
- Solvent (Park Tool CB-2)
- Chain Lubrication (Park Tool CL-1)
- Rags

There are more moving parts in the chain than any other part on the bike. Dirt and grit in the chain will wear on the rivets. Cleaning will add life to the chain and improve performance. Before cleaning the chain, brush clean the derailleur pulley wheels. It may be necessary to scrape the sides with a screwdriver if extremely dirty. Scrape rear sprockets with gear comb, such as the Park Tool GSC-1, or the blade of a thin screwdriver. Also wipe chainrings, if they are extremely dirty, before cleaning the chain.

Chain cleaning tools, such as the Park Tool CM-5 Cyclone Chain Scrubber, make cleaning the chain easier. Generally, these systems are boxes that hold solvent and brushes. The chain is cleaned by passing through the brushes and solvent. Follow manufacturer's directions for use. Expect some spray of dirt and solvent when using any chain cleaner. Using a diluted soap solution for a second

scrub will also help the cleaning process. To protect the floor, place newspaper or a drop cloth under the bike. Used as part of a regular cleaning schedule, these systems can add to the life of the chain. (6-6_Figure 1).

6-6_Figure 1

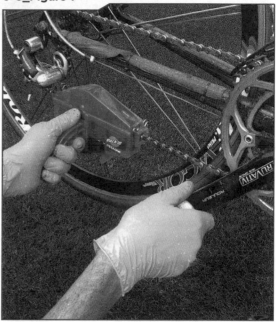

A chain cleaning system speeds chain cleaning

Chains can also be removed and cleaned off the bike. Use a pan or large can. Remove the chain, grab by one end and fold once in the middle. Lay the chain on a flat surface and coil the chain with loose ends in middle. Place chain in the pan and cover with solvent. Allow it to soak for some time. Use rubber gloves to protect the hands and work with adequate ventilation. Use a stiff bristle brush and scrub the plates on both sides of the chain. Unfold the chain and scrub downward on rollers and between side plates. Flip chain and scrub other side the same way. Rinse chain in solvent. Remove it from solvent and allow solvent to drip off as much as possible. Wipe with rag and allow to completely dry before lubricating. If available use compressed air to blow-dry the chain, especially between rollers. Wear safety glasses when using compressed air to blow dry the chain.

Dispose of old solvent properly. Contact your local hazardous waste disposal site, typically with the state or a county agency.

6-7 Chain Lubrication

TOOLS & SUPPLIES
- Chain lubricant (Park Tool CL-1)
- Rags

Chain rivets and link pivots require lubrication. The chain rivet and the narrower pair of chain plates rotate when traveling around a sprocket. Lubrication is required only at the rivet, not all over the outer plates. A drip applicator helps avoid applying too much lubrication, which can attract dirt. Proper lubrication will take time and patience. While lubricating, inspect the chain rollers and rivets.

It is best of course to begin with a clean chain. In any case, wipe chain off with a rag. Inspect chain for a master link or replacement rivet to act as a reference. Apply a drop of lubricant on each roller and at each side plate at the rivet (6-7_Figure 1). Lubricate each rivet between rear sprockets and front chainring. Turn pedals backwards to advance to the next section of un-lubricated chain. Lubricate this section and again advance chain. Continue until each rivet is lubricated once. Avoid over lubricating the chain.

6-7_Figure 1

Lubricate and inspect chain in the same procedure

After lubricating, turn pedals repeatedly to allow lubricant to work into pivots. Wipe outside of chain with a rag to remove excess lubricant. Repeat when chain appears dry.

Chapter 7

Derailleur Systems

Derailleur bicycles have several sprockets on the rear hub and multiple chainrings on the front cranks. By using different combinations, the cyclist will find low gears for going up hill and high gears for going down hill. The derailleur pushes, or "derails" the chain and moves it from one sprocket to another. The derailleur system consists of the shift levers, cable housing, derailleur cable, and either one or two derailleurs. The entire system requires maintenance and adjustment.

Some manufacturers have reference numbers on shift levers. These are arbitrary numbers and do not represent gear ratio order. For example, the number "6" showing on a lever does not mean the sixth gear out of the total number of ratios available. There is no agreement between manufacturers on these reference numbers and they will not be used here. This chapter will use the terms "inner" and "outer" sprockets, as well as "smallest and largest" sprocket.

> **NOTE:** For information on internal transmission hub systems, such as Shimano® Inter 7 and SRAM® Dual Drive, see Repair Help at www.parktool.com

7-1 Cable System

TOOLS & SUPPLIES
- Cable Cutter (Park Tool CN-10)
- Derailleur cable end caps
- Seal pick or pin
- Lubricant (Park Tool CL-1)

The connection between the shift lever and the derailleur is the cable system. The cable system consists of a derailleur cable and outer derailleur housing. The housing is the outer casing that routes the derailleur cable from the shift lever to the derailleur. Motion of the derailleur cable causes the derailleur to move. Dirty, rusty or worn derailleur cables and derailleur housing will not consistently and effectively transfer shift lever motion to the derailleur.

Derailleur cable systems generally use "compressionless" derailleur housing. Compressionless housing is stiffer than brake housing and offers better shifting performance. The derailleur cable runs inside a plastic liner,

which is surrounded by support wires that run longitudinally with the cable (7-1_Figure 1). Housing end caps must be used with all derailleur housing.

7-1_Figure 1

Compressionless derailleur housing with outer plastic cover cut away showing support wires inside

"Braided" or "woven" housing may be used for both brake and derailleur housing (7-1_Figure 2). The outer support wires are woven in a mesh around the liner.

7-1_Figure 2

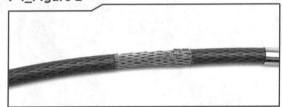

Braided housing useable for shift or brake housing

A third type of housing, called "articulated," uses small metal segments strung together over a liner (7-1_Figure 3). There is very little flex with the articulated housing.

7-1_Figure 3

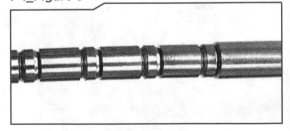

Articulated housing

Derailleur housing should be cut with bicycle cable cutters. The cutting jaws surround the cut and shear the multiple strands of compressionless housing, woven housing, brake cable and derailleur cable. Hold housing close to and square with the jaws and squeeze handle (7-1_Figure 4). Cutting may slightly deform the housing end. Use the reforming jaws section of the Park Tool CN-10 Professional Cable and Housing Cutter and gently re-shape the housing (7-1_Figure 5). If the housing liner is pinched closed, open liner with a sharp pointed object, such as a seal pick or safety pin.

7-1_Figure 4

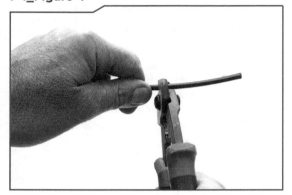

Hold compressionless housing square to jaws of cable cutter

7-1_Figure 5

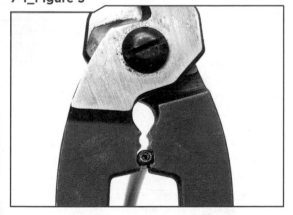

Re-shape compressionless housing after cutting

Derailleur cables are typically 1.1mm to 1.2mm in diameter, with a small cylindrical head on one end about 4mm ($5/32$") in diameter (7-1 Figure 6). The cable head will sit in a socket or carrier in the shift lever. The lever moves the carrier or socket, which pulls on the cable. High quality derailleur cables have a smooth outer finish to reduce drag in the derailleur housing. Some brands of derailleur cable are coated to help

reduce drag and friction. A derailleur cable should never be used as a brake cable.

7-1_Figure 6

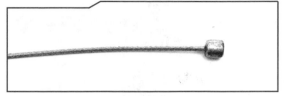

Derailleur cable with head

If the derailleur cable is cut anywhere between the lever and the cable pinch bolt, it should be replaced. Even the failure of a single strand of cable will eventually lead to breakage of the cable (7-1_Figure 7).

7-1_Figure 7

Inspect and replace cables with broken wires

7-1.1 Housing Lengths

Correct derailleur housing length will help insure that the bike shifts well. Generally, derailleur housing should be as short as possible, yet still approach the derailleur housing stops in the frame, adjusting barrel, shift lever and derailleur in a straight line. If the housing is too long, it will add friction because the derailleur cable passes through more housing and the housing makes excessive bends. If the housing is too short, it will mean excessive friction because the housing and end caps are kinked.

Examples of housing lengths at the rear derailleur are seen in the images below. Housing that is short will bend the housing end cap as it sits in the barrel adjuster (7-1.1 Figure 1). Housing that is too short will bend as it enters the barrel adjuster. Longer housing, in this situation, will enter the derailleur in a straight line, which will not bend the end cap (7-1.1_Figure 2).

7-1.1_Figure 1

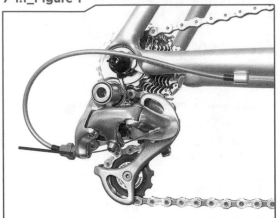

Housing does not enter the barrel adjuster in a straight line, indicating housing is too short.

7-1.1_Figure 2

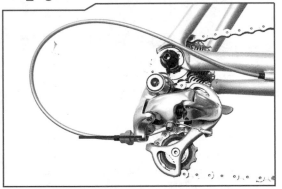

Housing enters derailleur adjusting barrel without a severe bend

On some bicycles, the front housing loops from the shift levers to the frame may be purposely switched from left to right sides. The left shifter housing is passed to the right side stop and vice versa. This is called "crossing-over" (7-1.1_Figure 3). The derailleur cable and housing must cross back over in order to arrive at the corresponding derailleur. Crossing-over reduces bends in the housing, creates a straighter line for the housing, and helps eliminate housing rub on the frame. However, crossing-over will not work well on all bikes. If the derailleur cables ends up rubbing on the frame, such as the down tube, or if there are severe bends down the system, do not cross over. It is acceptable for the derailleur cables to touch when crossing back.

7-1.1_Figure 3

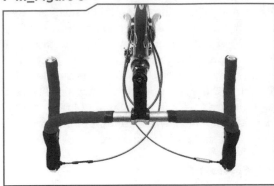

Crossing-over on a road bike

7-1.2 Cable Lubrication

If the cable system becomes dirty and rusty with exposure to water and mud, the derailleur cable will not move easily and shifting will be difficult. The derailleur cables can often be wiped clean and re-lubricated without taking them off the bike.

The procedure for re-lubrication of the cable system is as follows:

a.   Shift the rear derailleur to the sprocket with the tightest derailleur cable tension while turning the cranks. Stop pedaling the bike.

b.   Release derailleur cable tension by shifting the lever as if shifting to the other extreme sprocket. This slackens the cable.

c.   Push the derailleur body to further release tension on the derailleur cable.

d.   Pull housing ends from guides and stops (7-1.2_Figure 1). Wipe derailleur cable clean and apply light lubricant. If wiping does not remove rust, derailleur cable should be replaced.

e.   Push derailleur again to release tension in order to get housing back into the stops. Pedal the bike to shift the derailleur.

f.   Double check that housing is fully back into all stops.

NOTE NOTE NOTE **NOTE:** If the cable system uses a plastic liner from the shift lever to derailleur, no extra lubrication is required. "Gore-Tex®" type systems recommend no lubrication. These systems run housing from lever to derailleur. Do not remove cable system from stops. Simply inspect for rips in liner, especially at end caps. Replace as necessary.

7-1.2_Figure 1

Remove housing from stop to clean and lubricate cable

Some bicycle designs route the housing internally, through the frame tubing. Better designs use an inner guide to route the derailleur cable and/or housing in and out of the frame. If there is no guide inside, it can be difficult to get the housing through. Feed the housing through one end and then use a wire, such as a spoke, to help catch and guide the housing out the frame hole at the other end. To replace housing that is already in place, feed a derailleur cable into the back end of the housing and out the front. Pull the housing from the frame, leaving the derailleur cable in place to act as a guide when installing the new piece. Feed the derailleur cable into the new housing and push the new housing along the cable into the frame.

7-2 Shift Levers

TOOLS & SUPPLIES
- Hex wrenches (Park Tool-various models)
- Screwdriver for some models

The derailleur cable head will sit in a socket or carrier in the shift lever. The shift lever moves the carrier or socket, which pulls on the cable. Indexing shift levers use "clicks" or stops at pre-determined positions. Some bicycles use a "friction" system, where the lever has no pre-set stop, and the cyclist must listen and feel when the derailleur has reached the appropriate sprocket.

Some models of front derailleur shifters allow for "half" clicks, which allow the front derailleur to be "trimmed." This slight movement of the cage is used to prevent rubbing when the chain moves left to right on the rear sprocket combinations.

7-2.1 Flat Bar Trigger Shifters

Shimano®, Campagnolo®, and SRAM produce trigger shifters for flat handlebars. The Shimano® Rapidfire shift levers for flat bar bikes (mountain bikes, hybrid, etc.) are available as a brake/shifter set or as a shifter alone, without brake lever. The SRAM® trigger shifter is available as a shifter only (7-2.1_ Figure 1). If the lever is integrated with the brake (Rapidfire® or dual control), alignment preference should be given to the brake lever. Set levers at approximately a 45-degree downward slope from horizontal. The brake lever can be rotated by loosening the brake lever mounting bolt (7-2.1 Figure 2).

7-2.1_Figure 1

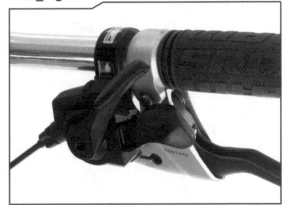

SRAM® trigger shifter

7-2.1_Figure 2

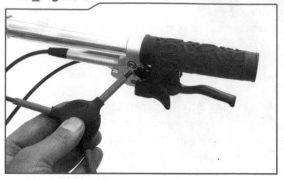

Align integrated shift lever for comfortable reach using the mounting bolt

Trigger shifter derailleur cable installation will vary with model and generation of lever. Inspect shifter for a plastic screw sealing the derailleur cable hole. Remove screw to access cable (7-2.1_Figure 3). Shift lever to the most relaxed derailleur cable position. Detach derailleur cable from derailleur.

7-2.1_Figure 3

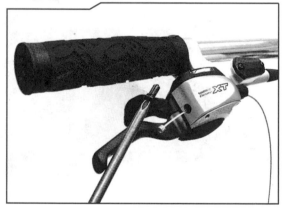

Install derailleur cable after removing cover

Some models may have a cover on the lever body that must be removed to see the derailleur cable attachment. There are both pry-out type covers and threaded type covers. For models using a threaded type cover plate, use a #1 Phillips tipped screwdriver to remove the two screws in the plate. It is helpful to rotate the bike upside down so the screw heads are pointing upward The screws are quite small, so use care when removing.. Remove cover. Shift the lever to the most relaxed derailleur cable position and install derailleur cable end in cable head carrier. The derailleur cable end is held in a

fitting that allows easy removal. There is a slot in the adjusting barrel and the body. Rotate the adjusting barrel so the slots align, and lift the derailleur cable outward. Install new derailleur cable into fitting and into adjusting barrel. Install cover plate and screws. Tighten screws until snug, but do not over tighten.

7-2.2 Twist-Grip Shifters

Twist-grip shifters mount to flat handlebars. The levers can be rotated around the handlebars. Levers mount to the handlebar between the brake levers and the grips. Check that shifters do not interfere with brake levers when brake levers are squeezed fully closed. Rotate shifter body so housing follows a smooth line to the frame stop. Look for a setscrew that locks the lever to the handlebars (7-2.2_Figure 1).

7-2.2_Figure 1

SRAM® Twist-grip shifter and location of setscrew

There have been different generations of twist-grip shift levers and installation of the derailleur cable can vary. A common style has an access hole with a plastic or rubber cover. Shift the lever to the most relaxed derailleur cable position and remove the cover. Detach the derailleur cable from the derailleur and then push the derailleur cable toward the lever. Some models may have a small setscrew over the derailleur cable end. Use a hex wrench to remove this screw. Other models use a small clip to hold the derailleur cable end. Use a small screwdriver to pry back the clip and then push the cable to remove it from the lever (7-2.2 Figure 2).

7-2.2_Figure 2

Use screwdriver to access cable

7-2.3 Above-The-Bar Shifters

The above-the-bar shifters are designed for flat handlebars. Placement should be close to the grip, and the body of the shifter should point downward at a slight angle (7-2.3 Figure 1).

7-2.3_Figure 1

Above-the-bar shift lever

Derailleur cable installation is relatively simple. The derailleur cable is fed through a hole in the shift lever and then through the housing.

7-2.4
Drop Bar Integral Brake & Gear Shifters

Shimano® STI and Campagnolo® Ergo drop bar levers combine shifting and braking into the same lever system. Brake lever placement will determine how the shift levers are aligned (7-2.4 Figure 1). For more on brake lever placement see Outline Item 8-1 Bar Levers.

7-2.4_Figure 1

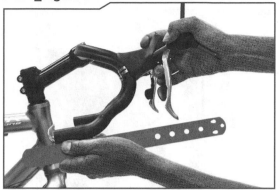

Align brake levers relative to handlebar drop

The derailleur cable end attaches to the shift lever by fitting through a small socket. The cable anchor pivot is sometimes difficult to see. Begin by shifting the smaller lever repeatedly. This places the socket in the most relaxed cable tension position.

For Shimano® shifters, feed the cut end of the cable through the socket, and pull it fully through until the head engages inside the socket (7-2.4_Figure 2).

7-2.4_Figure 2

Feed derailleur cable into the socket at top of lever

For Campagnolo® Ergo levers, begin by shifting the smaller lever repeatedly. Pull the rubber lever hood back to expose the cable anchor. Feed derailleur cable upward through anchor and out the top of the lever (7-2.4_Figure 3).

Housing and end cap enter lever from the top, and follow underneath the handlebar tape.

7-2.4_Figure 3

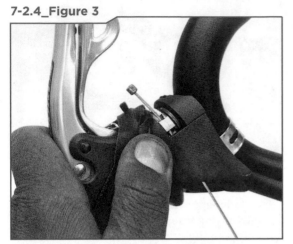

For Campagnolo® Ergo shifters, look under rubber hood when installing new derailleur cable

7-2.5 Down Tube Shifters

The shift fittings may be mounted on the down tube for some road bikes (7-2.5_Figure 1). The frame will have a fitting for the levers and there is no positioning adjustment for these levers.

7-2.5_Figure 1

Typical down tube shifters

Derailleur cable installation is relatively simple. The derailleur cable is fed through a hole in the lever and down below the bottom bracket to the appropriate derailleur.

7-2.6 Bar End Shifters

Bar end shifters are fitted into the ends of drop style handlebars, or to the end of "aero" handlebars. These levers secure inside the ends of the bars in place of end caps (7-2.6_Figure 1). The derailleur housing is then routed along the handlebar underneath the bar tape. Bar end shifters allow the rider to shift when on the lower part of the bars and without taking the hands from the bars. The derailleur cable is fed through a hole in the lever and through the housing.

7-2.6_Figure 1

Bar end shifter

7-3 Front Derailleur

TOOLS & SUPPLIES
- Hex wrenches (Park Tool—various models)
- Screwdriver
- Forth hand tool (Park Tool BT-2)

The front derailleur shoves the chain off one chainring and onto another. The derailleur uses a cage that surrounds the chain, and the cage is pulled in one direction by the derailleur cable. A spring in the derailleur returns the cage when the derailleur cable is relaxed. A properly adjusted front derailleur should shift the chain between the front chainrings but will not throw the chain off the chainrings. The basic adjustments for the front derailleur are the height, rotation, limit screw settings, and derailleur cable tension (index setting).

The common front derailleur secures to the seat tube with a clamp. The derailleur clamp must be compatible with the seat tube diameter. Clamp sizes are available in 28.6mm, 31.8mm, and 35mm diameters. Some clamp models are designed to use shims that will accommodate all of the common size tubes.

The Shimano® "E-plate" front derailleur models do not have height or rotation adjustments. These models mount on a plate and both height and rotation settings are pre-set.

Another front derailleur mounting system is commonly referred to as a "braze-on." A bracket is mounted to the seat tube and allows limited height and rotational settings.

Derailleur design will vary with the crankset type used. The common mountain bike triple crankset has a wide spread of chainring sizes and uses a cage with a relatively wide inner plate. The derailleur is called a "deep cage." Road bikes tend to have two front chainrings that do not require a wide plate, called a "shallow cage" derailleur (7-3_Figure 1). Consult a professional mechanic for the correct design for your bike.

placement of the parallelogram in relation to the derailleur clamp.

The top swing attaches with the parallelogram swinging above the clamp (7-3_Figure 3 and 7-3_Figure 5). The top swing derailleur clamp will end up lower on the seat tube as compared to a bottom swing derailleur. Some bike frames will only allow the mounting of a top swing derailleur, because there will be water bottle fitting or suspension fittings on the seat tube.

The "bottom swing" derailleur is designed so the parallelogram attaches and swings below the clamp (7-3_Figure 2 and 7-3_Figure 4). The clamp will end up higher on the seat tube as compared to a "top swing" derailleur.

The derailleur cable pulls the linkage of the front derailleur. The cable may come from the bottom bracket. These models are described as "bottom pull," as it is pulled from the bottom (7-3_Figure 4 and 7-3_Figure 5). If the cable comes down the seat tube, it is referred to as a "top pull" (7-3_Figure 2 and 7-3_Figure 3).

7-3_Figure 1

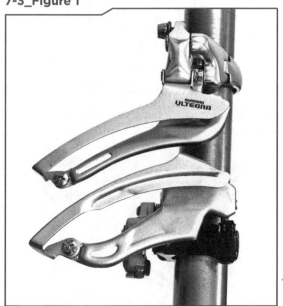

The shallow cage derailleur cage on top and the deep cage below

7-3_Figure 2

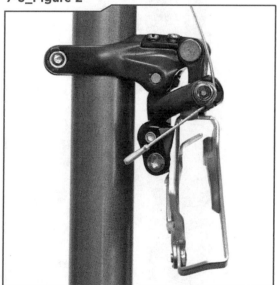

Top pull- bottom swing

Front derailleur cage is moved by a parallelogram. This linkage system allows the cage to move parallel to the chainring as it moves laterally. There are two basic linkage designs, the "top swing" and the "bottom swing". The top swing and bottom swing derailleurs differ in

7-3_Figure 3

Top pull-top swing

7-3_Figure 4

Bottom pull-bottom swing

7-3_Figure 5

Bottom pull-top swing

7-3.1 Derailleur Cable Attachment

The derailleur cable attaches to the front derailleur at the pinch bolt mechanism. Unthread the bolt and look for a groove in either the plate or derailleur arm. The derailleur cable will lay in this depression or notch (7-3.1 Figure 1). Inspect the groove and keep the derailleur cable in line with it. There may also be a tab system. The tab is used to prevent the washer from rotating. The derailleur cable is not usually routed around the tab.

While the bolt is loose, lubricate the threads. Pull the derailleur cable snug and secure the bolt. The typical torque for the pinch bolt is approximately 35 inch pounds. The derailleur cable will be flattened where it is pinched.

7-3.1_Figure 1

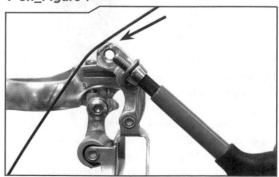

Derailleur cable is routed to pass through groove

7-3.2 Height Adjustment

If the derailleur cage is too far above the large chainring, it is will shift poorly. If the derailleur is too low, it may scrape against the chainrings and jam the chain when shifting. Height can be set with or without attaching the derailleur cable.

The procedure for setting front derailleur height is as follows:

a. Pull front derailleur cage plate until it is directly over outer chainring teeth. Use either the cable, or pull directly on the cage.

b. The gap between the teeth of the outer chainring and the lower edge of the outer cage plate should be 1-2mm, about the thickness of a US penny. Using the penny as a feeler gauge, fit it between the chainring teeth and the cage plate. It should just fit (7-3.2 Figure 1).

7-3.2_Figure 1

Set height for 1-2 millimeters at the closest point

c. To lower cage, release derailleur cable tension completely by shifting to innermost chainring.

d. Note angle of outer cage plate relative to the chainring.

e. Front derailleur clamps typically leave a mark on the frame, which is useful as a reference when changing height. Loosen the derailleur clamp bolt, change derailleur height, and return the cage to its original rotation relative to the chainring. Tighten clamp bolt. Move outer cage plate over outer chainring and check height again.

f. Repeat process until cage plate height is 1-2mm above outer chainring. Double check that the inner cage of the front derailleur clears the middle chainring. For triple chainring bikes, inspect that the inner derailleur cage plate is not striking the middle ring. It may be necessary to raise the derailleur slightly.

If the derailleur cannot be set to an acceptable height, it may be incompatible with the front chainring sizing.

7-3.3 Rotational Angle Adjustment

The front derailleur cage should be parallel to the chain. If the derailleur cage is rotated too far from this position, it will shift poorly. The chain angle moves, however, when the rear derailleur is shifted left and right. Use the outer most (smallest) rear sprocket when checking the cage rotation. Rotation of the braze-on mount or clamp mount derailleurs can be changed. There is no rotation option for the E-plate mounted derailleurs. The derailleur cable should be attached while inspecting rotation.

The procedure for setting front derailleur rotation is as follows:

a. Shift chain to outermost chainring and outermost rear sprocket.

b. Sight chain from directly above chainrings. Consider the chain as representing a straight line. Compare this line to the outer derailleur cage plate. Outer cage plate and chain should be parallel (7-3.3 Figure 1). Keeping the cage and chain parallel will minimize the risk of the chain jumping off the outermost chainring. If the cage is not parallel, there will be a relatively large gap at either the back or the front end of the cage, and the chain may overshift (7-3.3 Figures 2 and 3).

7-3.3_Figure 1

Acceptable cage rotation

7-3.3_Figure 2

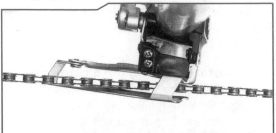

Misaligned cage, rotated too much clockwise. Notice end of cage is inward, toward the bike mid plane.

7-3.3_Figure 3

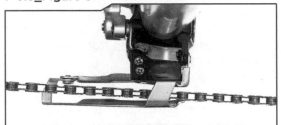

Misaligned cage, rotated too far counter-clockwise. Notice end of cage is outward relative to chain.

c.   If the derailleur cage must be rotated, note direction of desired rotation.

d.   Release derailleur cable tension by shifting to the innermost chainring.

e.   Many clamps leave a slight marking on the frame. Use a pencil to make two reference marks on the frame, one for height and a second, vertical mark, to reference rotation. Use the marks to avoid inadvertently changing height.

f.   Loosen clamp bolt and slightly rotate in correct direction. Use care not to change height. Tighten clamp bolt.

g.   Shift to outer chainring and observe rotation alignment.

h.   Repeat adjustment if necessary.

Although the above procedure usually creates the best alignment, there are situations where the back end of the cage is best rotated inward or outward. A derailleur that seems too slow when shifting inward, even after proper limit screws are set, may benefit from having the cage rotated clockwise slightly, as viewed from above the derailleur. This moves the back end

of the cage closer to the chain. In some cases, this can more effectively push the chain inward to the next sprocket. Double check all limit screw settings after any changes to rotation.

7-3.4 Limit Screw Adjustment

Limit screws stop the inward and outward travel of the front derailleur cage. Limit screws are marked "L" and "H." The L-limit screw will stop the inward motion of the derailleur toward the smallest chainring. The H-limit screw will stop the outward motion of the derailleur toward the largest chainring. The screws use a nylock fitting to prevent them from moving after adjustment. If the screws seem to move too easily, remove the screw and apply a mild thread locker.

L-limit screw

Although the limit screws stop the derailleur, it is the derailleur cable and derailleur spring that make the derailleur move. If the derailleur cable has too much tension, the derailleur will not rest on the L-limit screw stop. If the derailleur cable tension were to change, the derailleur inner limit would also change, possibly causing the chain to fall off the chainrings.

The procedure for adjusting the L-limit screw is as follows:

a.   Shift chain to innermost rear sprocket and innermost front chainring. Inspect derailleur for mark indicating "L" screw.

b.   Check derailleur cable tension. It should be fairly loose at this time. If derailleur cable is taut, turn barrel adjuster clockwise into lever. The barrel adjuster is typically located where the cable housing enters the shift lever. If barrel adjuster is already fully turned into the housing, loosen the derailleur cable pinch bolt, slacken the derailleur cable and retighten the bolt.

c.   Sight gap between the chain and inner cage plate. Only a small gap should be visible, about $1/16$" or 1mm, or about the thickness of a dime (7-3.4 Figure 1).

7-3.4_Figure 1

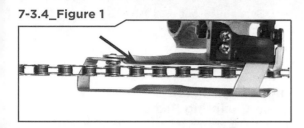

Sight gap from chain to inner cage plate

d. Pedal bike slowly and continue to sight gap. Set clearance at tightest point in chainring rotation. Adjust L-limit screw so there is a small gap between the inner cage and chain. Pedal the bike and check that chain is not rubbing cage as chainrings and chain turn.
1. If there is no gap and chain is rubbing cage, loosen L-limit screw ⅛ turn (counter-clockwise). Inspect for gap again and repeat until slight gap appears.
2. If the gap appears larger than 1mm at its widest point, tighten the L-limit screw, in small increments, until the gap closes.

e. Test the shift by shifting chain to next chainring then shift back to the innermost chainring. If chain shifts quickly, limit screw setting is adequate.

f. If the shift is slow (requires more than one pedal revolution to initiate shift), turn L-limit screw counter-clockwise ⅛ turn and repeat test. Repeat ⅛ turn increments until shifting is adequate. The gap will open wider than the 1mm target, but will still be as small as possible with adequate shifting.

g. If chain is shifting beyond the inner chainring and falls off the chainring, the gap may be too large or cage alignment may be off. Tighten L-limit screw ⅛ turn and check shift again. If chain ends up rubbing inner cage of derailleur, yet still drops off inner chainring when shifting, other problems such as chainline or derailleur rotation exist.

H-limit screw

The outward travel of the front derailleur is stopped by the H-limit screw. When viewing the H-limit screw adjustment, make sure there is enough tension on the derailleur cable by either keeping extra pressure on the lever, or by pulling the exposed derailleur cable taut by hand. Use a rag to protect your hand if pulling the derailleur cable.

The procedure for adjusting the H-limit screw is as follows:
a. Shift to outermost sprocket in rear and outermost front chainring. Inspect derailleur for mark indicating H-limit screw.
b. Pull derailleur cable with hand to increase tension to insure derailleur is against H-limit screw (7-3.4 Figure 2).

7-3.4_Figure 2

Pull derailleur cable tight to force derailleur cage to limit screw

c. Check gap between chain and outer cage plate. Only a small gap should be visible, about ¹⁄₁₆" or 1mm. Pedal bike slowly and continue to sight gap. Set clearance at tightest point in chainring rotation (7-3.4_ Figure 3).

7-3.4_Figure 3

View gap at closest point

d. If chain is rubbing cage, loosen H-limit screw ⅛ turn and pull on derailleur cable. Check gap again.

e. If chain is not rubbing, tighten H-limit screw repeatedly until chain does rub cage then loosen H-limit screw ⅛ turn and check again.

f. Test shift to the large chainring. Shift derailleur from next to largest to largest chainring using hand pressure on derailleur cable rather than shift lever. If shifting is slow, loosen H-limit screw ⅛ turn and repeat test. If chain shifts off the outside of the large chainring, the outer-limit is set too loose. Tighten H-limit screw limit and test shift again.

g. If chain ends up rubbing outer cage of derailleur, yet still drops off outer chainring when shifting, other problems such as chainline or derailleur rotation exist.

7-3.5
Index Adjustment
(Three Chainring Bikes)

The front derailleur system may have an index setting. If the shift lever has three distinctive stops or clicks, it is indexing. If the front shift lever is a friction type, there is no index setting. If the front shift lever has multiple clicks, such as some twist grip style shifters, it is shifted similar to friction levers. Set indexing only after completing limit screw setting. See Outline Item 7-3.4 Limit Screw Adjustments.

The procedure for adjusting the index shifting on three chainring cranksets is as follows:

a. Shift chain to middle chainring in the front and innermost rear sprocket.

b. View gap between inner cage plate and chain. Gap should be as small as possible without rubbing chain. To reduce gap, increase derailleur cable tension by turning barrel adjuster counter-clockwise. Check gap again.

c. If chain is rubbing cage, turn barrel adjuster clockwise.

d. If barrel adjuster is all the way in or out and no adjustment is possible, reset derailleur cable tension. Shift to innermost chainring and loosen derailleur cable pinch bolt. Pull derailleur cable with a fourth-hand tool and tighten pinch bolt. Begin adjustment of derailleur cable tension from "a."

e. Test shift front derailleur to all three front chainrings.

7-3.6
Index Adjustment
(Two Chainring Bikes)

If the shift lever has distinctive stops or clicks, it is indexing. If the front shift lever is friction, there is no index setting. Set the indexing only after checking and setting the limit screws. (Outline Item 7-3.4 Limit Screw Adjustments) If there is rubbing of the largest cage it will be the result of derailleur cable tension. Loosening limit screws will not move the cage.

The procedure for adjusting index shifting on two chainring cranksets is as follows:

a. Shift chain to outer chainring in the front and outermost rear sprocket.

b. View gap between outer cage plate and chain.

c. If outer cage plate clears the chain, index setting is adequate.

d. If plate is rubbing chain, increase derailleur cable tension by turning adjusting barrel counter-clockwise and check again.

e. If barrel adjuster is all the way in or out and no adjustment is possible, reset derailleur cable tension. Shift to innermost chainring and loosen derailleur cable pinch bolt. Pull the derailleur cable with a fourth hand tool and tighten pinch bolt. Begin adjustment of derailleur cable tension as in step "a."

f. Test shift front derailleur between front chainrings.

7-3.7 Front Derailleur Performance

There are limits to the performance of the front derailleur. There may be certain gear combinations that simply do not work well or cause problems. For example, when the bike is used with the smallest front chainring, and the smallest rear sprocket, the chain may rub against an adjacent chainring. This is called "cross-chaining." As a simple rule, if a gear combination causes a rubbing problem, avoid that gear (7-3.7_Figure 1). If there is no rubbing, the gear is useable.

7-3.7_Figure 1

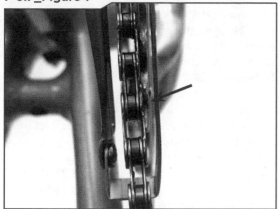

Rubbing chain-to-ring contact. No derailleur adjustment will prevent this.

Another chain rub problem can occur when pedaling in the largest front chainring and the smallest rear sprocket. Very hard pedaling will flex the frame slightly with each stroke, which may cause a chain to rub on the largest sprocket, even for properly adjusted bikes. Loosening the H-limit screw and tightening the index setting would move the front cage out more, and may stop the rubbing, but it may also cause the chain to shift over the largest chainring and come off. If all aspects of front derailleur adjustments are correct on this bike, the rider is simply exceeding the engineering and design capabilities of the machine. Front derailleur performance issues are related to chainline, which is discussed in Outline Item 7-5 Chainline.

7-4 Rear Derailleur

TOOLS & SUPPLIES
- Hex wrenches (Park Tool—various models)
- Screwdriver
- Forth hand tool (Park Tool BT-2)

Rear derailleurs "derail" the chain from one rear sprocket and move it to another. The upper derailleur pulley is also referred to as the G-pulley, or guide pulley. This pulley guides the chain to the sprocket, and when moved, pushes the chain to the next sprocket. The derailleur body is fitted with a spring that is pulled tight,

or relaxed, by the derailleur cable. Pulling the derailleur cable moves the derailleur cage and guide pulley in one direction and tightens the spring. Relaxing derailleur cable tension allows the spring to move the body and pulley in the opposite direction.

7-4_Figure 1

Derailleur and component parts
(A) Mounting bolt, (B) Body or B-screw,
(C) Limit screws, (D) Adjusting barrel,
(E) Derailleur cable pinch bolt,
(F) Upper pulley, (G) Pulley cage,
(H) Lower pulley

The rear derailleur attaches to the frame at a fitting called the derailleur hanger. The hanger has a tab that acts as a stop for derailleur rotation (7-4 Figure 2). Derailleur mounting bolts use a 10mm x 1mm thread. Grease the bolt before installing. When installing the derailleur, use care that any stop screw or plate on the derailleur clears the hanger tab. Hold the derailleur clockwise from its "normal" position while engaging the thread. The torque for the mounting bolt is modest, about 70 inches/lb for most makes. Test that the derailleur is freely pivoting on the hanger.

7-4_Figure 2

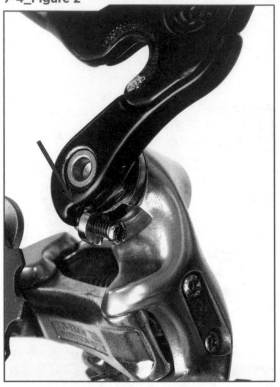

Derailleur stop screw contacting the hanger tab

7-4.1 Derailleur Capacity & Maximum Sprocket Size

The rear derailleur is usually selected to be compatible with sprocket sizing used on the bicycle. Derailleurs are made with specifications as to the "maximum sprocket size" and the "total capacity." The maximum sprocket size is the largest rear sprocket the derailleur is designed to work with. For example, a bike with a 32-tooth rear sprocket should use a rear derailleur with a maximum sprocket size of at least 32.

The total derailleur capacity refers to the derailleur's ability to take up chain slack as the derailleur shifts between different gear combinations. The capacity requirements of the bicycle are determined by the sprocket sizes. The difference between the smallest and largest chainring sizes is added to the difference between the smallest and largest sprockets of the rear sprockets. For example, a bike has a front crankset with 22-32-46 tooth chainrings. The spread between the front extremes is 24 teeth. If the rear sprocket sizing is 13-14-15-17-

19-21-23-26-30 teeth, the spread is 17 teeth. The total capacity requirements are then 17 plus 24, or a total of 41. A derailleur rated for a total capacity of 41 or greater would take up the slack for any gear combination. However, it does not mean that every gear combination will work well, only that the derailleur will take up the slack.

Derailleurs are available that do not take up chain slack in every gear combination. In the example above, if the bicycle is fitted with a derailleur with a rated capacity of 33, the derailleur will not be able to take up the slack in all gear combinations. The chain will hang slack when it is on the inner front chainring and in the 13, 14, 15, 17 or 19 rear sprockets. If the chain were shortened to accommodate these gear combinations, it would be too short when the bike is in the 46 tooth front chainring and the several of the larger sprockets in the back. When sizing a chain with a derailleur violating the total capacity needs of the bike, it is best to use the sizing method in Outline Item 6-1 Chain Sizing. This will allow shifting to largest rear and front sprockets, but the chain will hang slack is some small front chainring and small rear sprocket combinations. It will be necessary to avoid those gear combinations that cause problems in pedaling or shifting on these bikes.

Check with derailleur manufacturer for specifications on maximum sprocket size and total capacity. As a general rule, total capacity increases as the derailleur cage gets longer, and the distance between pulley wheels increases. Short cage derailleurs, those with approximately 50mm between pulley wheels, will have a capacity of about 29 teeth. Medium cage derailleurs (approximately 73mm) will have a capacity of approximately 33 teeth. Longer cage derailleurs (approximately 85mm), will have a capacity of approximately 45 teeth.

7-4.2 Derailleur Cable Attachment

The derailleur cable attaches to the rear derailleur at the pinch bolt mechanism. The derailleur cable is flattened by a plate and bolt (7-4.2 Figure 1). Unthread the bolt and look for a groove in either the plate or derailleur arm. The derailleur cable will lay in this depression or notch. Inspect the groove and keep the derailleur cable in line with it. There may also be a tab system. The tab is used to prevent the washer from rotating. The derailleur cable is not usually routed around the tab.

7-4.2_Figure 1

Derailleur cable flattened by pinch mechanism of plate and bolt

While the bolt is loose, lubricate the threads. Pull the derailleur cable snug and secure the bolt. The typical torque for the pinch bolt is approximately 35 inch pounds. Again, the derailleur cable will be flattened where it is pinched.

7-4.3 Limit Screw Adjustment

Derailleur pulleys are limited in both inward and outward motions by using the derailleur limit screws. The limit screws are usually marked "H" and "L." The H- limit screw controls the outermost limit of the derailleur, and the L-limit screw controls the innermost limit. The location of limit screws on the derailleur body may vary between manufacturers. Always look for the "H" and "L" marked adjacent to the screws.

Properly set, the derailleur will shift to both the extreme outward sprocket (the smallest in size) and the extreme innermost sprocket (the largest in size). The limit screws do not control the derailleur on the sprockets between the two extremes. The sprockets between the extremes are set using the barrel adjuster and tension on the derailleur cable during indexing adjustments.

Using the shift lever to adjust limit screws can cause confusion and problems because it tends to focus attention on the derailleur cable tension (indexing) rather than limit screw settings. Instead of using the shift lever, pull the derailleur cable with one hand to simulate shift lever action (7-4.3 Figure 1). This will help eliminate confusion between indexing problems and limit screw problems. Before adjusting the limit screws, practice shifting with this method.

7-4.3_Figure 1

Pull derailleur cable by hand to isolate limit screw performance

Turning the limit screws adjusts the travel limit of the pulleys. Tightening the screw restricts the travel, while loosening allows more travel. The purpose of the following procedure is to find the tightest H-limit screw setting that will allow a good shift to the outermost sprocket, and the tightest L-screw setting that will allow a good shift to the innermost sprocket.

It is normal for a chain to make some noise during a shift. The shift may appear subjectively "noisy," "loud," or "rough." Factors like the type of chain or sprocket, the wear on each, and the amount and type of lubrication will affect the noise a chain makes during shifting. The limit screws typically can do nothing to affect the noise during the shift between sprockets.

H-Limit Screw

When adjusting the H-limit screw, pay special attention to the outward shift from the second smallest sprocket to the outermost sprocket. Also notice how the chain rides on the outermost sprocket. However, do not be concerned with how the chain rides when it is held on the second sprocket. That is a function of derailleur cable tension, not limit screw settings. Do not become confused between issues of derailleur cable tension, which are index concerns, and limit screw setting. Again, when possible, simply pull the derailleur cable by hand rather then using the shift lever.

The procedure for adjusting the H-limit screw is as follows:

a. Shift chain to outermost (largest) chainring. Shift chain to outermost rear sprocket (smallest sprocket).

b. Check tension on rear derailleur cable. If derailleur cable appears to have any tension, it may interfere with the H-limit screw setting. Turn adjusting-barrel clockwise to eliminate derailleur cable tension.

c. Pedal bike at a quick cadence, approximately 60 rpm or more. Pull derailleur cable to shift derailleur one sprocket inward. Adjust pull on derailleur cable until chain rides quietly on second sprocket. Release derailleur cable quickly to shift back to outermost sprocket and note shift.

d. If the shift outward seems acceptable, tighten H-limit screw ¼ turn clockwise and repeat shift. Even if the shift appears acceptable, continue tightening H-limit screw by ¼ turn increments and checking shift until the shifting becomes slow or hesitant to the outer sprocket. The goal is to find the point at which the limit screw is too tight, then back it off until it is just right. Another symptom of a too tight H-limit screw is when the chain is on the smallest sprocket but makes a rattle from rubbing the second sprocket inward. View this last symptom by looking under the rear sprockets where the chain meets the sprockets. The inner plate of the chain will rub against the next sprocket inward, making the noise.

e. When symptoms of a too tight H-limit screw appear, loosen H-limit screw ¼ turn and check shift again. Repeat process of shifting and correcting by ¼ turn increments. When too tight symptoms disappear, H-limit screw is at tightest acceptable setting. The H-limit screw setting is done.

L-limit Screw

The L-limit screw stops the derailleur from moving inward (toward the spokes). The limit screw does not make the derailleur move, pulling the derailleur cable makes the derailleur move. The L-screw allows the pulley wheels to shift the chain to the innermost sprocket and yet not shift off the sprocket into the spokes. When adjusting the L-screw, be concerned with the inward shift from the second-to-innermost sprocket to the innermost sprocket. Additionally, notice how the chain rides on the innermost sprocket.

The procedure for adjusting the L-limit screw is as follows:

a. Shift bike to middle chainring of three chainring bikes, or smaller chainring of double chainring bikes.

b. Pedal bike at a normal riding cadence, approximately 60 rpm or more.

c. Pull rear derailleur cable by hand to shift derailleur inward from second to innermost sprocket to the innermost sprocket.

d. If shifting seems adequate, tighten L-limit screw ¼ turn and repeat shift. Continue to tighten L-screw until symptoms of too tight appear. The goal is to find the point at which the limit screw is too tight, then back it off until it is just right. The symptoms are that the chain will not complete the shift even with pressure on derailleur cable, the chain hesitates before shifting inward even with constant pressure on derailleur cable, or the chain rattles excessively when riding on innermost sprocket.

e. When symptoms of a too tight L-screw appear, loosen L-screw ¼ turn and check shift again. Repeat process of shifting and correcting by ¼ turn. When too tight symptoms disappear, L-screw is at tightest acceptable setting and limit screw setting is done.

NOTE NOTE NOTE NOTE: Shimano "Rapid Rise™" derailleurs use a reverse spring application. When the derailleur cable tension is completely relaxed, the derailleur sits on the innermost sprocket, which is reversed from other common derailleurs. When adjusting the H-limit screw, it is necessary to pull the derailleur cable until the chain is in the second to outermost sprocket then pull hard to shift to the outermost sprocket.

NOTE NOTE NOTE NOTE: Shimano "Rapid Rise™" derailleurs reverse the spring direction. To adjust L-screw, pull on derailleur cable and shift outward one sprocket. Release derailleur cable to shift inward. Tighten L-screw until shifting is slow, and then turn counterclockwise ¼ turn until good shifting is restored.

7-4.4 B-Screw Adjustment

After setting the L-screw, check the "B-screw" for an adequate setting. The B-screw controls the derailleur body (B) angle, hence the name, B-screw. Adjust the distance between pulley and sprocket when the chain is on the smallest sprocket in front and on the largest sprocket in back. This places the upper pulley and largest rear sprocket at their closest point.

Shimano®, SRAM® and some Campagnolo® derailleurs located the B-screw behind the upper mounting bolt (7-4.4 Figure 1).

7-4.4 Figure 1

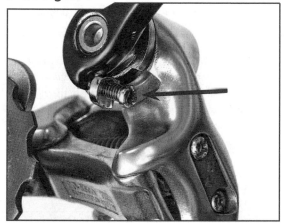

B-screw

If the indexing is already set, shift to the innermost sprocket. Otherwise, pull the rear derailleur cable and shift to the innermost rear sprocket. Hold tension and view the upper pulley relative to the largest sprocket. If the pulley is rubbing against the sprocket, tighten the B-screw to increase upper pivot spring tension, which pulls the pulley back and away from the sprocket. If there is a gap between the upper pulley and sprocket, loosen the screw. Back pedal to double check for rubbing. If the upper pulley rubs against the sprocket, it will wear out.

Campagnolo® model derailleurs may have a tension adjustment at the pulley cage, not at the upper pivot. The screw is basically a "rack and pinion" system. The cage spring plate rotates to increase or decrease tension of the cage. The tension of the upper pivot and lower cage pivot springs oppose one another. In this system, the upper spring tension is fixed (7-4.4 Figure 2). Increasing cage tension (turning

screw clockwise) in the cage will bring the upper pulley closer to the sprocket. Decreasing cage tension (turning screw counter-clockwise) will increase the distance between upper pulley and sprocket.

7-4.4_Figure 2

B-screw location for Campagnolo®

SRAM® brand derailleurs do not use a spring in the upper mounting bolt. A screw behind the upper mounting bolt adjusts the distance from the upper pulley to the largest sprocket. Adjust so there is approximately 6mm (¼ inch) gap between from the pulley and sprocket. Use a 6mm hex wrench to estimate this gap (7-4.4 Figure 3). Tighten the B-screw to pull body back, which will increase distance between sprocket and pulley. Loosen screw to decrease gap size.

7-4.4_Figure 3

Upper pulley to largest rear sprocket setting for SRAM® derailleurs

7-4.5 Index Adjustment

The indexing procedure here assumes that there are no unusual problems, such as bent derailleurs, bent derailleur hangers or excess derailleur cable friction from dirt in the housing. Additionally, manufacturers design shift levers and drive train components to work within their system. Mixing brands of components within the drive train may result in less then optimal shifting. Problems resulting from mixing different designs are referred to as incompatibility problems.

The rear indexing is adjusted by changing the derailleur cable tension. For conventional derailleurs (other than Shimano® Rapid Rise), increasing derailleur cable tension moves the rear derailleur inward, or toward the spokes. Decreasing derailleur cable tension allows the derailleur to move outward. The derailleur cable tension will not stop the derailleur at its extreme limits. The H-limit screw stops the derailleur at its outermost setting, and the L-limit screw stops the derailleur at its innermost setting.

Modern indexing shift levers use "dwell," which is a hesitation between movements in the lever. These hesitations are timed to match the movements of the derailleur and the spacing in the rear sprockets. The design of some derailleur and shift lever brands requires more of a push (or twist) of the lever to complete the shift. The amount of extra push or twist is not consistent between manufacturers and each rider must learn the particular attributes of his or her system. In other words, an index lever may, in some cases, need to be "finessed" to shift properly.

Changes to derailleur cable tension are made at the adjusting barrel. Adjusting barrels may be located either at the rear derailleur and/or the shift lever. The goal of adjusting the indexing is to find the tightest derailleur cable tension setting that will allow good shifting to the gears normally used. This setting will allow the longest lasting indexing adjustment as the system wears and the cable system stretches with use. To find the tightest derailleur cable setting, begin by purposely making the setting too tight and then relax tension slightly.

There are two basic symptoms for a "too tight" derailleur cable: a rattling noise from the chain rubbing against the next sprocket inward, or a slow or hesitant outward shift. These are symptoms for conventional rear derailleurs that sit outward when derailleur cable tension is released.

Noise from the chain as it rides on the sprocket is a useful symptom for setting indexing tension. There is, for any given bike, a "base level" of noise from the chain as it passes over the sprocket teeth. To demonstrate the "base level" noise, shift the bike to the second sprocket by pulling the derailleur cable. Continue to pedal and move the derailleur cable slightly to hear changes in the level of noise. The quietest level of noise may be considered the base or normal level for that bike. When the derailleur jockey wheel is out of alignment, the chain may make excessive noise.

The procedure for adjusting the rear index setting is as follows:

a. Set limits screws, if not already done (Outline Item 7-4.3 Limit Screw Adjustment)

b. Shift chain to outermost rear sprocket (smallest). Shift chain to outermost (largest) chainring in front.

c. Test initial derailleur cable tension. Pedal a normal cadence and shift rear derailleur with one click on lever. Use care to only move lever one position. If derailleur moves one sprocket, tension is adequate. Proceed to "e" below.

d. If derailleur fails to shift one sprocket, derailleur cable may be too slack. Return lever to relaxed derailleur cable position. Turn barrel adjuster fully into derailleur body (or shift lever) then turn counter clockwise two turns to allow for index adjustments. Loosen derailleur cable pinch bolt and gently pull on derailleur cable with fourth hand tool or pliers to remove slack (7-4.5_Figure 1). Tighten derailleur cable pinch bolt. Attempt shift again. If derailleur will not shift one sprocket after removing slack, return lever back to outermost sprocket position and increase derailleur cable tension by turning barrel adjuster counter-clockwise ¼ turn and attempt shift again.

7-4.5_Figure 1

Pull excessive slack from cable

e. Once derailleur and lever are on second sprocket, pedal the cranks and increase derailleur cable tension by continuing to turn adjusting barrel counter-clockwise until a definite rattling is heard. Rattle is from the chain scraping against the next sprocket

7-4.5_Figure 2

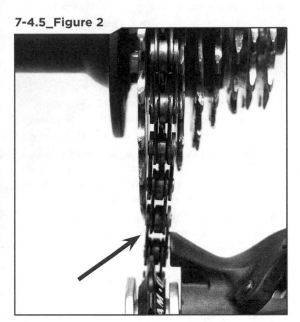

Look for rattle under rear sprockets

f. Once a too-tight rattle is achieved, turn barrel adjuster ¼ turn clockwise, to release derailleur cable tension, and pedal again. Listen and look for signs of scraping or rattling. Continue turning barrel adjuster ¼ turn clockwise at a time until rattle disappears.

g. Shift derailleur one sprocket inward at a time, listening for signs of rattle, indicating a too tight derailleur cable (7-4.5_Figure 2). Turn adjusting barrel ¼ turn clockwise to eliminate rattle. Continue shifting inward one sprocket at a time. Adjust only if rattling is heard and seen. Note: Do not attempt to shift to largest rear sprocket while in largest front sprocket. This gear is normally not used and adjusting tension to this shift may compromise other commonly used gears.

h. Shift to innermost (smallest) chainring and check shifting again. If no rattling is present, index adjustment is done.

NOTE: If adjusting limit screws and derailleur cable tension does not solve indexing problems, other drive train problems exist, such as a bent derailleur cage, worn cable system, worn derailleur, chainline problems, or incompatible components.

Shimano "Rapid Rise™" Derailleur— Indexing Adjustment

Shimano "Rapid Rise™" derailleurs use a return spring that puts the derailleur under the innermost rear sprocket when the derailleur cable tension is released. A loose derailleur cable will cause the chain to rub against the next sprocket inward.

The procedure for adjusting the indexing on Rapid Rise derailleurs is as follows:

a. Mount the bike in a repair stand.

b. Set limit screws (Outline Item 7-4.3 Limit Screw Adjustment).

c. Shift chain to the innermost rear sprocket and the middle chainring of a three chainring bike, or the smaller chainring of a double chainring bike.

d. Pedal and shift lever one position. If chain will not shift, release lever and increase derailleur cable tension.

e. When the chain is on the second to largest sprocket, pedal and turn barrel adjuster clockwise to relax derailleur cable tension until chain begins to rattle against next sprocket inward.

f. Turn barrel adjuster counter-clockwise ¼ turn until chain runs smoothly on second sprocket.

g. Shift outward one sprocket at a time, trying each gear. Turn barrel adjuster ¼ turn counter-clockwise if too-loose derailleur cable symptoms occur in other gears.

h. Shift to all other normal gear combinations and test adjustment. Make corrections as necessary in ¼ turn adjustments.

7-5 Chainline

Chainline is the relation of the front and rear sprockets to the center plane of the bicycle (7-5_Figure 1). The bike center plane is an imaginary plane running from front to rear through the middle of the bike. As an example, a front crankset and/or front derailleur might be designed to have a chainline of 50mm. This means the front derailleur will work best when the middle of the chainrings are 50mm from the bike centerline.

7-5_Figure 1

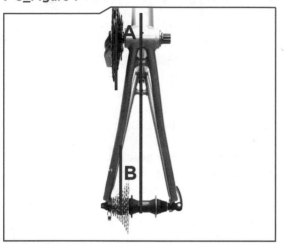

Chainline in relationship to the bike mid plane. (A) Distance from middle of front chainrings to mid plane, (B) Distance from middle of rear sprockets to mid plane

Chainline can also refer to the relative position of the front and rear sprockets to each other, without regard to the bike centerline. This is called "effective chainline." In 7-5_Figure 1, effective chainline is simply the difference between "A" and "B." However, distance "A" is not always designed to be equal to "B". For example, for most three chainring bikes, the middle of nine rear sprockets will be approximately 45mm from the bicycle mid plane, distance "B." The manufacturer's specified chainline of triple cranksets ranges from 47 to 50mm, distance "A." In this case, the front chainrings are not designed to align directly with the middle of the rear sprockets.

Drive train manufacturers do not generally consider all gear combinations to be useable. For example, a "27-speed" bike has three chainrings in front and 9 sprockets in the rear, for a total of 27 gears. There are likely to be several gear combinations that are exact or very close duplicates. It is also likely that the chain will rub the side of the middle chainring when

the chain is on the smallest sprocket in front and possibly 2 or 3 of the smallest sprockets in back. This is simply the limitation of the design. If the front crankset were moved outward until there was no rubbing in these combinations, there would likely be other shifting problems in other gear combinations, such as the largest chainring and several of the inner rear sprockets.

Sprocket combinations that should be avoided are termed "cross chaining." Drive train manufacturers vary on exactly which combinations should not be used. Generally, it is assumed that the smallest front chainring and smallest rear sprocket will not be used, nor will the largest rear sprocket in combination with the largest front chainring. As a practical matter, each bike may be different as to which exact gear combinations are un-useable.

As a simple rule of thumb, if the bicycle shifts well and does not have the symptoms described below, the chainline should be considered adequate:

• Chain jumping off large chainring when front derailleur is correctly adjusted for height, rotation and limit screw settings.
• Chain riding off lower derailleur pulley teeth when derailleur or hanger is not bent.
• Chain rattling on inner faces of front chainrings in what should be useable gears.
• Chain derailing off inner chainring when front derailleur is correctly adjusted for height, rotation and limit screw settings.
• Front derailleur cannot be adjusted to stop over shifts while still allowing good shifting.

Changes to chainline can be made by moving the front chainrings. By using different bottom bracket spindle widths, the chainrings can be moved inward or outward. Shorter spindles move the chainrings inward, and longer spindles move the chainrings outward. On some models, a thin spacer can be placed under the right side cup of the bottom bracket to move the chainrings outward. However, there are limits to this because it results in less thread engagement for the right side cup. There are limits to moving a derailleur inward, toward the bike mid plane. The chainrings may end up rubbing the frame. Additionally, the front derailleur may not work well with the front chainrings too close to the frame.

Chainline manipulation with the rear sprockets is generally more limited. The freehub mechanism cannot be moved laterally on the hub shell. If the hub uses a threaded axle, spacers may sometimes be moved under the cone locknut to shift the rear sprocket positions. If spacers are moved from the right side to the left side, double check that the chain will not strike the frame when on the smallest rear cog. It is important not to change the fit on the hub into the frame. Any change of axle spacing will also change the centering of the wheel rim over the hub. Double-check and correct dish if the spacers were manipulated. See Outline Item 4-2.3 Wheel Centering (Dishing).

The bicycle is designed for forward pedaling. There are times when a cyclist may want to pedal backwards, such as to set up the pedal orientation when entering a tight corner. When pedaling forward, the chain is guided to the rear sprocket by the upper derailleur pulley, which is very close to the sprockets. When a cyclist backpedals, the chain is guided to the rear sprocket by the front chainrings, which will be some distance away. The chain may disengage or become jammed when it is backpedaled because the front chainrings cannot keep the chain guided straight to the sprocket. Disengagement is likely to be worse in gear combinations where the chainline is offset the greatest. It may be possible to minimize back pedaling problems by changes to chainline, but again this may result in other problems.

7-6
Derailleur Hanger Alignment & Repair

TOOLS & SUPPLIES
- Derailleur Hanger Gauge (Park Tool DAG-1)
- Hex wrenches (Park Tool—various models)

The rear derailleur is mounted to the bike at the derailleur hanger. The hanger should be aligned parallel to the rear sprockets. A misaligned derailleur hanger will result in poor shifting performance (7-6_Figure 1). The derailleur hanger can become bent when the bike is crashed, bumped with force, or if something, such as a stick, becomes caught in the derailleur when riding. A bicycle may also simply be manufactured with a misaligned hanger.

7-6_Figure 1

A bent hanger from impacts to rear derailleur

It is often possible to repeatedly re-bend and align many derailleur hangers. This is because there is very little stress from riding the bike or shifting gears. As a rule of thumb, if a hanger survives a repair by bending, it will survive the riding.

To check alignment and repair the derailleur hanger, use a derailleur hanger alignment gauge, such as the Park Tool DAG-1 Derailleur Alignment Gauge. The tool extends the plane of the hanger and compares it to the rim. If the hanger is aligned to the rim, it will also be aligned to the rear sprockets.

NOTE NOTE NOTE: There are some hangers that do not repair well. Extremely thick hangers and titanium hangers are difficult and sometimes impossible to repair.

Bolt-on or replaceable hangers may be aligned (7-6_Figure 2). However, these types of hangers can be difficult to align if the clamping design of the hanger to the frame is inadequate. Replaceable hangers may move in the frame mount, which changes the alignment of the hanger and derailleur. Before checking alignment on replaceable hangers, double check security of hanger to frame bolts or screws.

7-6_Figure 2

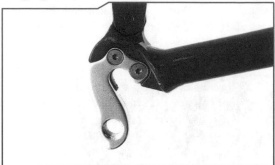

Replaceable type derailleur hanger

The procedure for derailleur hanger alignment is as follows:

a. Mount the bike in a repair stand. Level the bike, as it would appear on flat ground.

b. Check that the rear wheel is mounted straight in the frame.

c. Remove rear derailleur from hanger. Derailler may hang from housing.

d. Install DAG-1 into hanger and tighten handle. If the DAG-1 does not thread easily into the derailleur hanger, chase and clean the threads using a tap as necessary. Do not use the DAG-1 threads as a "chaser" of bad derailleur hanger threads.

e. Rotate the arm toward the left side of the rim, at the nine o'clock position. Rotate the tire valve to the same position. Use the valve on the rim as a constant reference point when checking the hanger (7-6_Figure 3). By checking the same point on the rim, wheel trueness or dish will not affect alignment.

7-6_Figure 3

Set DAG-1 to reference rim at the nine o'clock position

f. Loosen the sliding gauge knob and move the sliding gauge to contact the rim, then secure the knob.

g. Push gauge bracket toward hub before rotating arm. This prevents gauge from being forced against rim.

h. Rotate DAG-1 and rim valve 180 degrees to the three o'clock position. Slide indicator toward rim to same point near valve.

i. There are three possible results.

Condition A: The gauge barely touches the rim, or has a small gap less then 4mm. In this case the hanger is aligned horizontally.

Condition B: The pointer is away from the rim some distance. The hanger is misaligned (7-6_Figure 4). If the distance is greater then 4mm, the hanger will need re-alignment. Use a 4mm hex wrench to gauge the gap.

7-6_Figure 4

Gauge indicating misaligned hanger

Condition C: The pointer strikes inside the rim, indicating a misaligned hanger (7-6 Figure 5). It is easier to determine the error by seeing the gap between the rim and gauge. Re-set tool to rim contact at the 9:00 position and rotate back to the 3:00 position. There will be a gap between the rim and the gauge.

7-6_Figure 5

Reset gauge if it falls inside rim

j. Bend the derailleur hanger a small amount using the DAG-1 tool, then re-check both sides. Reset gauge and re-measure gap. Generally, it is best to bend with the DAG-1 arm next to the chainstay (7-6_Figure 6). This allows you to use the stay for leverage and to control the amount of bending either inward or out.

7-6_Figure 6

Use the frame to control bending of the hanger

k. Repeat bending and checking until the gap is less than 4mm. A 4mm gap at the rim means the hanger is off less than a millimeter at the sprockets, where the derailleur actually shifts. Use a 4mm hex wrench as a "go-no go" gauge.

l. When the horizontal positions are aligned, move on to check the 6:00 and 12:00 position. Set gauge to the 6:00 position, then check at the 12:00 position.

m. If the gap exceeds the 4mm tolerance, bend accordingly in small increments, re-checking and re-setting the gauge (7-6_Figure 7). When the gap is less than 4mm, keep the same setting and check at the 9:00 position. When three points that are 90-degrees apart are within 4mm, hanger is aligned.

7-6_Figure 7

Use a 4mm gauge to check the tolerance

n. Remove the tool and re-install the derailleur.

Check settings on both limit screws and check index settings (Outline Item 7-4.3 Limit Screw Adjustment and 7-4.5 Index Adjustment).

The threads of the derailleur hanger are commonly 10mm x 1mm. If the derailleur installs with difficulty, the threads of the hanger should be tapped. As a test of thread acceptability, fully tighten the derailleur. If the derailleur bolt does not strip, the hanger is useable. If the threads strip and fail, it is possible for a professional mechanic to install a coil thread, or a t-nut repair system (7-6_Figure 8). These repairs work well when properly done and allow the bike to be used as normal.

7-6_Figure 8

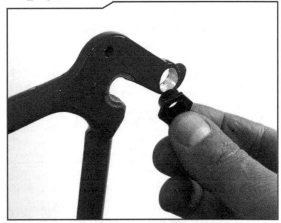

T-nut thread repair of a stripped hanger

7-7 Derailleur Inspections

Both derailleurs will eventually wear out with use, as play and excess movement develops at the pivots. Grab the lower cage of a rear derailleur and pull left to right to test play. It may help to compare the play in the old derailleur to new models. Replace the derailleur when the cage at the lower pulley has more then a ¼-inch (6mm) movement.

Chain travels over the pulleys and pulley teeth, causing wear. Worn pulley wheels will not engage well with the chain (7-7_Figure 2). The pulley wheels usually can be replaced.

7-7_Figure 1

Unworn pulley wheel on left and extremely worn pulley on right

The rear derailleur can be brushed off and lightly scrubbed with soap or solvent. Use care not to get solvent in the upper and lower pivots. A solvent in the cage pivots will ruin the grease inside. It is also possible to disassemble, clean, and re-assemble some rear derailleurs. Overhaul of the rear derailleur is not discussed in this book.

NOTE: For derailleur overhaul and pulley replacement, see Repair Help at www.parktool.com

The front derailleur can be flushed with degreaser, dried, and re-lubricated at the spring and all pivot points with a light lubricant. The pivots of the cage will eventually develop play and slop with enough use. Grab the back end of the derailleur and pull from side to side. Compare the old derailleur to the movement on a new derailleur. The cage may also be gouged or damaged from dragging on a chain. Front derailleurs typically have no replaceable parts and when the derailleur wears out, it is replaced.

7-8 Troubleshooting

Poor or inconsistent shifting can be the result of several problems or combinations of problems. It is often necessary to check each part of the shifting system to find the problem and solve it (Table 7-8 Troubleshooting Table).

Table 7-8 Troubleshooting Table

Shifting or Riding Symptom	Potential Problem	Potential Solution
Chain skips in all gear combinations	Poor indexing adjustment	Re-adjust indexing
Shifting is slow or hesitant for either inward and outward shifts	Friction in the cable system	Lubricate and or replace cable and housing
Shifting is slow or hesitant on inward shifts	Poor indexing adjustment with cable tension too loose (Rapid Rise® likely too tight)	Increase cable tension. Rapid Rise® decrease cable tension
Shifting is slow or hesitant on outward shifts	Poor indexing adjustment with cable tension too tight (Rapid Rise® likely too loose)	Decrease cable tension. Rapid Rise® increase cable tension.
Chain skips under pressure in only 1, 2 or 3 rear sprockets	Sprockets may be worn out	Inspect and replace sprockets and chain
Chain shifts off of largest front chainring	Front H-limit screw too loose, or rotation of cage is off	Inspect and correct cage rotation as necessary. Check H-limit screw setting.

Shifting or Riding Symptom	Potential Problem	Potential Solution
Chain shifts off of smallest front chainring	Front L-limit screw too loose, or rotation of cage is off.	Inspect and correct cage rotation as necessary. Check L-limit screw setting.
Chain shifts slow or not at all to largest front chainring	Front derailleur cable tension too loose, H-limit screw too tight, and/or rotation of cage Is off.	Check front index setting. Check derailleur rotation and H-limit screw setting.
Chain shifts slow or not at all to smallest front chainring	Front derailleur cable tension too tight, and/or L-limit screw too tight, and/or rotation of cage Is off	Check front index setting. Check derailleur rotation and L-limit screw setting.
Chain shifts well to largest front chainring but outer cage rubs after shift is completed	Front derailleur cable tension too loose	Increase front derailleur cable tension
Chain skips under load at front chainrings	Front chainrings worn	Replace chainrings

Chapter 8

Rim Caliper
Brake Systems

A good brake system is more than an emergency stopping system. Properly adjusted brakes give the user subtle control and modulation in bike handling and speed control. Many small details affect the control of the bike, including the placement of the levers, how the cable system is installed, and the alignment of the brake pads.

Derailleur bicycles commonly use rim caliper brake systems. The system includes the brake lever, cables and caliper. Rim calipers are attached to the frame and fork near the wheel rim. The calipers are attached by brake cables and housing to levers at the handlebars. Force is applied to the rim by the pads, converting the speed and energy of the bicycle into heat, which slows the bike.

Disc brakes use a rotor attached to the hub. Disc brakes may use either a cable or hydraulic tubing to actuate the caliper. Disc brakes are discussed in Chapter 9 Caliper Disc Brake Systems.

NOTE: For hydraulic rim brake service see Repair Help at www.parktool.com

8-1 Brake Levers

TOOLS & SUPPLIES
• Hex wrenches (Park Tool- various models)
• Straight edge (Park Tool SBC-1)

The brake lever is fitted to the handlebar with a clamp. The cyclist's hand pulls the lever, using the handlebar for leverage. Muscular force of the hand is then transferred to the brake pads via the cable system.

Flat Bar Brake Levers

Brake levers are clamped to the handlebars and should be positioned so they are easy and comfortable to reach. For flat bar brake levers, rotate the lever so it is in line with the rider's arm. A common standard is to set the lever at 45 degrees from the horizontal plane (8-1_Figure 1). This avoids bending the wrist to apply the brakes. Brake levers may be rotated on the bar by loosening the clamp-fixing bolt.

8-1_Figure 1

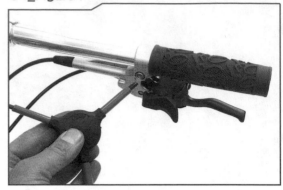

Rotate levers for comfortable reach from saddle

Flat bar levers commonly have a setscrew on the lever body that allows the lever to be set closer to the grip. The lever reach can then be set according to the rider's hand size and riding style. Tighten the setscrews to bring the levers toward the grip to accommodate smaller hands or shorter fingers.

Flat bar levers typically allow for easy installation of the cable end into the cable anchor of the lever. Pull the lever and inspect for the cable anchor. Inspect also for slots in the adjusting barrel. Align the slots, and then attach the cable to the anchor. Engage the brake cable between the slots in the barrel adjuster (8-1 Figure 2).

8-1_Figure 2

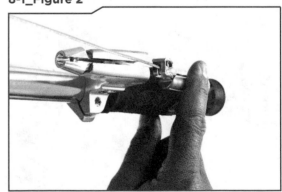

Use slots to engage cable end

Brake levers are designed to pull a certain amount of brake cable as the lever is squeezed. The distance from the cable head pivot to the lever pivot determines the amount of brake cable pulled. Linear pull brake levers will have a greater distance between cable end and lever pivot, approximately 30mm or more. Cantilever calipers will have a relatively shorter distance of less than 30mm. The brake lever should be compatible with the type of brake caliper used. Although the linear pull brake levers pull more cable, they pull with less force compared to the cantilever levers.

Some levers will adjust for either cantilever/side pull travel or the greater pull of the linear pull brake. Mechanical pulley systems, such as the Travel Agent®, are available that attach to the linear pull caliper. These allow the use of cantilever compatible levers with linear pull brakes.

Drop-Bar Brake Levers

Drop-bar brake levers may be moved up or down the curve of the bar for easier reach. Moving the lever down on the bar curve makes the levers easier to reach while riding on the drops. Moving the lever up on the bar makes them easier to reach when riding on the top of the bars. The handlebar tape must be removed to move the levers up or down (8-1 Figure 3).

8-1_Figure 3

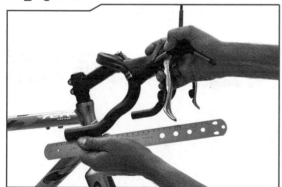

Adjust lever height for comfort

The brake lever uses a strap that pulls the body tight to the handlebar. The fitting to tighten the strap may be inside the lever body or on the side under the rubber hood covers. It may be necessary to pull the cover up in order to insert the hex wrench when tightening the strap (8-1_Figure 4).

The drop-bar lever should be tight to the handlebar. The user effectively uses the lever body as a "bar extension" when riding on the tops of the levers. If the levers were to move during use, it could result in a crash.

8-1_Figure 4

Inspect lever body for bolt tightening mounting strap

Brake cables are attached to the cable anchor in the lever. Pull the brake lever fully down and inspect inside. The anchor will have a socket fitting for the cable. The common aero-style lever will have a hole in the lever body for the cable end (8-1_Figure 5). Feed the cut end of the cable into the socket first, and route it out the back of the lever body. Pull the cable and check that the end is fully seated into the anchor. The housing will fit into the back of the lever body.

8-1_Figure 5

Insert brake cable from front of lever

8-2 Cable System

TOOLS & SUPPLIES
- Cable Cutter (Park Tool CN-10)
- Light lubricant (Park Tool CL-1)
- Seal pick

The cable system is made of the brake cable and housing. It connects the brake lever to the caliper. The brake cable is made of multiple strands of wire and a fitting on one end. This fitting sits in the lever. Cables often come double-ended, with a different shaped fitting on each end. One end is used and the other end is cut off using a cable cutter. The brake cable fitting sits in the brake lever, and the cut end of the cable is bolted into the caliper arm. Flat bar levers use a round disc shaped end about 7mm (⁹⁄₃₂") in diameter (8-2 Figure 1). Drop-bar levers use a "mushroom" or "tear-drop" shaped end (8-2 Figure 2). Brake cables have a minimum diameter of 1.5mm (¹⁄₁₆"), which is larger than derailleur cables.

8-2_Figure 1

Brake cable end for flat bar lever

8-2_Figure 2

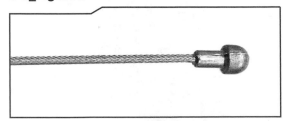

Brake cable end for drop bar lever

Housing allows the cable to bend around corners on the way to the brake caliper. Wound-type brake housing is made of a plastic liner tube around which support wire is wound. It is then covered by plastic to help prevent rust

(8-2 Figure 3). Wound housing differs from the compressionless housing used on derailleur systems. The support wires of compressionless housing do not hold up to the higher stresses of braking.

Replace housing if it is twisted, rusty, split, or too short. It is a good idea to replace the housing even if it is simply old, as there is a plastic tube inside the wound housing which becomes dirty and worn with use.

8-2_Figure 3

Common brake housing, with cut away to show inner support wire coil

"Braided" or "woven" housing is acceptable for either brake or indexing shift housing (8-2_Figure 4). The outer support wires are woven in a mesh around the liner.

8-2_Figure 4

Braided housing used for both braking and shifting

Another type is called "articulated housing." Small tubular segments are strung together over a plastic liner (8-2_Figure 5). Articulated housing may be used for both brake housing and indexing shift housing.

8-2_Figure 5

Articulated housing used for both braking and shifting

8-2.1 Cable Lubrication

To prevent rust and to insure smooth operation, apply a light lubricant to the brake cable where it passes through the housing. If the frame housing stops have a split, the housing and brake cable can be released from the stops for easier lubrication.

The procedures for lubricating cables already installed are as follows:

a. Release the brake caliper quick release to relax the cable tension.
b. Pull the housing back and out of the stop.
c. Slide the housing back to expose the cable. Wipe the cable clean with a rag and lubricate.
d. Re-install housing into the stops and close the caliper quick release.

If removing the housing from the stops is not possible, rotate the bike so lubrication can be dripped down the brake cable into the housing. Some housing systems use a liner to cover the entire length of cable from lever to caliper. (e.g Goretex® and Delta® systems). Do not lubricate the cable of these systems.

8-2.2 Cable Housing Length

When replacing housing, consider the housing length. Generally, housing should be as short as possible, yet still enter straight into the housing stops. If the housing is too long, it will pass an imaginary line created by the housing stop (8-2.2 Figure 1). If it is too short, it will create kinks or severe bends.

8-2.2_Figure 1

Housing passes housing stop, indicating housing is too long

8-2.2_Figure 2

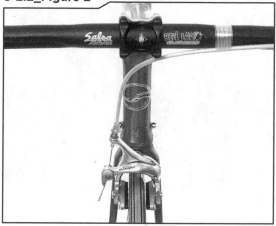

Housing enters stop in a straight line, indicating a good length

If the old housing was an acceptable length, cut new housing to the same length. If in doubt, cut housing longer and insert into stops, then inspect and cut shorter as required. For wound housing, cut with diagonal pliers. Bend brake housing where you wish to cut to open the wound coil (8-2.2_Figure 3).

8-2.2_Figure 3

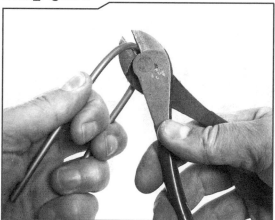

Flexing wound-type housing opens coils for the cutters

Wound housing is made of a single coiled wire. Any cutting tool tends to leave a sharp end or burr. The burr should be filed or ground smooth so the housing is flat (8-2.2 Figure 4).

8-2.2_Figure 4

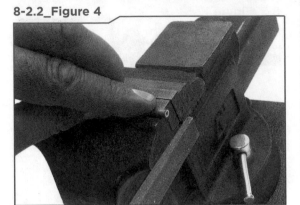

File brake coil smooth to eliminate burr from cutting

Woven or braided housing is cut with cable cutters, similar to index shift housing. Articulated housing is shortened similar to shortening a beaded string. Pieces are removed and the inner plastic liner cut with scissors.

Housing end caps should be used whenever possible (8-2.2 Figure 5). The end cap improves the fit of the housing into a cable stop. However, if an end cap will not fit into a brake cable stop, the stop has a tighter fit and the cap is not necessary. End caps are available in different designs. The end diameters vary to better mate with frame fittings, and some may have extensions for protective liners.

8-2.2_Figure 5

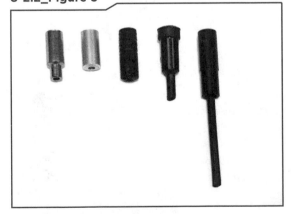

Various styles of housing end caps

After a brake cable is installed and the brake adjusted, the cable should be cut using a cable cuter, such as the Park Tool CN-10. A cable cutter is designed for multiple strand wires, such as brake cable, gear cable,

compressionless housing, and woven housing. The cutting jaws surround the cut and shear the wires. After cutting the brake cable, use a cable end cap to prevent the end from fraying (8-2.2_Figure 6).

8-2.2_Figure 6

Use a cable end cap to prevent fraying

The brake cable is fixed to the rim caliper arm by a plate and bolt. The brake cable is pulled with great force by the hand lever, and should not slip in the pinch bolt (8-2.2_Figure 7). The brake cable will become flattened with proper torque.

8-2.2_Figure 7

Pinch bolt and brake cable

If the brake cable is cut anywhere between the lever and the cable pinch bolt at the derailleur, it should be replaced. Even the failure of a single strand of wire will eventually lead to breakage of the cable (8-2.2_Figure 8).

8-2.2_Figure 8

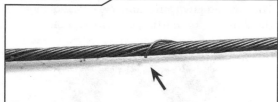

Inspect and replace cables with broken wire

8-3 Caliper Rim Brakes

Note: When rim calipers are discussed in this chapter, "right" and "left" will be from the mechanic's point of view, not the rider's point of view. In other words, the left caliper arm of the front brake is the left one seen when standing in front the bike. The left caliper arm of the rear brake is the one on the left side of the bike while standing behind the bike.

TOOLS & SUPPLIES	• Box or open end wrenches (Park Tool CBW-1 and CBW-4) • Hex wrenches (Park Tool-various models) • Fourth Hand (Park Tool BT-2)

The design of the brake caliper will determine how the brake pads are adjusted. Most caliper arms swing the pad on an arc as it approaches the rim. Certain caliper types swing the pad downward as it moves toward the rim, other types move the pad upward as it moves toward the rim. Before adjusting pads, begin by determining the basic type of caliper used. Move the caliper arm and watch how the pads move toward the arm. Arm movement will determine pad alignment. (8-3_Figure 1)

8-3_Figure 1

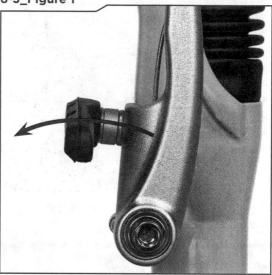

This pad will move downward as the caliper swings to the rim

Brake pads will wear with use and will require replacement. Some pads are made with a "wear line," which indicates the need for replacement. Age will also harden pad material, making it less effective. Inspect the brake pad and remove pieces of grit and foreign material as necessary.

Pads that are aligned too low on a rim will develop a lip on the low edge. This lip makes correct alignment impossible (8-3 Figure 2). Replacement pads should be compatible with the type of caliper. There are many after-market pads available, from all-round use to pads for wet conditions or specific rim compounds. Choose a pad set that meets your needs as a rider. A relatively soft pad, for example, will generally give high performance but will wear quickly.

8-3_Figure 2

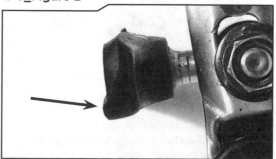

Worn pad, showing signs of low placement to rim

The brake pads may be replaced as an entire unit, with pad material and pad holder and fastener all together. Some pad systems use a "cartridge pad" that allows for the pad material to be changed, with the pad holder and fastener being re-used. To replace cartridge pads, inspect for and remove any screw or clip retaining the pad. Pull on the pad backwards, away from rim rotation direction (8-3_Figure 3). Install new pad by pushing it into holder, and re-install retaining screw or clip.

8-3_Figure 3

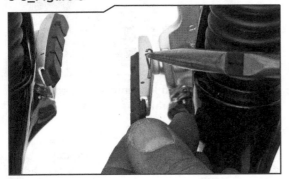

Pull cartridge pad toward back to remove it from pad holder

It is common for some cantilever and linear pull caliper brake pads to have the mounting stud placed off-center, so one end of the pad is longer (8-3_Figure 4). Look for manufactures' marking for direction of rim rotation and marking for "front" and "back."

8-3_Figure 4

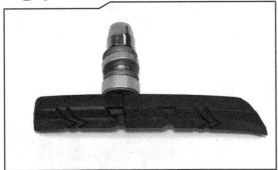

Off center brake pad mounting stud

Rim caliper pad adjustments depend upon the wheel being centered in the frame. A misaligned wheel will affect both pad centering and pad placement on the rim, and it is important that the wheel be centered before beginning pad adjustments (8-3_Figure 5).

8-3-Figure 5

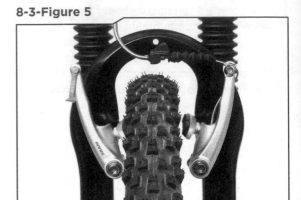

A misaligned wheel off to mechanic's left

A wheel can be misaligned from simply being placed in the frame incorrectly. Loosen quick release or axle nuts and pull wheel fully into dropouts. It is also possible the wheel rim is not properly centered over the hub. As a test, flip the wheel around left-to-right and inspect again. If the centering is good, wheel centering will look the same either way. A wheel may be purposely "mis-dished" to correct for minor frame or fork misalignment It is also possible the frame or fork was made with the left and right dropouts at slightly different heights. An effective solution is simply to hold the wheel centered when installing it, and then close the skewer tightly (or tighten axle nuts) to hold the wheel in place. Some frames have enough material that may allow filing to effectively raise one dropout. Consult a professional mechanic.

Brake pads are mounted to the caliper arms and are adjustable in several directions. There are four basic aspects to pad alignment: vertical height alignment, tangent alignment, vertical face alignment and pad toe. Not every brand or model of brake caliper has every adjustment, and sometimes it is necessary to compromise when setting pads.

Vertical Height Alignment

This is the setting up and down on the rim braking surface. The rim braking surface is the flat section of rim. View caliper face-on and move the arms, watching the pads move to the rim. If the pad moves on an arc moving down, it should be set to the upper edge of the rim braking surface (8-3_Figure 6). If the pad travels upward toward the rim, it should be set to the lower edge of the rim braking surface. As the brake pad wears, it gets thinner, and tends to move further upward or downward along its arc. Do not set pads so high that they strike the tire at any time, or so low that they are below the braking surface.

8-3_Figure 6

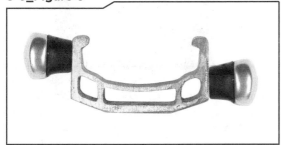

Pad on left is set at top of rim braking surface, while pad on right is at bottom of rim braking surface

Tangent Alignment

This is the setting of the pad tilt. Viewed from the side, the front and back of the pad should be parallel to the rim. One side should not be higher or lower than the other side (8-3_Figure 7). Use care when tightening the pad fixing bolt and hold the brake pad to keep it from rotating.

8-3_Figure 7

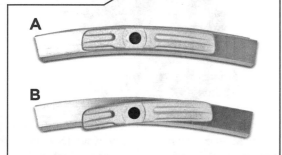

Front and back edge of pad should be square with rim (A) Proper alignment, (B) Improper alignment

Vertical Face Alignment

This is the setting of the pad's vertical surface relative to the rim's vertical surface. The vertical face of the pad should be set parallel to the face of

the braking surface (8-3_Figure 8). Most cantilever and linear pull calipers have an adjustment for vertical alignment. Many side pull and dual pivot caliper pad do not allow for vertical alignment. These pads will simply wear in with use, or they can be sanded or filed to shape.

8-3_Figure 8

Vertical face of both left and right pads are misaligned to rim braking surface

Pad Toeing

This is the setting of the pad angle as it touches the rim. Toeing refers to setting the pad so its front edge strikes first, with a slight gap of 0.25mm to 1mm at the back or trailing edge (8-3_Figure 9). Toe helps to reduce squeal during braking. Caliper arms have play in the pivots. Additionally, the mechanism flexes with the wheel when the brake is applied. This creates a "slip and stick" phenomenon, as the pads jerk backwards, then forward again. The affect is much like that of a bow on a violin string. The result is "harmonic resonance," or squealing. With systems that are more rigid, there is less flex and there tends to be less squealing. The stiffer the brake, the less it will tend to squeal, even without pad toe.

Generally, less toe angle is better then more, as too much angle will add to brake caliper flexing without providing power to the pads.

8-3_Figure 9

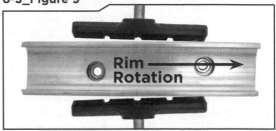

Toeing in pads

Some brake pad systems allow toe adjustment in the pad fixing bolt. Side pull and dual pull caliper arms can sometimes be bent slightly for pad toe. However, if the caliper arm is relatively thick, or seems difficult to bend, toe may be cut into the pad with a file. It is simplest to first ride the bike and see if toe is required.

Caliper Mounting

The brake caliper is secured to the frame or fork. Cantilever and linear pull calipers attach to separate frame or fork pivots on either side of the wheel rim. Attached to the frame or fork is a stud called the "braze-on." This stud is 16mm long and 8mm in diameter, with an internal thread for a 6mm bolt. Grease the surface of the braze-on before installing the calipers. Use a mild thread-locker inside the fitting and install the bolt to a relatively low torque. The cantilever should pivot freely when the bolt is secure. Over tightening may damage the fitting and cause the caliper to stick.

There may be several spring hole options in the braze-on as well as in the caliper (8-3 Figure 10). Mount left and right caliper springs into mirror image holes. Spring hole options allow changes in spring tension. Generally, select the middle option and move both sides symmetrically if changing tension.

8-3_Figure 10

Braze on for brake mounting

Dual pivot and side pull brake calipers secure in mounting holes in the frame and fork. These calipers secure to the frame with a single nut centered above the wheel (8-3_Figure 11). The front brake-mounting bolt has longer threads, while the rear brake bolt has shorter threads. When mounting a dual or side pull caliper, hold caliper centered to wheel and tighten bolt.

8-3_Figure 11

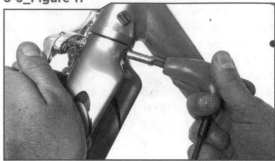

Mounting nut of a dual pivot or side pull caliper

8-3.1 Cantilever Caliper Adjustment

Cantilever calipers may be found on mountain bikes, cyclo-cross bikes and touring bikes. The pads move downward on an arc as they travel to the rim (8-3.1_Figure 1). Because of the downward arc, pads should be set high vertically on the rim, but without interfering with the tire. Pad height will lower as pad face wears, and the caliper arms get closer to the rim.

8-3.1_Figure 1

Pads travel downward as they move toward rim

Cantilever calipers may have either a "threaded stud" or a "smooth stud" brake pad. Smooth stud brake pads are secured by pressure from a "pad fixing bolt." Typically, a system of curved washers allows the brake post to rotate for setting toe (8-3.1_Figure 2).

8-3.1_Figure 2

Smooth stud pad with curved washer system

There are two basic systems for connecting the left and right calipers, the straddle wire carrier and the "link unit". The straddle wire carrier is centered over the wheel, and uses a pinch bolt to secure the cable coming from the brake lever (8-3.1_Figure 3). Place this type of carrier as low as practical, for the best mechanical advantage to the brake pads. The bottom of the carrier should be approximately even with the lowest part of the rear seat stay bridge or front fork crown.

8-3.1_Figure 3

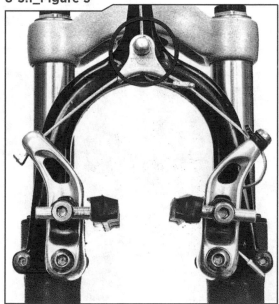

Straddle wire carrier for cantilever calipers

The link unit uses housing and a head that is a fixed distance above the tire (8-3.1_Figure 4). The height of the link unit determines the arm position. A longer link unit will allow more clearance above the tire.

8-3.1_Figure 4

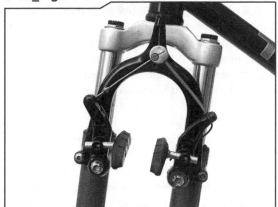

Straddle wire link-unit

The procedure for cantilever caliper pad and caliper adjustment is as follows:

a. Mount bike in repair stand.
b. For link units, attach cable to brake lever and to caliper arm. For straddle wire carriers, attach cable to brake lever, then attach cable to carrier and position the carrier above the tire. Secure carrier pinch bolt fully.
c. Turn brake lever barrel adjuster fully clockwise into lever body, then unthread two or three complete turns. This allows adjustment after setting pad placement.
d. Loosen brake pad fixing nuts on both sides of cantilever and lubricate threads, curved washers and washer-to-arm contact points.
e. Point pads down, away from rim, and gently snug nut. This allows proper alignment of caliper arms.
f. Position caliper arms parallel to one another (8-3.1_Figure 5). Adjust cable at cable pinch bolt. Use the Park Tool BT-2 Cable Stretcher to help adjust brake cable.

8-3.1_Figure 5

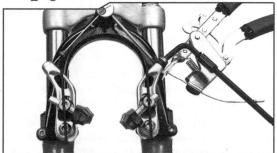

Adjust brake cable at pinch bolt until arms are close to parallel

g. View centering of caliper arms to rim. Most models use a centering setscrew on the caliper arm. Turning the setscrew changes spring tension in that arm. For example, to move both arms right, turn right side set screw clockwise. To move both arms left, turn counter-clockwise. Squeeze lever to work calipers and check centering again. Caliper arms should be centered to rim. Do not center pads to rim, view only arms relative to rim.

h. Attach a rubber band around backside of pad. This is used in pad alignment only and is later removed (8-3.1_Figure 6). The rubber band creates a shim to give "toe" to the brake pad. Some pads may have a built in toe-feature at the back end of the pad. Do not use a rubber band on these pads. Simply align the built in toe-feature flush to the rim.

8-3.1_Figure 6

Adjust one pad at a time, using a rubber band to create toe

i. Adjust pad alignment to rim. Push one pad until it is contacting rim. Use care not to move caliper arm. Align pad correctly for four positions. Height, with pad close to top edge of braking surface. Tangent, with front and back edge even to rim. Vertical face, with pad face and rim parallel. Toe, with slight gap at trailing edge of pad. The rubber band acts as a shim to hold the back of the pad out slightly.

j. Hold mounting bolt with hex wrench and tighten mounting nut. Pad should contact rim after adjustment.

k. Remove rubber band from rear and view

toe. There should be a slight gap at back of pad. Double check pad alignment by viewing from top, bottom, front and side.

l. Loosen other pad and repeat steps h-k. Both pads should be contacting rim when pad adjustment is completed.

m. Squeeze lever multiple times to seat brake cable and test brake cable pinch bolt. Cable should not slip.

n. Set clearance at lever for rider preference. If brake feels tight, turn barrel adjuster clockwise to loosen brake cable tension. If brake feels loose, turn barrel adjuster counter-clockwise to tighten brake cable tension.

o. If barrel adjuster is all the way engaged at lever and brake lever is still too tight, loosen brake cable pinch bolt and allow slack to feed through pinch plate. Tighten pinch bolt and test again. Adjust at brake lever.

p. View pad centering to rim. If not adequately centered, use centering set screw on arm (8-3.1_Figure 7).

8-3.1_Figure 7

Use spring tension to center pads to rim

q. Inspect that the pads are not rubbing the tire. Re-adjust if necessary. Use care not to move brake pad stud in or out from caliper arm as this changes centering. Move pads only up/down.

NOTE
NOTE
NOTE
NOTE:
Some brands and models of cantilever calipers have no centering setscrew or other system of centering. In this case, move pad stud laterally as necessary in pad fixing bolts. Some brands use adjustable spring tension on each caliper at the mounting bolt. Spring tension can be changed on either arm.

The cantilever may have a threaded stud brake pad. The arms cannot be moved until both are parallel. The threaded stud uses a ball and socket system

The process for threaded stud brake pad cantilevers is as follows:

a. Mount bike in a repair stand.

b. Use straddle wire to bring pads to rim and secure pinch bolt.

c. Align pads correctly for four positions. Height, with pad close to top edge of braking surface. Tangent, with front and back edge even to rim. Vertical face, with pad face and rim parallel. Toe, with slight gap at trailing edge of pad.

d. Turn adjusting barrel into lever to clear pads from rim. Squeeze lever and set lever clearance as desired.

8-3.2
Linear Pull Caliper Adjustment

TOOLS & SUPPLIES
- Box or open end wrenches (Park Tool CBW-1 and CBW-4)
- Hex wrenches (Park Tool— various models)

Liner pull brakes are similar to cantilever brakes. The arms pivot on frame or fork mounted studs at one end and are pulled at the other end. There is no extra straddle wire as with cantilevers. The primary cable from the brake lever passes through a cable housing stop called the "noodle." The noodle is fitted to one arm and the cable attaches to the second arm. Pulling the lever pulls the arms together, forcing the pads into the rim braking surface.

"Linear Pull" brakes and Shimano V-brakes® are common on many mountain bikes and hybrid bikes (8-3.2_Figure 1). The caliper arm shares the same frame mounting system with cantilevers.

8-3.2_Figure 1

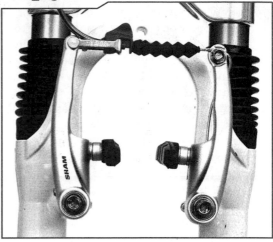

Linear pull brake

Linear pull calipers move the pads on an arc moving downward toward the rim. Pads should be set high vertically on the rim, but without interfering with the tire. Pad height will lower as pad face wears.

Linear pull brake pads often use a washer system to set caliper arm position to the rim. Push both arms together until pads are touching rim and view caliper arms. Arms should be close to parallel with one another. If arms are forming a wide "V," swap the wide spacers inside the caliper for the narrower spacers outside the caliper. If the arms tilt inward when the pads are striking the rim, swap the narrow spacers inside the calipers for the wider spacers outside the calipers (8-3.2_Figure 2 and 8-3.2_Figure 3).

8-3.2_Figure 2

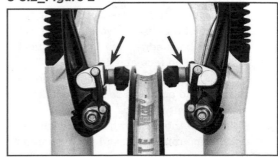

Spacers inside caliper will set arms wide apart

8-3.2_Figure 3

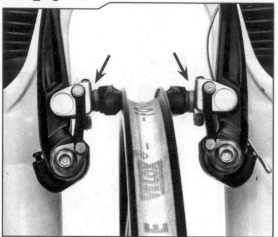

Move wide spacers to outside of arms to narrow calipers

Some models of the Shimano® XTR, XT and LX brakes use a moving parallelogram for the pad-to-rim motion. These are called V-brakes® and differ in pad placement from other linear pull models. The parallelogram allows the pads to move straight toward the rim, not on an arc. In this design, the brake pad is not mounted directly to the caliper arm. The pad is mounted to a moving plate attached to the caliper arm with a linkage system (8-3.2_Figure 4). Set pad height to strike in the middle of rim height for these brakes.

8-3.2_Figure 4

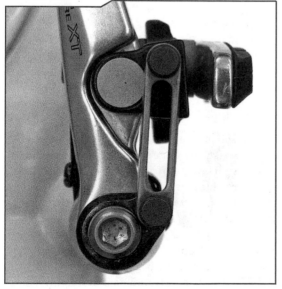

Linkage system of Shimano® V-brake system

Linear pull calipers, like cantilevers, are attached to the frame or fork at the braze-on. Grease the outer surface of the braze-on before installing the calipers. Use a mild thread-locker inside the fitting and install the bolt to a relatively low torque. The cantilever should pivot freely. Over tightening may damage the fitting and cause the caliper to stick.

Most models of linear pull calipers use a threaded stud brake pad. A threaded bolt is fixed into the pad. The bolt is sandwiched to the caliper arm by a series of convex and concave washers. This "ball and socket" system allows the bolt and pad to move in the caliper arm for toe and vertical face alignment (8-3.2_Figure 5). To change pad angle, loosen the bolt and move pad to desired position. Hold pad while securing nut/bolt.

8-3.2_Figure 5

Ball and socket system of threaded brake pad

The procedure for linear pull caliper adjustment is as follows:

a. Attach brake cable to brake lever and through housing. Feed cable through the "noodle" and through the rubber boot, if available. Finally, feed brake cable through pinch mechanism and secure.

b. Push both arms together until pads are touching rim and inspect caliper arms. Arms should be close to parallel with one another. Move washers as necessary to position arms, as described above.

c. Adjust one pad position to the rim at a time. Loosen pad nut/bolt and lubricate curved washers and thread. Install rubber band shim at back edge of pad (8-3.2_Figure 6).

8-3.2_Figure 6

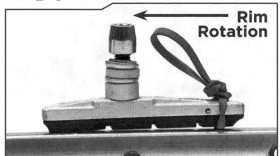

Using a shim to create toe

d. Push caliper arm to rim and view pad alignment. If practical, unhook spring from arm to make alignment easier. Align pad correctly for four positions. Height, with pad close to top edge of braking surface. Tangent, with front and back edge even to rim. Vertical face, with pad face and rim parallel. Toe, with slight gap at trailing edge of pad. The rubber band acts as a shim to hold the back of the pad out slightly.

e. Tighten pad nut and remove rubber band. Inspect pad alignment again.

f. Repeat pad adjustment on other side of caliper.

g. Squeeze lever hard several times and set pad clearance at lever for rider preference. If brake feels tight, turn barrel adjuster clockwise to loosen brake cable tension. If brake feels lose, turn barrel adjuster counter-clockwise to tighten brake cable tension. If barrel adjuster is all the way engaged at lever and brake lever is still too tight, loosen brake cable pinch bolt and allow slack to feed through pinch plate. Tighten pinch bolt and test again. Adjust at brake lever.

h. Inspect pad centering to rim. Use set screw on sides of caliper to center pads to rim. Tighten setscrew on arm with pad that is closest to rim (8-3.2_Figure 7).

8-3.2_Figure 7

Use screw to change spring tension when centering pads to rim

i. Inspect that pads are not rubbing tire. Re-adjust if necessary.

If the linear pull caliper uses the smooth stud brake pads, the procedure is similar to cantilever calipers. Use the cable to set arms close to parallel, and adjust pads. Use the barrel adjuster to back pads off rim for clearance.

8-3.3 Dual Pivot Caliper Adjustment

TOOLS & SUPPLIES
- Box or open end wrenches (Park Tool CBW-1 and CBW-4)
- Hex wrenches (Park Tool—various models)
- Fourth Hand (Park Tool BT-2)

Dual pivot calipers are popular on many road bikes. They appear visually very similar to side pull brakes. However, the left side and right side dual pivot brake caliper arms move on separate pivots, and the two arms arc in different directions. As seen from the mechanics point of view, the left pad swings downward toward the rim, while the right pad swings upward. As with other calipers, the swing of the arm determines pad height.

8-3.3_Figure 1

Dual pivot brake

Some dual pivot brakes allow for only height and tangent alignment adjustments to rim. Toeing or vertical face alignments are possible with pads using a ball and socket system only. Dual pull caliper arms can sometimes be bent slightly for pad toe. However, if the caliper arm is relatively thick, or seems difficult to bend, toe may be cut into the pad with a file. It is simplest to first ride the bike and see if toe is required.

The procedure for dual pivot caliper and pad adjustment is as follows:

a. Feed brake cable through brake lever and through housing.

b. Attach brake cable to pinch bolt and secure.

c. Loosen and lubricate threads of pad bolt/nut.

d. Squeeze both pads to rim and adjust pads for height and tangent. Right pad should be set to lower edge of braking surface. Left should be set to upper edge of braking surface. Vertical face alignment to rim and toe alignment are not typically adjustable on dual pivot calipers. If desired, toe may be set by slightly bending arm. Grasp arm with small adjustable wrench and bend arm as needed. Use rag on arm to protect finish if surface scarring is a concern.

e. Tighten pad fixing bolts.

f. Squeeze lever to test pad clearance.

g. Use barrel adjuster to adjust pad clearance. Set clearance for approximately 3-4mm (⅛") per side from pad to rim. Draw slack from system using brake cable pinch bolt if barrel adjuster is set out to its limit.

h. View pad centering to rim. If left pad appears closer to rim, tighten setscrew. If right pad appears closer, loosen setscrew (8-3.3_Figure 2).

8-3.3_Figure 2

Center pads to rim with setscrew in brake bridge

NOTE: For more detail on adjustments to arm pivots of dual pivot caliper arms see Repair Help at www.parktool.com

8-3.4 Side Pull Caliper Adjustment

TOOLS & SUPPLIES
- Box or open end wrenches (Park Tool CBW-1 and CBW-4)
- Hex wrenches (Park Tool—various models)
- Fourth Hand (Park Tool BT-2)

Road-type bikes may also use a side pull brake. Side pull calipers at first glance look like dual pivot calipers. However, each arm shares a single pivot bolt in the middle of the brake. The bolt for mounting the brake and for the arm pivot is centered over the rim. Both pads swing downward on an arc toward the rim and should be set high on the braking surface.

8-3.4_Figure 1

Side pull caliper

The side pull caliper arm pivot can be adjusted if there is play (knocking) between the arms, or if the caliper arms bind from being too tight. There are two basic types of pivot bolt systems, the double nut system, and the safety pivot system. While the pivot adjustment is important to the brake performance, the adjustment process is not covered in this manual.

NOTE: For more detail on side pull caliper pivot adjustment see Repair Help at www.parktool.com.

The procedure for side pull caliper adjustment is as follows:

a. Feed brake cable through lever and through housing.

b. Loosen each pad fixing nut and lubricate threads.

c. Push one arm to rim and set pad alignment. Adjust pad to strike upper edge of braking surface. Pad front and back edges should be level. Most side pull pads adjust only for height and tangent. Vertical face alignment is not typically adjustable. Tighten pad fixing bolt.

d. Repeat adjustment with other pad and tighten pad fixing bolt.

e. Attach brake cable to pinch mechanism. Squeeze pads to rim and draw slack from cable. Secure brake cable pinch bolt.

f. Squeeze lever hard several times to test brake cable pinch bolt.

g. Check lever clearance to handlebar. Squeeze lever gently until pads contact rim. Gap to handlebar should be no less than one inch (25mm) at this point. Use adjusting barrel to change lever clearance to rider preference.

h. Check brake pad centering to rim.

i. If pads are not centered to rim, hold caliper arms with one hand while loosening rear nut. Move caliper so pads are centered to rim and tighten rear nut. Some models are fitted with a wrench flat in the center bolt. Use one wrench on the stud and another wrench on the mounting nut, and move wrenches the same direction and the same amount (8-3.4_Figure 2). One pad may contact the rim before the other when squeezed to the rim. This is not an issue

with side pull calipers. It is only important that the pads are centered to the rim when they are fully open.

8-3.4_Figure 2

Centering sidepull with centering flats on brake stud

j. Set toe if necessary. Test ride bike and apply brakes. If brakes do not squeal, toe is not necessary. If desired, toe may be set by slightly bending arm. Grasp arm with small adjustable wrench and bend arm as needed. Use rag to protect arm if surface scarring is a concern.

Chapter 9

Caliper Disc
Brake Systems

Disc brake systems use a caliper mounted near the dropouts of the frame or fork ends, and a rotor (disc) mounted to the hub. The brake pads are housed in the caliper and are forced into the rotor. Disc caliper brakes slow the bike by converting the speed and energy of the bicycle into heat. Disc brakes can be effective in wet weather where mud, dirt and water are a concern in braking. The system can generate significant heat from slowing the wheel and bike. Allow rotor and caliper to cool before servicing.

Disc brake systems can be mechanical, hydraulic, or hydro-mechanical. Mechanical systems use calipers that are cable actuated, similar to rim caliper brakes, with an inner brake wire and housing pulled by a brake lever (9_ Figure 1). Hydraulic systems use sealed tubing to push brake fluid (9_Figure 2). The mechanical-hydraulic systems use a brake inner wire that actuates a piston in the caliper.

9_Figure 2

Hydraulic disc brake

9_Figure 1

Mechanical disc brake

Disc brake calipers mount to fittings on the bicycle frame and fork. The common standard is referred to as the International Standard. This standard uses two mounting holes spaced 51mm apart and the caliper mounting bolts are positioned perpendicular to the rotor face.

A less common mounting system is the post mount. The mounting bolts of the post mount are parallel with the rotor face and the mounting holes are spaced 74mm apart. Brake calipers designed for the post mounting system can be fitted with adapters to work with the International Standard.

Brake pads for both mechanical and hydraulic systems are available in various compounds. Generally, a softer resin material will tend to squeal less. It will also offer the user more modulation, or the ability to brake lightly. However these types of pads will also wear more quickly. The harder metal or semi-metallic pads will last longer, especially in wet and muddy conditions (9_Figure 3).

9_Figure 3

(A) Semi-metallic disc brake pads, (B) Resin disc brake pads

9-1 Rotor

TOOLS & SUPPLIES
- Hex wrenches
- T25 Torx wrench (Park Tool PH-T25, TWS-I)

The rotor or disc of the disc brake system secures to a disc-specific hub. The common system uses six bolts. Use a mild thread locker on the threads, and secure the bolts. Many brands use rotor bolts requiring the use of a Torx T-25 wrench (9-1_ Figure 1). A Torx fitting is a special 12-point socket head bolt. Secure rotor bolts to manufacturer's torque specifications (Appendix C).

9-1_Figure 1

Secure bolts using Torx driver

The rotor diameter may vary between models and brands. Common rotor diameter sizes are 145mm, 152mm, 160mm, 185mm, and 203mm. The brake caliper and rotor diameter must be compatible.

Shimano® also has a splined fitting system with a lockring, similar to a cassette lockring. The spline system of the rotor matches splines at the hub. Use the Park Tool FR-5 to secure the lockring to 350 inch-pounds (9-1_Figure 2).

9-1_Figure 2

Shimano XTR lockring system for rotor mounting

The rotor and brake pads should be kept clean of oils and grease. If pads become contaminated, it is best to replace them. When cleaning the rotors or washing the bike, remove wheel and remove pads from bike. Use isopropyl alcohol or similar solvent when cleaning rotor surface of dirt or film. Do not use a solvent or cleaner that contains oils or leaves an oily residue.

Rotors may become bent or warped with use and abuse. Some re-bending may be possible. It is generally best to bend at the rotor arm, not at the braking surface directly. The Park Tool BT-3 Brake Tool makes a useful tool to grab the rotor arm for bending (9-1_Figure 3). It can be useful to number the rotor arms to better track the repair progress. Mount the bike in a repair stand and spin the wheel. Watch the wobble at the caliper, or hold the BT-3 at the caliper as a rub indicator. Stop the wheel and notice the location and direction of the rub. Find the arm or arms corresponding to this area and bend slightly. Spin the wheel and check rotor again.

9-1_Figure 3

Re-bending a warped rotor

Front disc brakes place a load on the front hub in a direction that tends to remove it from the fork. It is especially important to properly tighten the front skewer on bikes with disc front brakes.

9-2 Hydraulic Disc Brakes

Hydraulic brake systems use a piston at the hand lever called the "master" piston. The piston pushes brake fluid through sealed brake tubing to another set of pistons at the caliper called the "slave" pistons. The slave pistons push the pads to the rotor. Because the hydraulic fluid does not compress or flex, hydraulic systems are considered higher performance than mechanical systems.

With use over time, brake fluid will become contaminated with dirt and moisture and should be replaced. It is critical to use the correct type of fluid for the specific brake. Some manufacturers use mineral oil as the fluid, while others use an automotive brake fluid. The manufacturer will specify the type of fluid. The different types of brake fluid should never be mixed. Using the wrong fluid is likely to cause seals to fail, resulting in brake failure.

Automotive fluids are DOT (Department of Transportation) approved and are generally polyglycol fluids. The D.O.T. fluids have different ratings, such as 3 or 4. Contact the manufacturer for a specific recommendation. Automotive brake fluids are caustic and toxic.

Work with care to avoid fluid contact with the outside of the lever or caliper, the bike, or your skin. When available, use protective gloves, such as Park Tool MG-1 Mechanic Gloves.

Hydraulic systems should be inspected at all fittings and hose connections for fluid leakage and seepage. Additionally, the bike should not be stored or turned upside down, as air may enter the brake lines. If the bike has been upside down, allow it to sit several minutes before use, and test the levers by pulling with force.

NOTE: Never squeeze the brake lever of a hydraulic lever when the wheel and rotor are out of the caliper. Use plastic blocks supplied by manufacturers, or re-install wheel before working lever.

9-2.1 Brake Lever Adjustment

The hydraulic brake lever is positioned on the handlebar similar to conventional or non-hydraulic levers. Set the angle for comfortable reach when the cyclist is in the saddle. The brake lever reach is adjusted behind the lever pivot. Tightening the screw moves the lever closer to the handlebars (9-2.1_Figure 1).

9-2.1_Figure 1

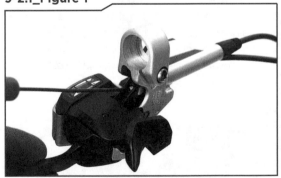

Reach screw adjustment on the Shimano® brake lever

Brake manufacturers design the hydraulic cylinders at the calipers to be compatible with the cylinder at the brake lever. The diameter of the cylinder and the distance it will move (the stroke) may vary between brands. Check with the manufacturer before mixing different levers and calipers.

As the brake fluid heats, it expands. Hydraulic disc systems use a reservoir system that contains a bladder to allow for the expansion of the brake fluid. Some models use an enclosed bladder in the lever, while others use an "open system" (9-2.1_Figure 2). The master piston is sealed when the lever is pulled, but is open to the reservoir when the lever in fully open.

9-2.1_Figure 2

Reservoir and bladder

In all hydraulic systems, it is important that there is no air in the tubing or lines between the caliper and the lever piston. Air bubbles in the line will compress, causing the brake to feel "soft" when the lever is pulled with force.

9-2.2 Brake Caliper Alignment

TOOLS & SUPPLIES

- Hex wrenches, 3mm and 5mm
- T-25 torx wrench, Park Tool PH-T25
- Phillips screwdriver, #1 and #2
- 7mm wrench or small adjustable wrench
- Bleed tube- plastic tubing with 3/16 inch inside diameter
- Plastic bag for catching brake fluid
- Brake rotor blocks (substitute a clean shim of 10mm thick, such as a hex wrench)
- Brake pad block (substitute clean steel shim of 2mm thick, such as a cone wrench)
- Lint free cleaning rag

For any disc system, it can be difficult to view the pad to rotor alignment. Place a white paper or white rag behind the area you are viewing. If possible, shine a flashlight on the rag for a highlighted background (9-2.2 _Figure 1).

9-2.2 _Figure 1

Use a white background to help in viewing pad to rotor alignment

There are two different caliper mounting systems for the Shimano® hydraulic brake caliper. The caliper body may bolt directly to the rotor mounts of the frame or fork (9-2.2 _Figure 2). Alternatively, the caliper body may bolt to a bracket, and the bracket is bolted to the frame or fork. In either case, the hydraulic systems have very close tolerances between pads and rotor. Alignment of the caliper to the rotor is critical to the performance of the brake.

9-2.2 _Figure 2

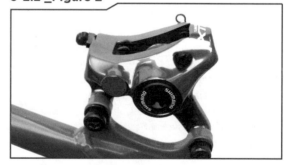

Caliper bolted directly to frame

The procedure for Shimano® Hydraulic XTR, XT, Deore, Saint caliper alignment using an adaptor bracket is as follows:

a. For bracket mounted calipers, fully loosen caliper mounting bolts. This will allow the caliper to move sideways.

b. Depress the brake lever to secure pads against the rotor and maintain pressure. This will move caliper so pads are aligned to rotor. Inspect caliper and brake pad pistons. Push caliper left or right until pistons appear centered over rotor. Maintain pressure on the rotor and tighten the caliper mounting bolts (9-2.2 _Figure 3).

9-2.2 _Figure 3

Align caliper and pads to rotor, then tighten caliper mounting bolts

c. Release lever and inspect this initial pad alignment. Ideally, the pads should clear the rotor with no rubbing. In some cases, however, a light rubbing may occur and will not generally be an issue with performance. If the wheel seems to slow when it is turned, re-adjust the pads by loosening the caliper mounting bolts to reposition the caliper. Fine-tune the pad alignment by fully loosening one mounting bolt while keeping the ot her bolt snug. This will allow you to push the caliper while pivoting off the snug bolt.

If the brake caliper is bolted directly to the mounts, it is necessary to use thin washers and shims to adjust the caliper. A washer with a post, called a "banjo washer," can be placed between the frame or fork mount and the caliper body (9-2.2 Figure 4). Install washers and secure mounting bolt. View pad to rotor alignment, then add or subtract washers as necessary.

9-2.2 _Figure 4

Add banjo washers to move caliper and pads

9-2.3
Brake Pad Removal and Replacement

Brake pads wear thin with use. Most manufacturers list specifications for minimum pad thickness. For Shimano® pads, replace when pad material (not including pad holder) is less then 0.9mm thick. Inspect old pads when removing. If pads are worn unevenly, it may be a sign that the caliper is misaligned to the rotor (9-2.3_Figure 1). New disc pads have a "burn in" period. Solvents from manufacturing are burned off from the heat of braking. Braking performance will improve after the burn in period.

9-2.3_Figure 1

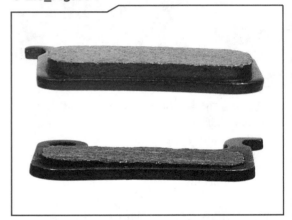

The pad above is new, while the used pad below shows signs of misalignment to the rotor

As the pads wear, the pistons reposition closer to the rotor. It will be necessary to remove the rotor and push the pistons away from the center before installing new pads.
The procedure for Shimano® XTR, XT, Deore, Saint pad replacement is as follows:
a. Mount bike in repair stand.
b. Remove wheel(s).
c. Rotate lever on handlebar until top surface of reservoir is parallel with the ground.
d. Clean lever of dirt and wipe around reservoir cover.
e. Remove reservoir cover. This will allow excess fluid to spill from reservoir.
f. Remove pad fixing bolt clip and unscrew pad fixing bolt (9-2.3 _Figure 2).

9-2.3 _Figure 2

Remove bolt after removing clip

g. Remove pads by pushing them outward, away from hub axle. Notice orientation of pad return spring between pads. This spring assists pad release from rotor during braking.

h. Wipe piston area clean. Use a clean rag and a mild solvent such as isopropyl alcohol to clean the piston faces and inside the caliper body.

i. Using a plastic lever, such as a tire lever, push both pistons into the caliper body. Push near center of piston and avoid pushing edge of piston (9-2.3_Figure 3).

9-2.3_Figure 3

Push pistons back into caliper body

j. Place pad return spring between new pads. (9-2.3_Figure 4)

9-2.3_Figure 4

Pad return spring is placed between pads

k. Install pads into caliper. Orient eyehole in pads and spring to align with pad fixing bolthole.

l. Install and secure pad fixing bolt.

m. Install pad fixing bolt clip.

n. Install reservoir cover and secure screws.

o. Install wheel and test brake by squeezing lever with force. If lever feels soft, system will require bleeding.

p. If pads drag or are misaligned, reset the pads as described in Outline Item 9-2.4.

9-2.4
Brake Fluid Bleeding & Replacement

Bleeding a hydraulic system is removing trapped air from the lines and calipers. Shimano brake systems use mineral oil. Never use an automotive D.O.T. brake fluid in a system requiring mineral oil. Remove the brake pads before bleeding or replacing fluid so they do not become contaminated with brake fluid. When servicing hydraulic brakes, work in clean conditions if possible. Use care to keeps hydraulic pieces, such as the bladder, clean and away from dirt.

The procedure for bleeding Shimano® XTR, XT, Deore, Saint brake fluid is as follows:

a. Mount bike in repair stand.

b. Remove wheels.

c. Remove brake pads to avoid contamination by brake fluid.

d. Install Shimano® brake block #Y8CL18000 in place of pads. If blocks are not available, substitute a block of about 10mm wide (⅜ inch) to prevent piston from extending. Substitute a clean 10mm hex wrench if the brake block is not available (9-2.4_Figure 1).

9-2.4_Figure 1

Install a block to prevent piston movement

e. Rotate bike as necessary until tubing has a continuous upward slope from the brake caliper to the reservoir (9-2.4_Figure 2).

9-2.4_Figure 2

Rotate bike and lever for continuous upward slope

f. Rotate lever on handlebar until top surface of reservoir is parallel with the ground.
g. Attach bleed tubing to end of bleed nipple at caliper. Attach plastic bag to end of tubing to catch waste fluid (9-2.4_Figure 3).

9-2.4_Figure 3

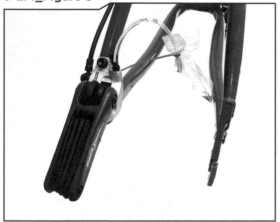

Bleed nipple with tubing and bag for excess fluid

h. Clean dirt from lever and wipe around reservoir tank cover. Unthread screws at reservoir tank cap. Remove reservoir cap and bladder. Fill reservoir to top.
i. Loosen bleed nipple, at caliper body, ⅛ turn.
j. Operate lever repeatedly. Bubbles will

appear in reservoir tank, and fluid level may drop. Keep reservoir filled with fluid. Use a non-metallic lever to tap along brake line to encourage any air trapped in the line to rise toward the reservoir.

9-2.4_Figure 4

Keep reservoir tank filled with fluid

k. When oil begins to come out of bleed tube, close bleed nipple at caliper body.
l. Test lever by pulling. Lever will eventually become stiff and firm when pulled. If there is no resistance to lever, open bleed screw and continue to operate handle and pump oil into the system.
m. When lever resistance stiffens, close bleed nipple. Hold lever closed and maintain pressure (9-2.4_Figure 5).

9-2.4_Figure 5

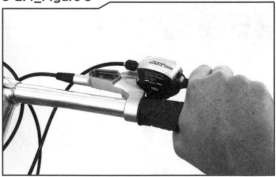

Hold pressure at lever

n. Using a 7mm wrench, or a small adjustable wrench, loosen bleed nipple to open system. Open and close system within one second, noticing if any of the expelled fluid contains air bubble (9-2.4_Figure 6).

9-2.4_Figure 6

Open system briefly to expel air bubbles

o. Release lever. Check reservoir tank and add fluid.

p. Operate lever repeatedly. If lever feels stiff with resistance at the end of its travel, line contains no air and is fully bled. If lever feels soft, repeat steps "m" through "o."

q. Check that reservoir tank is filled to top. Install reservoir bladder and cap. Expect some excess fluid to spill from lever. This is normal and insures no air is below bladder. Tighten cap screws.

r. After bleeding, disconnect hose from bleed nipple. Wipe lever and caliper of any fluid.

s. Install brake shoes and wheel.

Brake fluid can become dirty with use and may become contaminated with moisture. If the bike is used extensively, the fluid should be replaced once a year.

The procedure for changing fluid is as follows:

a. Proceed with steps "a" through "j" above.

b. Operate lever to pump fluid through the hose, adding more fluid as level in reservoir tank drops.

c. Continue to pump lever until fluid appears clear at the bleed hose. Again, check fluid and add as the level drops at the reservoir tank.

d. Close nipple and proceed with the bleeding process "m" through "s" above.

9-2.5 Resetting Brake Pads

If the pads seem to rub on the rotor, and re-alignment will not prevent this, the pistons may need to be reset. The procedure requires the use of a shim in the caliper for the adjustment. Shimano® supplies this shim, part #Y8CL1200, with the brake set when purchased new. Alternatively, use a hard, flat material that

is the thickness of the rotor. Park Tool cone wrenches, such as the Double-Ended Cone Wrench DCW 1-4, match the width of rotors and can substitute for the pad spacer.

The procedure for resetting Shimano® XTR, XT, Deore, Saint pads is as follows:

a. Remove wheel(s) from bike.

b. Remove pad retention screw and remove pads. Use a clean rag and a mild solvent such as isopropyl alcohol to wipe clean the piston faces and inside the caliper body.

c. Use a plastic lever, such as a tire lever. Push each piston back into caliper body. Notice if the piston moves after being positioned back into caliper body. If a piston moves after being reset, there may be excess fluid in the system. Remove cover of reservoir. Allow excess fluid to spill out of the reservoir as the pistons are pushed into the caliper body. If reservoir cap was removed, re-install cap. Wipe oil from lever.

d. Install pads, pad return spring, and pad retention screw.

e. Install floating shim (Shimano part number Y8CL1200) or a shim of equivalent thickness (9-2.5_Figure 1).

9-2.5_Figure 1

Install shim of equal thickness to rotor

f. Squeeze lever repeatedly. Pistons will automatically center to caliper body.

g. For bracket mounted caliper bodies, loosen caliper mounting bolts fully.

h. Install wheel. DO NOT squeeze lever at this time.

i. Inspect pad alignment to rotor. For bracket mounted caliper bodies, position caliper body to center pads over rotor. Tighten caliper mounting bolts and inspect.

j. For caliper bodies mounting directly to the frame, use washers to center pads to rotor. Secure mounting bolts fully

k. Squeeze lever and inspect pad alignment. Fine tune pad alignment as necessary.

9-3 Mechanical Disc Brakes

Mechanical disc calipers use two brake pads, one on each side of the rotor. Depending upon the design of the caliper, both pads may move to contact the rotor. However, alternative designs have one pad being fixed, with only one pad moving to contact the rotor.

9-3.1 Brake Lever Adjustment

Flat handlebar brake levers used with mechanical disc calipers are compatible with the linear pull caliper rim brakes. The lever should be set for a comfortable reach and secured to the bar. The brake housing and brake wire are the same as with rim caliper brakes. Prepare housing and wires as with rim caliper brakes. See Outline Item 8-1 Brake Levers and Outline Item 8-2 Cable System.

9-3.2 Brake Caliper Adjustment

TOOLS & SUPPLIES
• Hex wrenches (Park Tool—various models)
• Flash light

Avid® mechanical calipers use an outer pad that moves toward the rotor when the caliper-actuating arm is pulled by the brake wire. The inner pad can be adjusted toward or away from the rotor with a pad-adjusting knob, but it is fixed during braking. The moving pad flexes the rotor toward the fixed pad when the brake is operated. The moving pad also uses an adjusting knob to position the pad relative to the rotor (9-3.2_ Figure 1). The dial uses an indent system, with 16 "clicks" per revolution. One complete revolution moves the pad approximately 1mm. The Avid® mechanical disc brake for MTB bikes uses a brake lever designed for linear pull brakes.

9-3.2_Figure 1

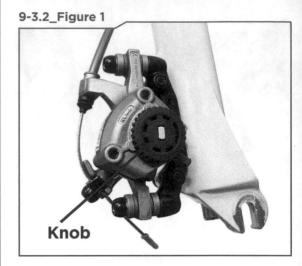

Knob

Pad adjusting knob moves pad position relative to rotor

Avid® disc caliper brakes use a ball-and-socket system for the caliper mounting bolts. This fixing system is similar to many brake pads on linear pull caliper rim brakes (9-3.2_ Figure 2). This system allows easy alignment of the brake caliper to the rotor.

9-3.2_Figure 2

Ball and socket system for pad and caliper alignment to rotor

The caliper body position over the rotor is very important to braking performance. Compare the gap from the rotor to the caliper. The gap from the caliper body to the rotor on the inside (fixed pad side) should be approximately twice as much as the gap from the caliper body to the rotor on the outside (9-3.2_Figure 3).

9-3.2_Figure 3

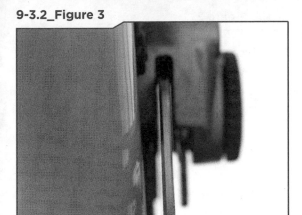

Gap from fixed pad to rotor is larger then gap from moving pad to rotor

The procedure for Avid® mechanical caliper pad alignment is as follows:

a. If the caliper is attached to a bracket, check that the bracket is fully secured to the frame or fork.

b. Loosen caliper-mounting bolts so caliper is loose on bracket. Caliper·adjustment is made at caliper to bracket interface, not at bracket to frame/fork interface.

c. Loosen brake wire pinch bolt if it is secured.

d. Check that both pad adjusting knob dials are turned fully counter-clockwise to move pads fully away from rotor.

e. Turn the inner pad adjusting knob clockwise approximately 1¾ turn (about 24 "clicks").

f. Turn the outer pad adjusting knob clockwise until pad fully secures rotor. This aligns pads and caliper body to rotor.

g. Snug each caliper mounting bolt. Then alternatively tighten first one bolt, and then the other until both are fully secure.

h. Draw slack from the brake wire and secure pinch bolt. Do not allow caliper arm to move upward when drawing slack from brake (9-3.2_Figure 4).

9-3.2_Figure 4

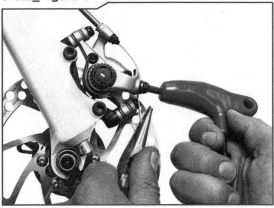

Pull slack from cable, but do not move caliper arm

i. Set pad clearance. Inner pad (fixed pad) should have twice the gap to the rotor as the outer pad (moving pad). Loosen fixed (inner) pad adjusting knob 2-3 clicks counter-clockwise. Loosen moving pad adjusting knob 4-6 clicks counter-clockwise.

j. Squeeze lever to test caliper brake. Adjust lever modulation setting by moving pads inward or outward from rotor by using both pad adjusting knobs. To maintain the 2:1 ratio, turn the fixed pad adjusting knob twice as many clicks as the moving pad adjusting knob. For example, if a looser modulation is desired, turn the fixed pad adjusting knob counter-clockwise 4 clicks, and the moving pad adjusting knob counter-clockwise only 2 clicks.

The caliper actuating arm is designed to operate from a fully open position. Set cable tension at the adjusting barrel so actuating arm is fully opened or returned.

9-3.3
Mechanical Brake Pad Removal & Replacement
Do not use the brake lever adjusting barrel or cable pinch bolt to account for pad wear. Caliper arm may bottom out on caliper body, preventing pads from pressing on rotor.

As pads wear, use pad-adjusting knobs to move pads closer to rotor. Turn the fixed pad adjusting knob clockwise twice as many clicks as the moving pad adjusting knob to maintain the 1:2 ratio of pad to rotor spacing.

For example, if the fixed pad adjusting knob is turned clockwise two clicks, turn the moving pad adjusting knob one click.

Brake pads should be removed and replaced if the pad thickness, including the metal holder, is less than 3mm.

The procedure for Avid® mechanical caliper pad removal and replacement is as follows:

a.   Remove the wheel.

b.   Loosen each pad adjustment knob an equal amount.

c.   Grab lever at end of pad and push toward center of caliper body, pulling pad outward and away from caliper (9-3.3_Figure 1). Repeat process for second pad.

9-3.3_Figure 1

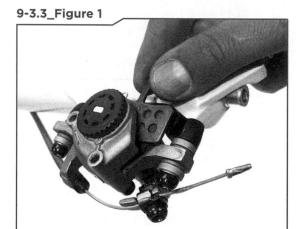

Push lever to center of caliper body and lift to remove

d.   Note orientation of pad return spring and remove spring from pads.

e.   Place new pads over pad return spring (9-3.3_Figure 2). Spring should be sandwiched between new pads. Installation lever is set asymmetrically on pad. Align bridge of spring with caliper boss locators.

9-3.3_Figure 2

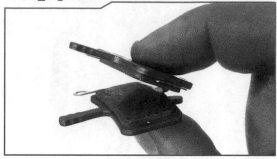

Place spring between brake pads

f.   Gently squeeze return spring and pads. Engage pads into caliper body. Pad installation lever orients away from brace bolts. Push return-spring and pads into place (9-3.3_Figure 3). Pad locator will engage bosses in caliper boss.

9-3.3_Figure 3

Push pads into caliper body

g.   Install wheel.

h.   Refer to Outline Item 9-3.2 Brake Caliper Adjustment for proper caliper pad alignment.

Chapter 10

Handlebars, Stems, Saddles & Seat Posts

The handlebars, stem, saddle, and seat post are critical to the cyclist's safety and performance because they are important contact points on the bike. They should be adjusted to the rider's body and be securely attached to the frame. Some changes in angle and height are possible to stems, bars, and saddle. Different models and styles can also be installed to fit individual needs.

NOTE: To record your body position on the bike, see Repair Help at www.parktool.com

10-1 Handlebar Adjustment

TOOLS & SUPPLIES
• Hex wrenches (Park Tool- various models)
• Straight edge (Park Tool SBC-1)

Flat Style Bars

Fat style bars are commonly used on mountain bikes and hybrid bikes. The handlebars typically have a slight bend to either side. Generally, these bars should be aligned to point straight back, so the bars are level to the ground (10-1_Figure 1). However, the bars can be rotated in the stem for different hand positions. If the bars are rotated, it will affect brake and shift lever rotation as well. The mountain bike handlebar can also have a rise built into the bar to bring the rider's hands higher. The flat bar uses a 22.2mm outside diameter at the ends for securing brake levers, shift levers, and bar-end extensions.

10-1_Figure 1

Flat bars rotated to a level position

Handlebars are secured in the stem. There are two standards for the flat handlebar center. The traditional size is 25.4mm where it tightens to the stem. There is also a larger bar center standard of 31.8mm. The two standards are not interchangeable.

Bar-ends, mounted either internally or externally to the ends of the handlebars, give the rider another hand position option (10-1_Figure 2). Bar-ends may take nearly the entire body weight of the rider during use and should be very secure on the bar. However, external bar-ends may crush the end of thin handlebars. If the inside diameter of the bar is greater than 19mm, a plug is required to provide internal support to prevent damage. Consult a professional mechanic or the manufacturer if in doubt.

10-1_Figure 2

Secure bar ends so they do not slip under load

Grips vary in shape, color, compounds, size and length. However, all are designed to fit the 22.2mm bar diameter. Grips should not slip or move during the ride. With much use and time, grips tend to expand and will loosen on the bar. It is possible to help the grip bond to the bar using adhesive glue and/or wire tying. Bar grips are typically rubber compounds. Gluing rubber to a metal bar is a difficult bond for most adhesives. Contact cement and tubular tire cements are good choices for glue. If you are using glue, use a thin layer inside the grip rather than on the bar. Grips will eventually wear out and should be replaced.

For new grips, glue is typically not required. Make sure the levers are positioned to allow the grips to slide fully onto the bar. It can help to lubricate the inside of the grip with non-oily liquids, such as rubbing alcohol, hair spray, or window cleaner (10-1_Figure 3). Do not use oil of any type, as this will prevent the grip from holding fast to the bar.

10-1_Figure 3

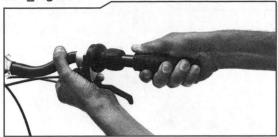

Wet grips with fluid and quickly push into place

If the old grips are worn out and are being replaced, they may be cut off the bar. It is also possible to remove and re-use the grips if they are in adequate condition. Use a long, flat tipped screwdriver worked gently under the inside edge of the grip. Drip or spray liquid such as window cleaner, hair spray, or rubbing alcohol in the gap. Work the solvent around the grip to loosen the bond, and slide the grip off the bar.

If the grip had a sealed end, it is also possible to remove it with compressed air. Use a blow tip and place inside end of grip. Wiggle grip while pulling as blown air loosens grip from bar. It may be necessary to have someone plug the exposed bar end to remove second grip.

Drop Style Handlebars (Road)

Drop style bars curve downward, forming hooks for the hands. Bars will vary in width, reach of the drop, and shape of the bar. Select a bar for comfort. There are now several bar center diameter standards. None should be considered interchangeable. Sizes may be 25.4mm, 26.0mm, 26.4mm, 31.7mm, or 31.8mm. When in doubt, the size should be checked with a measuring caliper.

The stem should match the standard of the bar center. For example, using a stem made for a 26.0 bar center with a 25.4 bar will mean the bar will not properly secure in the stem. This would be a very dangerous situation for the user, as the bar would slip and move when used. A difference of 0.1mm between stem and bar is considered acceptable.

Drop style bars can be rotated for comfort. There are rotational limits (10-1_Figure 4 and 10-1_Figure 5). Too far up or down can sacrifice performance and safety. Drop bars experience a significant amount of stress at the clamp, and it is important that the drop bar be fully secure.

Refer to Appendix C and with manufacturers for torque values.

10-1_Figure 4

Low limit of drop bar rotation

10-1_Figure 5

Upper limit of drop bar rotation

Drop handlebars are typically wrapped with bar tape. Bar tape will vary in thickness, comfort and durability. Wrapping is a skill that takes practice and patience.

NOTE: For more detail on bar wrapping, see Repair Help at www.parktool.com

There are several "aero" bar attachments available, with each system offering different positions (10-1_Figure 6). It is important the bars be fully secure before riding. A loose bar could cause the rider to lose control.

10-1_Figure 6

"Aero" clip-on handlebars

10-2 Stem Adjustment

TOOLS & SUPPLIES
- Hex wrenches (Park Tool - various models)
- Straight edge or ruler
- Grease (Park Tool PPL- 1)

Stems connect the handlebars to the steering column. Stems are available with different lengths and rises, measured from the center of the bar clamping area to the center of the steering column. A stem may compress the handlebar using either a faceplate, or a one-piece pinch clamp. All binder bolts in the stem should be lubricated and secured tight. However, do not get grease or oil in the area where the bar meets the stem or column.

The removable faceplate of the stem presses against the bar center when the stem binder bolts are tightened. It is important that the top and bottom gaps between the face plate and the stem body are the same. If the gap size is different, the head of the bolt may be stressed as it rotates during tightening (10-2_Figure 1).

10-2_Figure 1

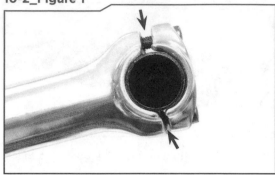

Faceplate gaps are uneven

The two basic types of stems are "quill" and "threadless."

Quill Stems
Quill stems are used on bikes with threaded headsets (10-2_Figure 2). The "quill" refers to the vertical post of the stem that inserts into the inside of the threaded steering column. A bolt draws up a wedge or cone to jam the stem tight in the column. The stem binder bolt, bolt head, wedge and outside of the quill should be greased before installing and tightening.

10-2_Figure 2

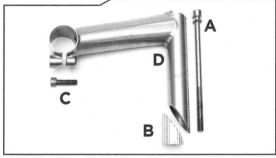

Quill type stem. (A) Stem binder bolt, (B) Stem wedge, (C) Handlebar binder, (D) Quill

It is important that the stem quill diameter is a correct match for the inside diameter of the steering column. The quill is slightly smaller than the inside of the column. There are several different steering column sizes found on bikes. Quill stems of 22.2mm are used in the 1" (25.4mm) steering column. Quill stems of 25.4mm are used with the 1⅛" (28.6mm) column, and a 28.6mm quill is used in the 1¼" (31.8mm) column.

To change stem height on a quill type stem,

loosen the stem binder bolt. The headset locknut is not used to move the stem. Attempt to move the stem by twisting after loosening the binder bolt. If it will not move, strike the top of the stem binder bolt with a hammer or mallet to free the wedge. If the stem is raised it may affect cable housing length. The stem must not be raised too high. Inspect the stem for a "max height" line and do not raise the stem past this mark (10-2_Figure 3).

10-2_Figure 3

Stem is too high, "max height" must not be visible

Align the stem with the front wheel. If this proves difficult, use a straight edge to help. Alternatively, the handlebars provide a straight edge to help align the stem. Align the bars parallel to the front hub. It is useful to place a straight edge on the fork blades. Compare this line to the handlebar near the stem. If the two lines appear parallel, the stem is straight (10-2_Figure 4 and 10-2_Figure 5).

10-2_Figure 4

Straight edge shows bars and stem are not aligned

10-2_Figure 5

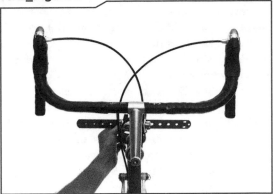

Straight edge is parallel to bar, which makes stem aligned

Tighten the stem binder bolt after aligning the stem. It is important to not over tighten the bolt. Too much force on the wedge can deform the steering column. The handlebars should be difficult to rotate in the column after tightening.

Threadless Stems

Threadless stems clamp around the outside of the steering column (10-2_Figure 6). The headset is adjusted using the adjusting cap at the top of the steering column. Do not confuse this cap for part of the stem. The threadless stem should be mounted only to a threadless steering column.

10-2_Figure 6

Common threadless stem. (A) Handlebar binder bolts, (B) Stem binder bolts

The threadless stem standard is determined by the outside diameter of the steering column. There several standards in use, the 25.4mm stem for 1" steering columns, the 28.6mm stem for 1-⅛" columns, the 31.8mm stems for 1-¼" columns, and 38.1mm stems for 1½" columns.

A few bike companies do not use these industry standards. They have proprietary stem and bar design fits. Replacement stems or handlebars are typically available only from that specific company.

It is possible lower threadless stems by removing extra spacers that are below the stem, and stacking them above the stem. However, if after lowering the stem there is an excessive amount of steering column above the stem, the column may be shortened. See Outline Item 11-3.6.1 Unthreaded Steering Columns.

To raise a threadless stem, it is commonly necessary to install a different stem with more rise. Simply adding spacers below the current stem may compromise the stem-to-steering column engagement, making the bike unsafe. The steering column must have good engagement inside the threadless stem. The steering column should be slightly recessed below the stem top (10-2_Figure 7). For most top caps, a 3mm gap between top of stem and column is adequate.

10-2_Figure 7

Threadless steering column must be recessed below threadless stem

Align the stem in line with the front wheel. If this proves difficult, use a straight edge to extend the line of the fork blades, as with quill stems described above. (10-2_Figure 8)

10-2_Figure 8

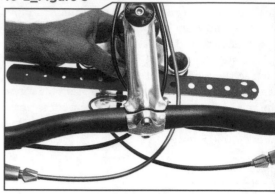

Stem is misaligned when bars are not parallel to fork blades

10-3
Saddle & Seat Post Adjustment

TOOLS & SUPPLIES
- Hex wrenches (Park Tool-various models)
- Lubricant (Park Tool PPL-1 and CL-1)

Most bicycle saddles have two rails mounted beneath the seat mold. There are, however, designs of saddle and posts that use a single rail system. The rails are secured to the seat post by saddle rail binder clamps (10-3_Figure 1). Lubricate saddle rail binder bolts of post before tightening.

10-3_Figure 1

Saddle rail binder bolts

Saddles can be changed and upgraded. To change the saddle, begin by noting the position of the current saddle. Place a straight edge on the saddle and measure the saddle tilt or angle using an angle finder. Note how far back the saddle is on the rails. Unbolt the old saddle from the seat post cradle. Lubricate saddle rail binder bolts with a light lubricant. Install the new saddle on the post clamp and secure binder bolts. Using an angle finder, measure saddle angle and position on the rails as compared to the previous saddle. Change position as necessary. The clamps can be adjusted so the saddle may point either up or down. Generally, begin with the saddle level, and then make changes in small increments upward or downward as necessary (10-3_Figure 2).

10-3_Figure 2

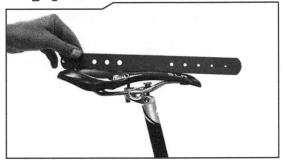

Use straight edge to extend saddle line

Hard use and crashing may bend the saddle rails. Riding with bent rails may lead to breakage of the rail. Repair of bent rails is very difficult and often impossible. Damaged saddles should be replaced.

Seat Post

Seat posts hold the saddle, and secure inside the seat tube of the frame. Typically, the frame has a slot cut into the top, which is pinched by a seat post binder bolt. Remove and lubricate threads of binder bolt. The seat post binder bolt does not require a great deal of tension to hold the post tight. Generally, only tighten the binder until the saddle will not rotate when pressed with one hand. If it will not rotate with one hand, it is unlikely to slip downward (10-3_Figure 3).

10-3_Figure 3

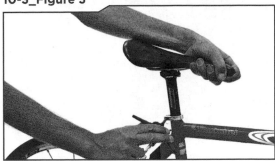

Test saddle rotation with only one hand, not two

Frames are made with many different sized seat tubes and different seat post diameters are available. The seat post size may range from 22.2mm to 32.4mm. The post diameter should be approximately 0.1mm smaller than the inside frame diameter. Generally, if the frame is steel, titanium or aluminum, it is necessary to grease or anti seize inside the seat tube to prevent rust and corrosion from seizing the post However, if either the seat post or frame is carbon, grease or oil is not recommended. Many manufacturers of carbon frames recommend installing the post dry, without any treatment.

Seat posts are usually marked with a "maximum extension" or "minimum insertion" line (10-3_Figure 4). Do not raise the post above this line, or the danger of breakage is greatly increased. Generally, always keep the end of the post inserted below the frame lug or weldment. Seat posts can bend from impact and heavy use. A bent seat post is not repairable and should not be used. Replace immediately.

10-3_Figure 4

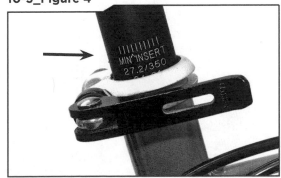

Post is too high, insert post so "max line" is not seen

Chapter 11
Headsets

Two wheeled vehicles, such as bicycles and motorcycles, make small self-corrections in steering while traveling forward. The headset is the bearing system that connects the bicycle fork to the main frame and allows the front wheel to steer smoothly while riding. If the headset is pitted or worn, the rider cannot make these corrections smoothly and handling suffers. Very worn headsets tend to "lock up" when the front wheel is pointing straight. Pick up the front of the bike and gently swing the handlebars back and forth from center. Pitting in the cups will cause the headset to stick as it passes through the center position. A pitted headset should be replaced.

The upper and lower bearing races in a headset rest on the support surfaces of the head tube. If the support surfaces are not machined parallel, the bearings will bind as the fork is rotated. This can lead to premature bearing wear and poor adjustment. The head tube can become deformed by welding, or by inadequate manufacturing techniques. If necessary, the head tube can be machined (faced), so the surfaces are parallel, by using the head tube reaming and facing tool (11_Figure 1).

11_Figure 1

Facing the head tube for better bearing alignment

The base of the fork steering column should also be cut square to the fork. If it is not properly machined, the fork crown race will not sit square to the steering column and will add to the binding effect. The fork can be machined with a crown race cutter (11_Figure 2). Facing the head tube and fork crown is best left to professional mechanics. Generally, the headset can be installed and then simply adjusted. If it adjusts well, with no binding, the machining is adequate.

11_Figure 2

Machining the fork crown race

> **NOTE:** For more on frame machining, see Repair Help at www.parktool.com

11-1 Headset Types

There are two basic types of headset groups, termed threaded and threadless. The threaded headsets use a threaded bearing race and locknut that secure onto a threaded steering column (11-1_Figure 1). A quill stem insets down inside the steering column. See Outline Item 10-2 Stem Adjustment.

11-1_Figure 1

Bike with threaded headset

The threadless headset features a steering column with no threading (11-1_Figure 2). The adjustment is done using a non-threaded race that slides onto the steering column. It is pushed into the bearing by pressure from an adjusting cap at the top of the column. Pinch bolts on the stem lock the adjustment and secure the stem.

11-1_Figure 2

Bike with threadless headset

The threaded and threadless headsets described above will be referred to as "conventional." These have been the traditional headset designs. They use cups pressed into the head tube. The bearing races may be caged ball bearings, loose ball bearings, or cartridge bearings. With the conventional design, the bearings sit outside, or above and below, the head tube faces.

Threadless headsets have several variations. The "low-profile," "internal," and/or "zero stack" threadless systems use a relatively large diameter head tube, approximately 50mm outside diameter (11-1_Figure 3). These are simply different names for the same headset system. Shallow headset cups are pressed into the lower and upper parts of the head tube. The bearings may be either caged balls or cartridge bearings. The bearings do not sit above and below the head tube faces, rather, the bearings sit almost level with the head tube faces.

11-1_Figure 3

Bike with low-profile threadless headset

Integrated headsets are another variation of the threadless headset category (11-1_Figure 4). Integrated headsets use cartridge bearings

that are slip fit into the frame, which means the cartridge bearing simply drops into place. The low-profile headset is not considered an integrated design, because cups are pressed into the frame. When a new low-profile headset is purchased, new cups as well as bearings are included. For integrated headsets, only the cartridge bearings and top cap parts are included.

11-1_Figure 4

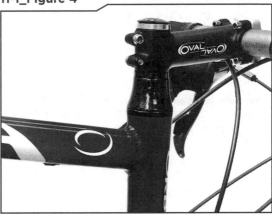

Bike with integrated threadless headset

There are several non-interchangeable industry standards for headset designs. It is important to know which standard the bike uses in order to get the correct replacement parts. See Outline Item 11-3.1 Headset Replacement & Installation for more discussion.

11-2 Headset Service

TOOLS & SUPPLIES

- Hex wrenches
- Headset wrenches, for threaded headsets only (Park Tool HCW-15)
- Large adjustable wrench, for threaded headsets only
- Grease (Park Tool PPL-1)
- Rags
- Solvent (Park Tool CB-2)

The front wheel throws dirt and water directly up at the lower headset bearing. An overhaul can extend the life of the headset by removing this dirt. If the headset feels gritty when turned, it should be overhauled. However, if the headset seems to stop as it rotates, the races are dented, and the headset should be replaced, not overhauled. Like any overhaul, taking notes during disassembly will help during reassembly.

The handlebars are in the way when servicing the headset. It is best to disconnect the cables from the brake calipers and derailleur, and completely remove the bars. This will prevent damage to housing and inner wires. See Outline Items 7-2 Shift Levers and 8-3 Caliper Rim Brakes. Additionally, it is best to remove or disconnect handlebar-mounted computers to avoid damage to the wire.

The pressed races may be left in the head tube and on the fork unless the headset is being replaced. Clean all bearings and races with a solvent. Use care on suspension forks not to get solvent into lower sliding legs.

11-2.1
Threadless Headset
Disassembly & Assembly

The threadless headset service here will include low-profile and integrated headsets. If the headset uses a cartridge bearing rather then caged ball bearings, simply replace the cartridge bearing as a unit. It is possible to use a seal pick and remove the seals of some cartridge bearings and to clean and re-grease the bearings. However, if the bearing is pitted or rough, the new grease will not solve the problem.

The procedure for threadless headset disassembly and assembly is as follows:

a.   Loosen stem bolts, and remove stem from steering column. Remove any washers/ spacers from steering column.

b.   Pull fork from bike. It may be necessary to use a mallet and tap the top of the steering column, driving fork downward (11-2.1_ Figure 1). Once the fork is driven down a little, lift it back up and remove center cone from adjusting race.

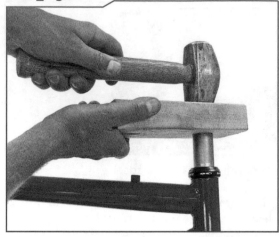

If necessary, drive fork downward to remove fork

c.   Remove fork from frame and note orientation of cage bearing retainers or cartridge bearings as they sit in headset (11-2.1 Figure_2).

Inspect bearing retainer orientation before removing

d.   Clean and inspect parts. View races for pitting and damage, looking for gouging and small evenly spaced pits (11-2.1_ Figure 3). Use a ballpoint pen to trace the bearing path. Roughness and wear will be felt as the small ball of the pen passes over bad areas. Wear in the races will not become smooth with new grease. Any worn parts should be replaced.

11-2.1_Figure 3

Pitted headset cup

e. If the ball bearings have a shiny silver color and appear smooth, they can be re-used. If the ball bearings appear discolored, they should be replaced. The ball bearings are generally the last part of the system to wear out.

If the headset is using bearing caged ball retainers, check the orientation of the retainers in relation to the races before installing. Retainers have only one correct orientation. The open side of the ball retainer should face the cone shaped race, not the cup shaped race. If in doubt, place bearing into headset. Use mating race and press downward on bearings with your hand and rotate race side to side. If bearing orientation is wrong, race will have a rubbing feeling. If orientation is correct, race rotates on balls and will feel smoother.

The procedure for threadless headset assembly is as follows:

a. Grease bearing retainers and bearing race cups. For cartridge bearing headsets, drop cartridge in place.

b. Install bearing retainers into upper and lower cup shaped races.

c. Install fork steering column through head tube.

d. Install race-centering cone onto column. Press centering cone into adjusting race to help hold fork.

e. Install spacers and accessories as appropriate.

f. Install stem and snug stem bolts. Check for adequate clearance from top of column to top of stem (11-2.1_Figure 4). 2-3mm of clearance is recommended for clearance, add spacers as necessary. Spacers may be placed either below or above the stem.

11-2.1_Figure 4

Column must be recessed below top of stem

It is possible to replace retainer ball bearings with loose ball bearings of the same diameter. Loose balls, especially in the lower racer, can move about which helps prevent the pitting that commonly ruins headsets. Installation and assembly with loose bearings is more difficult. It is important that the bearings stay aligned in the cup as the headset is assembled.

To use loose ball bearings, grease cups to hold bearings. Place balls into cup shaped races. Leave a gap equal to two to three ball bearings (11-2.1_Figure 5). Do not attempt to fully fill cup with ball bearings. If possible, rotate bicycle upside down in the stand to assist assembly before installing fork. After assembly with loose ball bearings, rotate fork to check smooth rotation. Any popping or sudden change in feeling indicates a bearing out of place.

11-2.1_Figure 5

Loose balls bearings in the headset cup. Leave a gap so balls can roll freely

11-2.2 Threadless Headset Adjustment

Threadless headsets, including low-profile and integrated, all operate on the same principal. The bearing races must press against the bearings. The bolt in the top cap will put pressure on the stem, which presses on washers below the stem, which press on the bearing races, which press against the bearings (11-2.2_Figure 1). The stem is secured to maintain this pressure on the bearings.

The cap and bolt at the top of the threadless systems are used for bearing adjustment only. These caps do not secure the stem onto the steering column. The stem uses binder bolt(s) to secure the stem from moving once the adjustment is made.

If not already inspected in assembly, remove the top cap to inspect the star nut or plug inside the steering column. The cap bolt threads into this fitting and pulls on the fork against the headset bearing surfaces, which acts to tighten the adjustment.

11-2.2_Figure 1

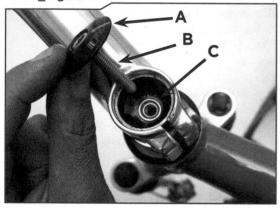

The top cap, bolt and star nut used for bearing adjustment. (A) Top cap, (B) Bolt, (C) Star nut

Note the height of the steering column relative to the stem. It should be about 2-3mm (⅛") below the level of the stem. The stem needs to press down on the spacers in order to adjust the bearings. If the steering column is level with the top of the stem, it will be unable to add any load to the bearings. Spacers can be added either above or below the stem to achieve a gap. (11-2.2_Figure 2)

11-2.2_Figure 2

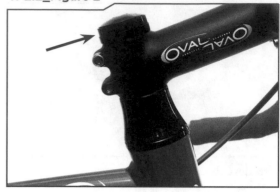

Spacers added to increase clearance between top cap and column

The procedure for threadless headset adjustment is as follows:

a. Remove top cap bolt to inspect steering column. Lubricate bolt and re-install cap and bolt gently. Do not tighten cap bolt.

b. Loosen stem bolt(s) that secure stem to the steering column. Lubricate these bolts if they are dry.

c. Wiggle the stem side to side to see that it is loose. If the stem is jammed or rusted frozen to the steering column, no adjustment can be made.

d. Align stem straight to wheel and gently secure the top bolt. Stop when resistance is felt (11-2.2 _Figure 3).

11-2.2_Figure 3

Make bearing adjustment only when stem bolts are loose

e. Tighten stem bolt(s) and check for play by pulling back and forth on fork. Turn the handlebar in different directions while checking for play. There may be play at this early setting. Grab the upper portion of suspension forks because the legs may have play.

f. To adjust bearings, loosen stem bolt(s).

g. Turn adjusting bolt in center cap ⅛ turn clockwise.

h. Secure stem bolts, check for play again.

i. Repeat adjustments as above until play disappears. Remember to loosen stem bolts before turning adjusting bolt in cap.

j. Check alignment of stem and tighten stem binder bolts fully.

Another test of play is to place the bike on the ground and grab the front brake tightly. Press downward on the handlebars and rock the bike forward and back. A knocking sensation may indicate a loose headset. In effect this does the same thing as grabbing and pulling on the fork. However, play in the brake caliper arms may cause a knocking. Front suspension forks may also have play in the legs, which can cause a knocking.

If a bearing adjustment cannot be found to be acceptable, there may be other problems in the headset. Bearing surfaces may be worn out, the ball bearing retainers may be upside down, or a seal may be improperly aligned. If play always seems present no matter the adjustment, the steering column may be too long and may be pressing into the top cap. Add spacers as necessary. Another source of play can be a loose press fit, either in the head tube or on the fork crown race. See Table 11-3.3 Interference Fit Guidelines.

11-2.3
Threaded Headset Disassembly & Assembly

The threaded race of a headset requires a narrow headset wrench. Use either the Park Tool HW-2 Headset Locknut Wrench, or a large adjustable wrench on the top locknut when possible. These wrenches allow more purchase of the top nut.

The procedure for threaded headset disassembly is as follows:

a. Loosen stem binder bolt. Attempt to move the stem by twisting. If stem will not move, strike the top of the stem binder bolt with a hammer or mallet to free the wedge (11-2.3_Figure 1). Attempt to twist stem again.

11-2.3_Figure 1

Drive stem binder downward to free stem

b. Pull stem and handlebars from fork.

c. Install wheel into fork to act as a lever. Stand in front of bike and hold the wheel between your knees while working with the locknut and race.

d. Hold lower threaded race with thin headset wrench. Loosen and remove top locknut with second wrench, preferably large adjustable wrench or Park Tool HW-2 Headset Locknut Wrench.

e. Remove wheel.

f. Remove any spacers or brackets from under the locknut.

g. Unthread and remove the threaded race. Note orientation of upper and lower bearing retainers.

h. Pull fork from bike.

i. Clean and inspect parts. View races for pitting and damage, looking for gouging and small evenly spaced pits (11-2.3_Figure 2). Use a ballpoint pen to trace the bearing path. Roughness and wear will be felt as the small ball of the pen passes over bad areas. Wear in the races will not become smooth with new grease. Worn parts should be replaced. If the ball bearings have a shiny silver color and appear smooth, they can be re-used. If the ball bearings appear discolored, they should be replaced. The ball bearings are generally the last part of the system to wear out.

11-2.3_Figure 2

Inspect for wear and pitting marks on the bearing races

Threaded headsets commonly use a spacer with a notch or "tooth" on the inside diameter. This notch is designed to sit inside a groove running vertically in the column. However, these types of spacers will often rotate, causing damage as the notch cuts into the threads. This is especially the case when the spacer is made of steel, and is relatively thin. Wide, aluminum spacers do not tend to damage fork threads. Inspect the threads of the fork. If any damage is present, file out the notch, or get a new spacer without a notch

If the headset is using bearing retainers, check the orientation of the retainers in relation to the races before installing. Retainers have only one correct orientation. The open side of the ball retainer should face the cone shaped race, not the cup shaped race (11-2.3_Figure 3). If in doubt, place bearing into headset. Use mating race and press downward on bearings with your hand and rotate race side to side. If bearing orientation is wrong, race will have a rubbing feeling. If orientation is correct, race rotates on balls, and will feel smoother.

11-2.3_Figure 3

Open side of bearing cage should face the cone shaped adjusting race

The procedure for threaded headsets assembly is as follows:

a. Grease bearing retainers and bearing race cups. Grease threads of steering column.

b. Install bearing retainers into upper and lower cup-shaped races.

c. Install fork steering column through head tube.

d. Thread on top race.

e. Install spacers and accessories as appropriate.

f. Thread on locknut. Inspect that steering column does not touch inner lip of locknut. Add spacers as necessary.

It is possible to replace retainer ball bearing with loose ball bearings of the same diameter. Loose balls, especially in the lower racer, can move about which helps prevent the pitting that commonly ruins headsets. Assembly with loose bearings is more difficult. It is important that the bearings stay aligned in the cup as the headset is assembled.

To use loose ball bearings, grease cups to hold bearings. Place balls into cup-shaped races. Leave a gap the size of two to three ball bearings (11-2.3_Figure 4). Do not attempt to fully fill cup with ball bearings. If possible, rotate bicycle upside down in the stand to assist assembly before installing fork. After assembly with loose ball bearings, rotate fork to check for smooth rotation. Any popping or sudden change in feeling indicates a bearing out of place.

11-2.3_Figure 4

Leave gap in loose headset ball bearings so balls can roll freely

11-2.4 Threaded Headset Adjustment

Threaded headsets are adjusted using a top locknut and threaded race. The stem has no affect on the bearing adjustment. The best bearing adjustment is as loose as possible, but without bearing play or knocking. To achieve this, the following procedure will first create play in the adjustment and then proceed to incrementally tighten the race until play is gone.

The procedure for threaded headset adjustment is as follows:

a. Make sure headset locknut is loose. Use a headset wrench to hold threaded race. Use a large adjustable wrench or the Park Tool headset wrench HW-2, on the locknut

b. By hand, turn threaded race clockwise until it contacts ball bearings. Turn race back counter-clockwise at least ¼ turn from this setting. Hold threaded race with headset wrench and tighten locknut. Tighten locknut fully (11-2.4_Figure 1). This early setting is intended to have play.

11-2.4_Figure 1

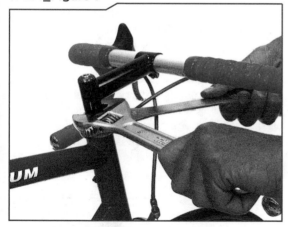

Secure locknut before checking bearing play

c. Check for play by pulling back and forth on fork. A knocking sensation indicates play. Turn the handlebars in different directions while checking for play. There should be play at this early setting. If headset feels tight, loosen adjustment further until play is found. Grab the upper portion of suspension forks because the legs may have play.

d. Grab front wheel between knees and hold it in line with top tube. Front wheel will act as a lever to hold steering column. Threaded race will need to be adjusted

slightly clockwise. Use a wrench to hold race and note orientation of wrench relative to front wheel.

e. Loosen locknut and rotate threaded race clockwise ¹⁄₃₂ of a turn relative to wheel.

f. Hold threaded race securely with wrench and tighten locknut fully. Check for play by rotating fork and moving fork forward and back at different positions.

g. If play is present, repeat steps "e and f" above until play disappears. Adjustment is finished when there is no play in any position as the fork rotates and locknut is fully secure.

Another test of play is to place the bike on the ground and grab the front brake tightly. Press downward on the handlebars and rock the bike forward and back. A knocking sensation may indicate a loose headset. In effect this does the same thing as grabbing and pulling on the fork. However, play in the brake caliper arms may cause knocking. Front suspension forks may also have play in the stanchion and sliding legs, which can cause knocking.

If an acceptable bearing adjustment cannot be found, there may be other problems in the headset. Bearing surfaces may be worn out, the ball bearing retainers may be upside down, or a seal may be improperly aligned. Another source of play can be a loose press fit, either in the head tube or on the fork crown race. See Outline Item 11.3.3 Pressed headset installation. If the headset seems well adjusted at one position, but binds when rotated to another position, the head tube may require facing to improve bearing alignment. Consult a professional mechanic.

11-3
Headset Replacement & Installation

TOOLS & SUPPLIES

- Hex wrenches (Park Tool—various models)
- Headset wrenches, for threaded headsets only (Park Tool HCW-15)
- Head cup remover: (Park Tool RT-1)
- Bearing Press: (Park Tool HHP-2)
- "Star" nut setter (Park Tool TNS-1)
- Crown race installer (Park Tool CRS-1)
- Ball peen hammer
- Punch
- Measuring Caliper

The headset may be replaced when worn or when upgrading to a better model. After installing the new headset, assembly and adjustment is the same as in Outline Items 11-2.2 Threadless Headset Adjustment or 11-2.4 Threaded Headset Adjustment.

There are several standards for headsets found on bicycles. When selecting a new headset, it is important to get one that will fit the bike. There are currently over one dozen headset standards that do not interchange. Table 11-3 Headset Fit Standards reviews some of these standards, but the table is not exhaustive, as some unusual and proprietary standards exist. It will usually be necessary to remove the headset to know exactly what standard is being used. If in doubt, consult a professional mechanic for the correct standard for your bike.

It is sometimes possible to use a smaller steering column than the head tube was designed to use. Reducing rings are available and are pressed into the head tubes of the larger standards, allowing the bike to use smaller headset standards and steering columns. Reducers are available to size the 1.5 standard head tube down to the 1⅛ inch standard, and to reduce the 1⅛ inch standard down to the 1-inch "European" standard. It is not possible to convert a bike upward. A larger steering column cannot be used than the head tube was designed to accept.

The integrated headset systems use the frame to act as a holder for cartridge bearings (11-3_Figure 1). Unlike conventional headsets, there are no pressed bearing races in the head tube.

The integrated systems use cartridge bearings with an angular contact to fit inside the frame.

11-3_Figure 1

Head tube of an integrated headset bike

There are several non-interchangeable standards of cartridge bearing diameter and contact angle. There are commonly two numbers listed on the cartridge bearings. The first number is the contact angle of the inner race, commonly 36-degrees. This is contact to the fork race and compression ring. The second number is the contact angle of the outer race, which is the race surface contacting the frame. For example a bearing marked 36-45 has a 36-degree contact angle for the inner race, and a 45-degree contact angle for the frame contact.

To service an integrated headset, simply dismantle the headset. Cartridge bearings are lifted out by hand and a new bearing is placed in the headset, again by hand (11-3_Figure 2). The adjustment procedure is the same as for a conventional threadless headset.

11-3_Figure 2

Removing the integrated headset bearing

Table 11-3 Headset Fit Standards

Standard name	Steering Column: Threaded Or Threadless	Pressed Cup	Steering Column Outside Diameter	Pressed race or Cartridge Bearing Outside Diameter
Conventional 1" Japanese Industrial Standard (JIS)	Threaded and Threadless 1"	Pressed races	1" (25.4mm)	30.0mm
Conventional 1" "European" Standard	Threaded & Threadless 1"	Pressed races	1" (25.4mm)	30.2mm
Integrated 1"	Threadless	Slip fit	1" (25.4mm)	30.2mm
Conventional 1 1/8" Standard	Threadless & Threaded	Pressed races	1 1/8" (28.6mm)	34.0mm
Conventional 1 1/4" Standard	Threadless & Threaded	Pressed races	1 1/4" (31.8mm)	37.0mm
One-point-five® (1.5 standard)	Threadless	Pressed races	1 1/2" (38.1mm)	49.8mm
IS (Integrated Standard)	Threadless	Slip fit	1 1/8" (28.6mm)	41mm
Campagnolo® Hiddenset Integrated Standard	Threadless	Slip fit	1 1/8" (28.6mm)	42mm
Low-Profile (45-47mm head tube)	Threadless	Pressed races	1 1/8" (28.6mm)	41.4mm
ED-36	Threadless	Slip fit	1 1/8" (28.6mm)	41.5mm
Microtek®	Threadless	Pressed races	1 1/8" (28.6mm)	42.0mm
Integrated 36° by 36° contact	Threadless	Slip fit	1 1/8" (28.6mm)	44.0mm
Low Profile (50mm head tube)	Threadless	Pressed races	1 1/8" (28.6mm)	44.0mm pressed cup (if used, cartridge bearing is 41mm)
Perdido®	Threadless	Pressed races	1 1/8" (28.6mm)	44.5mm pressed races

11-3.1 Headset Stack Height

Headsets vary between brand and model in stack height. Stack height is the amount of steering column length the headset will occupy (11-3.1_Figure 1). The steering column is always longer than the head tube. Headset stack height does not include the stem of threadless headsets, nor any sizing washes used to give extra rise to the stem.

11-3.1_Figure 1

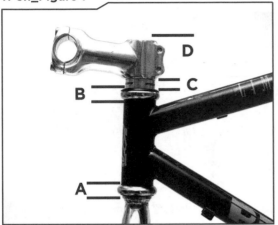

Headset stack height equals (A) plus (B). Note stem height (D) and spacer width (C) are not included in the stack height as listed by headset manufacturers.

A new headset will have the stack height listed on the box or instructions. Generally, when replacing a headset, select one of equal or smaller stack height. Using a headset with more stack height may result in the column being too short for the bike, or you may need to remove spacers from under the stem, if that is an option.

11-3.2 Headset removal

Begin headset replacement by removing the wheel, handlebars and fork as with Outline Item 11-2 Headset Service. To remove pressed races, use a race removal tool such as the Park Tool RT-1 Race Tool. Install tool with smaller end first through the headset cup. Squeeze sides of prongs and pull tool fully into head tube. Do not press prongs with hand as prongs will close and pinch flesh. A clicking sound will be heard as tool prongs engage head tube cup. Use a steel hammer at the small end of the RT-1 and drive cup from head tube (11-3.2_Figure 1). Use care

as cup approaches end of tube; the tool may fall to ground on the last blow of the hammer. Place RT-1 with small end first through remaining cup and repeat process to remove second race. A long punch can also be used to remove the head tube races. Alternate tapping left to right to "walk" out the race.

11-3.2_Figure 1

Removing the pressed race

The fork crown race must be removed from the fork. Professionals will use the Park Tool CRP-1 Crown Race Puller (11-3.2_Figure 2). An alternate procedure is to use a punch or other tool that will engage race. In some cases this may scar the fork and crown race. Place the fork column downward on soft material such as wood to protect top of column. Using a hammer, tap race alternately first on one side, then the other side, driving the race off the crown seat (11-3.2_Figure 3).

11-3.2_Figure 2

Park Tool CRP-1 Crown Race Puller removing fork crown race.

11-3.2_Figure 3

Carefully tap alternate sides repeatedly
to remove

11-3.3 Pressed Headset Installation

Conventional and low-profile headset bearing
races or cups require a press fit into the frame.
The press, or interference, fit occurs when
parts are held together by internal and external
surfaces forced together. There must be a slight
diameter difference between the two pressed
surfaces. This tension is what keeps the cups
tight in the frame. Generally, the difference in
the press fit should be between 0.1mm and
0.2mm. A professional mechanic will be able to
ream the head tube to improve the fit.

Use a caliper to measure the outside diameter
of the cups. Next, measure the inside diameter
of the head tube in two places, each 90 degrees
from the other. Average the two readings
(11-3.3_Figure 1). The difference between the
outside diameter and inside diameter is the
amount of interference fit.

11-3.3_Figure 1

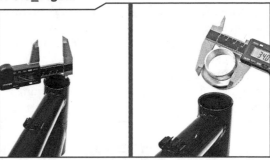

Measure and compare the inside diameter of
the head tube to the outside diameter of
the headset

Table 11-3.3 Interference Fit Guidelines

Difference between race outside diameter and head tube inside diameter	Result and action required
0.26mm or greater	Too great of press fit difference. Ream head tube inside diameter to improve fit.
0.1mm to 0.25mm	Acceptable tolerances for press fit.
0.01mm to 0.09mmm	Unacceptably small interference. Get a new race with larger diameter. It is also possible to use a retaining compound.
0mm or any negative number	No interference fit at all, headset is smaller than head tube. Use a different race if possible. Retaining compound may be tried if no other option is available.

Significant force is required to press headset races into the head tube. Additionally, the races should be pressed square to one another. It is best to use a bearing press (Park Tool HHP-2 Bearing Press) for the head tube races. The HHP-2 Bearing Press comes with a pair of cup guides (#530-2) to help maintain cup alignment during pressing. The cup guides fit most 1-inch and 1-⅛-inch conventional headset races.

> ⚠ Before using the cup guide, insert the guide into the race. If guide appears to jam or is a tight fit, do not use for that particular headset cup. Do not use cup guides if they press on any pre-installed cartridge bearing (ex. Chris King® headsets). For headsets not fitting #530-2 cup guides, use the threaded press plate and sliding press plate only. Press one cup at a time.

The procedure for installing head tube races is as follows:

a. Determine the acceptability of the headset press fit as described above.
b. Adjust threaded press plate of HHP-2 until top is flush with end of hex shaft thread.
c. Remove sliding press plate and install cups onto guides.
d. Place upper headset cup on top of head tube. Hold guide onto top threaded press plate and lower assembly through upper headset cup.
e. Install second cup guide on sliding press plate and place lower cup onto guide (11-3.3_Figure 2). If guides do not fit headset well, press one cup at a time using only the press plates.
f. Engage sliding press plate onto hex shaft, and push plate upward until headset cup meets head tube. Release lever. Sliding press plate lever must be engaged in one of seven hex shaft notches. Pull downward on lower press plate to test engagement.

11-3.3_Figure 2

Arrangement of cups and pressing guides for the HHP-2

g. Turn handle clockwise slowly and inspect alignment of cups as cups enter head tube. Press cups fully into head tube.
h. Inspect for full seating where cups meet frame. A gap between the frame and cup indicates incomplete pressing. (11-3.3_Figure 3).

11-3.3_Figure 3

This cup is not fully seated into frame

i. Remove HHP-2 from bike. Unthread handle 1 turn, press lever of sliding press plate and remove tool from bike.

> **NOTE:** Never use a "cheater" bar to extend leverage of handles. If cups will not press using handle, other press fit issues are present and should be addressed.

It is sometimes possible to press a headset without the headset press. Substitute a large threaded rod, called all-thread, of ½ inch diameter with thick flat washers and two nuts fitting the rod. Press one cup at a time, use care when turning the nut with a large adjustable wrench.

11-3.4 Fork Crown Race Installation

The fork crown race is pressed to a crown race seat on the fork. Because the fork race is smaller than the crown race seat, it expands as it is pressed. Crown races are commonly made of bearing hard steel, which are very hard and brittle and do not expand to the same extent as the head tube when the headset race is pressed. Measure the difference between the inside diameter of the fork crown race and the outside of the fork crown. The crown race seat should be larger then the race by only 0.1mm to 0.15mm. Greater differences then this between race and seat may stress and crack the bearing race. When the crown race seat is too large for the fork crown race, the crown race seat may be cut smaller. A professional mechanic will use a crown race seat cutter such as the Park Tool CRC-1. If the crown race seat is only slightly larger than the race (0.02 to 0.09mm) use a strong retaining compound. If the crown race seat is equal to or even smaller than the race, use a different race if possible, and consult a professional mechanic.

The fork crown race must be pressed to the fork crown. Determine acceptability of press fit as described above. The Park Tool CRS-1 crown race setter will drive on the race. Place race on fork crown and select most compatible Park Tool CRS-1 aluminum ring. Place ring on tool and insert over fork. Use a steel hammer and strike top of tool until race fully seats (11-3.4_Figure 1). The sound of the hammering will change as it seats. Inspect sides of race for full seating against fork.

11-3.4_Figure 1

Pressing the fork crown race

There are some models of headsets using cartridge bearings that use a lower race made with a split ring. These races press on and remove by hand. The race does not directly ride on the rotating bearings, but inserts into the cartridge bearing race.

11-3.5
Star Nut or Compression Plug Installation

Threadless headsets are adjusted by pressure on the top-bearing race. Pressure is applied when the bolt in the top cap is tightened. The bolt is threaded into either the "star nut" or a compression plug (11-3.5_Figure 1).

11-3.5_Figure 1

Star nut on the left and compression plug on the right

Compression plugs are a threaded system installed into the steering column. A socket fitting is tightened to hold the plug secure. These plugs have an internal thread for the top cap. The plug diameter must be compatible with the diameter of the steering column. The compression plug is removable.

The star nut system is designed not to pull upward after installation. In other words, it is meant not to be removable. The star nut has flanges with an outer diameter slightly larger than the inside diameter of the fork column. This allows the flanges to bite into the fork walls and hold tight.

To install a star nut, use a tool such as the Park Tool TNS-1 Threadless Nut Setter. The tool will drive the star nut about 15mm (⁹⁄₁₆") below the top of the steering column. This allows the adjusting bolt to thread fully into the nut for adjustment pre-load. Mount the nut with concave side toward tool thread. Hold TNS-1 over steering column. Use care to align TNS-1 with the column. Tap squarely on top of TNS-1 with steel hammer. Continue until TNS-1 is fully seated (11-3.5_Figure 2).

11-3.5_Figure 2

Seating the star nut

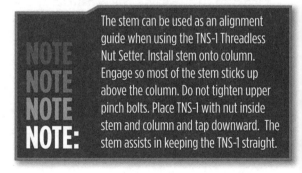

NOTE NOTE NOTE NOTE: The stem can be used as an alignment guide when using the TNS-1 Threadless Nut Setter. Install stem onto column. Engage so most of the stem sticks up above the column. Do not tighten upper pinch bolts. Place TNS-1 with nut inside stem and column and tap downward. The stem assists in keeping the TNS-1 straight.

An alternate technique to the TNS-1 is to create a driving system. For example use a short wooden dowel to drive in the star nut. It will require careful use of the hammer to tap the nut in straight. Another alternative is to thread the bolt into the nut, then tap the bolt to drive in the nut.

11-3.6 Fork Sizing and Cutting

The steering columns on new forks are typically longer than required and the column is cut to fit. Threadless columns must be long enough to fit the stem and any spacers. Threaded columns must be long enough to engage the locknut. Steering columns that are too long will prevent bearing adjustment.

11-3.6.1 Unthreaded Steering Columns

TOOLS & SUPPLIES

- Saw guides (Park Tool SG-6)
- Hex wrenches (Park Tool— various models)
- Hack saw, good quality blade of 24 TPI (32 TPI for carbon)
- Files, flat and round
- Tape measure
- Caliper
- File
- Scribe or marker
- Bench vise (substitute repair stand to hold column if necessary.)

For threadless steering columns, the column length will limit the height of the stem and handlebars. When installing a new fork, consider where you would like the handlebars to be. It is possible to cut a threadless column relatively long and to use spacers under the stem to raise the bars. However, there are limits to how far the stem can safely be raised above the headset. For steel and aluminum steering columns, do not exceed 40mm between the stem and headset. If you feel you require more stem and bar height than this limit will allow, consider purchasing a new stem with more height or rise.

It is also possible to cut a column purposely too long, and stack spacers above the stem to allow bearing adjustment.

Carbon fiber steering columns also have limits on the height of spacers. Generally, manufacturers recommend no more than 20mm additional stack height between stem and upper race. Contact the fork manufacturer for limits in regards to your fork.

The safest and most practical method to determine column length is to install the fork first without cutting. Mark the fork at the appropriate point and then remove it for cutting. When cutting unthreaded columns, use the Park Tool SG-6 Saw Guide.

The procedure for cutting threadless steering columns is as follows:

a. Assemble steering column into the head tube with bearings and parts in place. Install stem and all desired spacers.

b. Press downward on stem to simulate an adjusted headset and snug stem bolts. Remove what play you can, but the adjustment need not be perfect.

c. Scribe or mark steering column at top of stem (11-3.6.1_Figure 1).

11-3.6.1_Figure 1

Mark column for cutting

d. Remove fork from bike. Measure an additional 3mm from mark toward fork crown, and mark column. This will be the cut line. This allows the top of the column to sit slightly below the top of the stem.

e. Place fork inside Park Tool SG-6 Saw Guide. Loosely secure handle. Move SG-6 saw guide opening over mark on column and secure handle. Place SG-6 Saw Guide in vise. (If no vise is available, hold column in repair stand jaws.)

f. Cut through column using proper hacksaw technique (11-3.6.1_Figure 2). Apply pressure forward, with the direction of cutting teeth, and release pressure drawing the blade backwards.

11-3.6.1_Figure 2

Cut the fork square using the SG-6 Saw Guide

g. Loosen handle and push column further into SG-6 Saw Guide.

h. Use a flat file to finish and bevel end of steel or aluminum columns. Hold file at approximately a 45-degree angle to bevel the end of the column. Use a round file or de-burring tool to remove the sharp inside edge of the column.

i. Remove fork from SG-6 Saw Guide and install on bike.

Steel columns tend to be relatively thin. A pipe cutter can substitute for the hacksaw technique described above. The cutting wheel will leave a burr at the end of the tubing, which must be filed off.

Alternatively, if no SG-6 Saw Guide is available, it is possible to use a hacksaw and steel radiator hose clamps for a guide. Measure and mark the column. Mount and secure one clamp on each side of the mark, leaving a gap wide enough for the hacksaw blade. After cutting, finish the end flat and square with a file.

For carbon fiber steering columns, a fine 32 TPI blade is recommended. Carbon dust is a potential health risk due to the small size of the dust particulates. Take normal precautions of wearing a dust mask and working in a well ventilated area. Additionally, to minimize dust from the carbon, keep the blade wet. If using a "diamond rod blade," it is possible to install washers to widen the guide slot of the SG-6 Saw Guide. Use a fine emery cloth to finish the end, again wetting the paper.

11-3.6.2 Threaded Steering Columns

TOOLS & SUPPLIES

• Saw guide- (Park Tool SG-1 for 1" fork or SG-2 for 1 1/8" fork)
• Hex wrenches (Park Tool— various models)
• Hack saw, good quality blade of 24 TPI
• File
• Tape measure
• Caliper
• Scribe or marker
• Bench vise (Substitute repair stand to hold column if necessary)

The threaded steering columns require enough thread for the threaded race to press on the bearings. However, the column should not have too many threads. The threads should never extend past the depth of the quill stem. If the column cannot be shortened to permit the quill to extend past the threads, a new fork should be installed with less threading.

The procedure for cutting and sizing threaded steering columns is as follows:

a. Assemble the threaded fork in the bike with all spacers.

b. Measure how much steering column extends past the top spacer and write this number down.

c. Turn the locknut upside down and measure the amount of depth of locknut to "lip" at the end of the nut. This is the amount of available threading in the nut. The steering column should not contact this inner lip when the locknut is secured (11-3.6.2_Figure 1). Deduct an additional millimeter from this number, to allow a small gap between nut and column.

11-3.6.2_Figure 1

Cut away of locknut on threaded column. Locknut lip should not contact top of column.

d. Deduct the available threaded height in the locknut from the amount of steering column extending past the spacers. For example, a steering column is extending 27mm above the spacers. The threaded locknut measures 7mm down to the lip. Deduct one millimeter from the nut, making only 6mm of threading available. Cut 21mm off the column.

e. Use a saw guide such as the Park Tool SG-1 Saw Guide (1" column), or SG-2 (1-1/8" column) to insure that the cut is square to the fork. Thread fork into saw guide until it reaches desired cut length at the gap for the blade. Clamp the guide in a vise. If no vise is available, hold column in repair stand jaws. Use a hacksaw and cut fork.

f. The threads at the end of the fork will require extra finishing after the cut. Thread the fork further into the guide to expose freshly cut threads. Hold a flat file at approximately a 45-degree angle to bevel the threads at the end of the fork (11-3.6.2_ Figure 2). Rotate the fork into the file as the file is pushed forward. Use a round file to finish the inside of the fork, removing any sharp edges or burrs.

11-3.6.2_Figure 2

Bevel end of fork thread

If no Park Tool Saw Guide is available, it is possible to use a steel threaded race as a saw guide. Thread race on column and measure exposed threads. Hold column in bike repair clamp. Press race to clamp so it cannot move. Cut the column using a hacksaw, holding the blade against the face of the race. Finish the cut with a file to bevel the end of the column.

Many threaded columns are made with a machined groove running along the axis of the threads. Many threaded headsets come with spacers with a notch or "tooth" on the inside diameter. The groove is for this notch. Shortening a fork may remove the groove. Do not attempt to extend or create a new groove for the notched washer. If the spacer is made of steel and is narrow, file out the notch or get a new spacer without a notch.

Chapter 12

BIKE WASHING

TOOLS & SUPPLIES

- Repair stand
- Chain cleaner (Park Tool CM-5 Cyclone® Chain Scrubber)
- Buckets of warm water (minimum of 2)
- Water hose and nozzle (optional)
- Sponges (medium and small sizes)
- Brushes, a variety of shapes (Park Tool BCB-4 Bike Cleaning Brush Set)
- Solvent (Park Tool CB-2 Citrus ChainBrite)
- Lubricant (Park Tool CL-1 Synthetic Blend Chain Lube)
- Cotton rags
- Rubber gloves (Park Tool MG-1 Mechanics Gloves)

Cleaning the bike adds to its life and performance by removing dirt, grime, salt and grit. Washing also allows you to more closely inspect the frame and component parts. Keeping the bike clean also adds to one's feeling of wellbeing. Although cleaning helps the bike's performance,

overzealous washing and rinsing can wash out grease from bearings. Avoid using high-pressure car washes or blasting the bike with streams of water from the hose.

It is possible to clean the bike by wiping off the frame and parts using rags. This is a slower process and will also consume a lot of rags. Use a mild cleaning solvent such as a window cleaner or furniture polish to cut grime on the frame.

Cleaning with soap and water is very effective but messy, just like washing a car. Bike washing is common with race mechanics, which must clean many bikes that are often very dirty. Washing is best done outdoors in a place where the water can drain. Wear appropriate clothing and rubber gloves. It is always best to use biodegradable cleaners whenever possible (12_Figure 1). Avoid using diesel or kerosene as a cleaner.

For the most detailed cleaning, it is

12_Figure 1

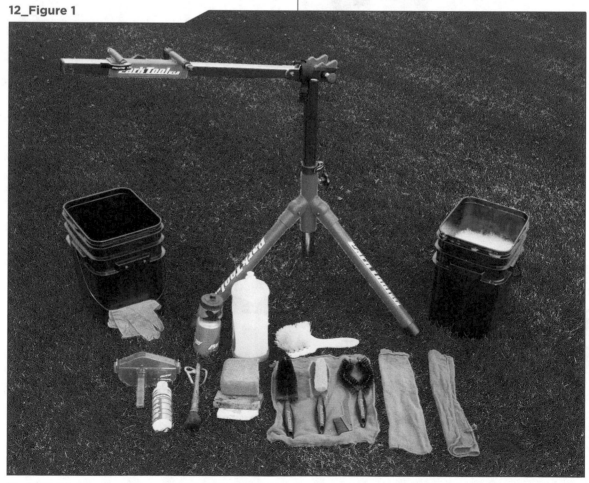

Useful equipment and supplies for bike washing.

best to remove wheels from the bike. It is also a good idea to remove frame pumps, water bottles, and clip-on accessories.

The procedures for washing the bike is as follows:

a. Begin by filling both buckets with warm water. Just like when washing dishes, warm water cleans better. Mix a biodegradable soap, such as for dishwashing, into one of the buckets. Use the other bucket for clean rinse water if no water hose is available.

b. Sponge the area to be clamped clean of dirt and grit. This will prevent marring the finish where it is clamped. Also clean the jaws of the clamp. (12_Figure 2)

12_Figure 2

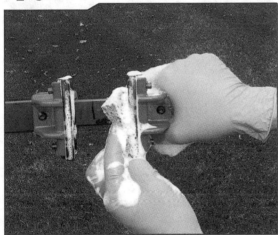

Clean jaws before clamping

c. Clamp the bike in the repair stand.

d. Apply the degreaser to the chain and allow it to soak in. Also apply degreaser to chainrings if they are very dirty.

e. Designate one stiff bristle brush and one of the smaller sponges as "drive train" only tools. These will become quite dirty and should not be used on other parts of the bike. Apply degreaser to brush and brush other components, such as the derailleurs and brakes, if they are very dirty. Brush chainrings and rear pulley wheels with the stiff bristle brush and degreaser. (12_Figure 3) Also scrub the rear sprockets with the stiff bristle brush. If necessary, use a flat tipped screwdriver to scrape dirt from pulleys. Use care not to get degreaser into

bearings such as the bottom bracket, hubs or headset.

12_Figure 3

Scrub chainrings with solvent on the brush

f. Use chain cleaner if available, following manufacturer's instructions (12_Figure 4). If no chain cleaner is available, use a stiff bristle brush. Shift the chain to the largest chainring and scrub outer side plates at chainring. Turn pedals to move the chain through chainring. Move to left side of bike and scrub left side chain plates. Next, scrub rollers from the top between the bottom of the rear cogs and the chainrings.

12_Figure 4

Chain cleaners can thoroughly and quickly clean the chain

g. Clean the degreaser from the drive train before moving to the rest of the bike. Wrap the small drive train sponge around the chain and pedal the bike, flushing the chain clean with soapy water. The sponge will become contaminated with oils and should not be used on the rest of the bike. Repeat until the water falling from the chain is relatively clean looking. Use the same sponge to wipe off the chainrings, derailleur, and rear pulley wheels. Drip soapy water over the rear cogs. To wipe between cogs, use a rag pulled taut.

h. Wipe down the frame with soapy water using the non-drive train sponges and brushes (12_Figure 6). If the brakes are extremely dirty, use the drive train sponge to clean, then follow up with other sponges.

i. Wash hub center. If available, use a "bottle brush". (12_Figure 7)

12_Figure 6

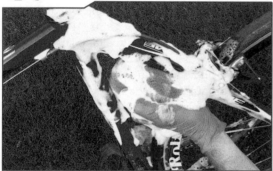

Clean frame with soapy sponge

12_Figure 7

Use bottle brush to clean hub

j. Wash rims and rim braking surfaces. Use care not to scrape or harm the tire sidewall (12_Figure 8). For glued tubular tires, use damp rag to clean rim, but do not soak or scrub tires.

12_Figure 8

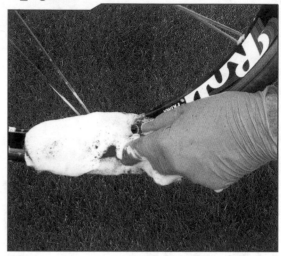

Wash rims but do not scrub at tire sidewalls

k. If no hose is available, use a discarded water bottle or plastic tub to rinse using the second bucket of clean water. Rinse from the top of the bike down. Spin the wheels and chain to help remove excess water.

l. If rinsing with a hose, use gentle spray. Do not blast the bike using a jet stream of water.

m. Remove the bike from the stand.

n. Bounce bike on the ground to shake off water. If no air compressor is available, use a rag to wipe the chain dry. If an air compressor is used, blow dry the chain, but use care not to blast air at the bearings as it may remove grease.

o. Lubricate chain and all accessible pivot points with light lubricant. Use care not to lubricate axle bearings or bottom bracket bearings with the liquid lubricant.

Chapter 13

On-the-Ride Repairs

Mechanical problems can and do occur while riding on the trail or road. The best way to prevent these problems is to regularly clean, lubricate and inspect the bike. Keeping your bike well maintained will prevent many of the mechanical problems described below, even when riding off-road.

13-1 Tool Choices

Should problems arise, be prepared by carrying a few tools. When selecting tools for the ride, consider the type of bike components being used by you and others in your group. Consider the weight of the tools and the amount of space available for carrying. Your budget and level of mechanical skill will also affect your choice of tools.

There are numerous possibilities for tool options and pre-packaged tools kits. One versatile tool choice is the "multi-tool." These contain several tools, including hex wrenches, screwdrivers, spoke wrenches, tire levers, and others in one unit. This type of tool is compact and cost effective. You may assemble your own take-a-long kit of tools. The list below outlines recommended tools for a typical MTB or road ride.

Item Description	Park Tool No.
Multi tool	MTB-3, MTB-7, PPM-3 (includes several functions of tools listed below)
Chain tool	CT-5, or CT-6
Tire levers	TL-1 or TL-2
Patch kit	GP-2 or VP-1
Screwdriver	
Spoke wrench	Park Tool SW-7
Tire boot	TB-1
Inner tubes	Match valve and size of existing tube
Hex wrench set	AWS-10, AWS-9
Chain "master link" or Shimano® replacement pin	

13-2 Repair Procedures

Repairs made during the ride have some limitations. The right tools or parts are not always available. Some bikes can simply be flipped upside down to work on them, but be careful to not damage shift and brake levers or housing. Additionally, some hydraulic brake systems should not be turned upside down. If it is necessary to turn a hydraulic brake system upside down, allow it to sit upright several minutes after the repair, then test the brake to insure no air has entered the brake line. The following text outlines problems that may occur on the ride and gives suggestions for addressing them. If a repair seems questionable, walk the bike home or call for a lift. Do not ride an unsafe bike.

13-2.1 Flat Tire

Always carry a spare tube. On long rides or big group rides, carry two tubes if possible. A patch kit is also essential (Outline Item 2-6 Repairing Inner Tubes). To clean the tube before patching, carry a foil sealed alcohol wipe. These are available in drug stores.

13-2.2 Cut or Ripped Tire

Use a tire boot such as the Park Tool TB-1. (Outline Item 2-7 Temporary Repair of Tire with Tire Boot). Replace the tire as soon as possible.

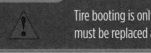

Tire booting is only a temporary fix. Tire must be replaced as soon as possible.

13-2.3 Broken Spoke

The only permanent repair for a broken spoke is to replace the spoke and re-true the wheel (Outline Item 4-3 Replacing Broken or Damaged Spokes). If a single spoke is broken, the lateral true can be improved by loosening the two spokes immediately adjacent to the broken one. This will somewhat bring the wheel back into lateral true. It may be possible to continue the ride. If the wheel has 28 or fewer spokes, having one spoke missing or broken may make the wheel unsafe to use. Bent spokes, even severely bent ones, are less of a problem. If the wheel is still adequately true, continue the ride. True the wheel as necessary, and then replace the spokes after the ride. See Outline Item 4-2 Truing Procedures.

13-2.4 Dented Rim

Rims can become dented from striking objects on the ground. First determine the extent of the dent. If the braking is not badly affected, it may be best to leave it alone and finish the ride. Have the rim repaired or replaced after the ride. With rim caliper brakes, severe dents will be felt during braking and may lock up the wheel unexpectedly. A badly dented rim can also affect the seating of the tire bead. In either of these cases, it is best to not ride the bike.

13-2.5 Broken Chains

A broken chain can usually be shortened as an emergency repair. If you have extra links, these may be added, but the chain will be compromised and should be replaced with a new chain as soon as possible. Note that outer plates must be joined to inner plates and remove links accordingly. If the chain was shortened, use care not to shift into the largest rear sprocket and largest front chainring combination. The most common cause for a broken link is improper installation. When installing a chain, inspect all pins and links to prevent on-the-ride chain problems. Additionally, if a chain has broken on a ride, inspect all rivets and links after repairing. If there was one bad link, there are likely to be more. For chain link cutting, see Outline Item 6-2 Chain Cutting.

13-2.6 Chain Suck

Chain suck occurs when a chainring will not release the chain at the six o'clock position. The chain gets stuck on a tooth and continues upward with the chainring and eventually jams into the frame. If it is not too jammed, grasp the chain at the bottom, and pull down while turning the crank backwards. Scarring of the paint and frame is likely. If pulling the chain will not dislodge it, it may be possible to disconnect a link of chain, and unthread the chain from the frame and re-install correctly. The last option is to remove the right crank, which requires a crank puller. Inspect the chain after pulling it free. The chain may have become twisted or damaged. Inspect the chainring teeth as well, which may be the cause of the problem. If a tooth is bent, avoid using that chainring if possible.

13-2.7 Twisted Chain

Chains can twist from being shifted into the spokes or from jamming against the frame during chain suck. It may be possible to twist the chain back using a pair of pliers, but it is difficult to do so by hand. Isolate the twisted section and use the rear cog to hold one end of the chain. Twist the chain back using pliers at the end of the twist. Replace the chain as soon as possible after the ride.

13-2.8 Squeaky and Noisy Chain

A squeaky chain is caused by the lack of lubrication in the links. It is usually not necessary to carry chain lubricant on shorter rides if the chain has been lubricated as part of regular maintenance. If the ride is especially wet, the lubricant may wash away. In this case, almost anything that will penetrate the link will provide some temporary lubrication. Sunscreen oils or creams, bug repellent creams and cooking oils can provide some short-term relief from a noisy chain. Clean and lubricate the chain properly after the ride.

13-2.9
Rear Derailleur Shifting into the Spokes or Frame

This problem is typically the result of improper limit screw settings. The limits of the rear derailleur act as a stop to the derailleur body. If the derailleur or derailleur hanger is bent, the previous limit screw settings will no longer be appropriate. View the derailleur from the back and sight that the pulley wheels are parallel to the cogs. If the derailleur hanger or pulley cage appears to be pushed inward toward the spokes, something has been bent. It may be possible to pull the derailleur back. Insert a hex wrench in the mounting bolt and pull upward until the derailleur appears parallel with sprockets (13-2.9_Figure 1).

13-2.9_Figure 1

Bend hanger back until visually straight

Check shifting and reset H-limit and L-limit as necessary. Take the bike to a professional shop for proper hanger alignment after the ride or see Outline Item 7-6 Derailleur Hanger Alignment & Repair to do it yourself.

13-2.10 Derailleur not Indexing Properly
The common cause of derailleurs not indexing properly is poor derailleur cable tension adjustment. Apply the same skills and procedures as with routine derailleur adjustment (Outline Item 7-4 Rear Derailleur). Have someone hold the bike by the saddle while you pedal and make adjustments to the barrel adjuster.

13-2.11
Broken Derailleur Body, Cage, or Hanger
If the rear derailleur body, pulley wheel cage, or derailleur hanger has broken, shifting is no longer possible. The bike may be converted to a single speed to get back home.
a. Remove the chain. For procedures see Outline Item 6-2 Chain Cutting.
b. Remove the derailleur or other affected parts.
c. Choose a gear. For triple chainring bikes, use the middle ring and one of the middle rear

sprockets. For two chainring bikes, use the smallest ring.
d. Run the chain from the chosen rear sprocket to the front chainring and determine the correct pin to remove in order to shorten the chain. It may be necessary to change rear sprocket choices to get better chain tension.
e. Cut the chain and connect the links. The chain should be tight enough so it does not come off the front sprocket.
f. Pedal the bike and bounce the chain up and down to check tension.

13-2.11_Figure 1

By-pass derailleur to create a make–shift one speed

13-2.12 Missing Derailleur Pulleys
Look for missing parts if possible on the trail or road behind you. If parts are not available, convert to a one-speed as described in Outline Item 13-2.11 Broken Derailleur Body, Cage, or Hanger.

13-2.13
Front Derailleur Cage Bent or Twisted
The front derailleur cage can get twisted if a chain jams during a shift, or if it is struck. Realign the cage if it has twisted, see Outline Item 7-3 Front Derailleur. Outer cage should be approximately straight to chainrings. The derailleur may not properly shift after the re-alignment, so select the preferred chainring and use cable tension or limit screw to keep the derailleur on that chainring.

13-2.14 Crank Falling Off

If the crank has completely fallen off, the bolt may be missing. In this case, walk the bike back. It would be dangerous to attempt riding it with the arm simply shoved back in place. If you have the bolt, re-install the arm. The torque for crank bolts is relatively high, around 300 inch-pounds. Basically, tighten as much as you feel the tool will be able to withstand.

13-2.15 Pedals Falling Off

A loose pedal may be secured with a correct fitting wrench. Park Tool RW-1 and RW-3 Road Wrenches are small pedal wrenches made specifically for on the ride use. The Park Tool MTB-3 Rescue Tool also comes with a short pedal wrench. If no wrench is available, it is best to walk the bike. Riding with a loose pedal in the crank may cause the thread to pull out of the arm, resulting in a catastrophic crash for the rider.

13-2.16 Bent Crank

If a bike has crashed with much force, the crank may bend. The pedal surface and your foot will then oscillates as the bike is ridden. If the crank clears the frame, it is best to finish the ride by riding lower gears and going slowly. Replace the arm. If the crank does not clear the fame, walk the bike or get a ride. Attempting to re-bend a bent arm may lead to failure.

13-2.17
Bottom Bracket Loose or Falling Apart

Depending on the specific bottom bracket, there may be very little repair that is possible. It is impractical to carry bottom bracket tools on the ride. If the bottom bracket is so loose that the cranks strike the frame, do not ride the bike.

13-2.18 Broken Derailleur Cable

If a derailleur cable has become frayed between the lever and cable pinch bolt, it is more likely to fail. Avoid using the derailleur if possible. Broken gear cables usually mean a non-functioning derailleur.

   If a front derailleur cable has broken, and a spare is not available, consider the remainder of the ride, then chose the most comfortable chainring for completing the ride. Typically the middle chainring is best. Pull the cage up to the middle ring by hand and tighten the L-limit screw. For rear derailleurs, again consider the remainder of the ride. Choose one of the middle cogs and tighten the H-limit screw to hold the derailleur in that position. Broken cables will tend to get caught in moving parts. Remove the old cable and store until it can be properly disposed.

13-2.19 Broken Brake Cable

Do not attempt to patch together broken brake cables. If the cable were to fail again when needed, the consequences could be disastrous. Ride the remainder of the ride with caution, and replace the cable as soon as possible. Walk the bike rather than ride if in doubt as to safety. Remove and store the broken brake cable until it can be properly disposed. For brake cable installation see Outline Item 8-2 Cable System.

13-2.20
Twisted or Bent Handlebars or Stem

Handlebars may become misaligned from crashing. To re-align, stand in front of the bike and grab wheel firmly between knees. Loosen stem binder bolt(s) and pull stem back into alignment until bars appear parallel with front hub, and stem is aligned with wheel. Re-secure binder bolt(s). It will likely be necessary to re-adjust the headset if the binders of a threadless stem are loosened. For headset adjustment see Outline Item 11-2.2 Threadless Headset Adjustment. It is possible to ride with a slight misalignment in the bars. If the crash has actually bent the bars or twisted the stem, it is best not to continue riding. A bent bar or stem may fail without warning. Replace it as soon as possible.

13-2.21 Bent Frame or Fork

Very severe crashes may bend either the frame or fork. Inspect the frame, especially behind the head tube. Look for paint cracks, and wrinkles in the metal, indicating bent frame tubing (13-2.21_Figure 1). If the frame is bent, it should be considered unsafe. Do not ride this bike.

   Fork blades and fork crowns can also bend. View the bike from the side to see if the alignment looks odd. Again, a bent fork makes the bike unsafe to ride.

13-2.21_Figure 1

Bent frame at head area

13-2.22 Bent Saddle or Seat Post

If the saddle has come loose on the post, it may simply be re-aligned and tightened. For saddle security see Outline Item 10-3 Saddle and Seat Post Adjustment. If the clamp is broken, it will be difficult to repair away from home. In this case, remove both entire seat post and the saddle. Simply removing the seat and leaving the post installed is inviting an accident to happen.

Appendix A-C

Appendix A : Tool List

Appendix B : Glossary

Appendix C : Recommended Torque
for Bicycle Components

The tool list below will stock a very complete "home mechanic shop." The list does not duplicate a professional shop. For example, there are no bottom bracket taps, head tube reaming tools and other tools a full service center at a retail bicycle shop would use.

There are often several choices for a particular piece of equipment. It will be necessary to research these choices to make the best decision for your specific circumstances.

TOOL	PARK TOOL OPTIONS
Repair stand	**PCS-1** Home Mechanic Repair Stand
	PCS-2 Bench Mount Home Mechanic Repair Stand
	PCS-4 Deluxe Home Mechanic Repair Stand
	PCS-9 Home Mechanic Repair Stand
	PRS-2OS Deluxe Double Arm Repair Stand
	PRS-3OS Deluxe Single Arm Repair Stand
	PRS-4OS Deluxe Bench Mount Repair Stand
	PRS-4W Deluxe Wall Mount Repair Stand
	PRS-7 Bench Mount Repair Stand
	PRS-15 Professional Race Stand
	PRS-20 Team Race Stand
Floor pump	**PFP-2** Professional Mechanic Floor Pump
	PFP-3 Home Mechanic Floor Pump
Spoke wrenches	**SW-0** Professional Spoke Wrench (3.23mm nipples)
	SW-1 Professional Spoke Wrench (3.3mm nipples)
	SW-2 Professional Spoke Wrench (3.45mm nipples)
	SW-7 Triple Spoke Wrench (3.23mm. 3.3mm, and 3.45mm nipples)
Truing stand	**TS-2** Professional Wheel Truing Stand
	TS-8 Home Mechanic Wheel Truing Stand
Spoke tension meter	**TM-1** Spoke Tension Meter
Dishing tool	**WAG-3** Portable Wheel Dishing Gauge
	WAG-4 Deluxe Wheel Dishing Gauge

TOOL	PARK TOOL OPTIONS
Spoke ruler	**SBC-1** Spoke, Bearing, and Cotter Gauge
Tire levers	**TL-1** Tire Lever Set
	TL-2 Tire Lever Set (thin, flat type)
	TL-5 Heavy Duty Steel Tire Lever Set
Valve core remover	
Inner tube patch kit	**VP-1** Vulcanizing Patch Kit
	GP-2 Pre-Glued Super Patch Kit
Tire Boot	**TB-1** Tire Boot
Bottom bracket tools	**BBT-2** Bottom Bracket Tool for 20-tooth internally splined Shimano® (and other) bottom brackets.
	BBT-5 Bottom Bracket Tool for 12-tooth internally splined Campagnolo® bottom brackets
	BBT-4 Bottom Bracket Tool for 6-notch Campagnolo® bottom brackets
	BBT-8 Bottom Bracket Tool for 8-notch Shimano®, Truvativ®, and Bontrager® bottom brackets
	BBT-9 Bottom Bracket Tool for Shimano, FSA, and Truvative 16-notch external bearing bottom brackets
Fixed cup spanner-36mm	**HCW-4** 36mm Box End Spanner / Pin Spanner
Lockring spanner	**HCW-5** Double-Sided Lockring Spanner
Pin spanner	**SPA-2** Pin Spanner
	SPA-6 Heavy Duty Adjustable Pin Spanner
Bearing cup press	**HHP-2** Bearing Cup Press
Fork crown race setting tool	**CRS-1** Crown Race Setting System
Headset race remover	**RT-1** Head Cup Remover
Fork crown race remover	**CRP-1** Crown Race Puller
Fork saw guide	**SG-6** Threadless Saw Guide
Threadless star nut setter	**TNS-1** Threadless Nut Setter for 1" and 1 1/8"

TOOL	PARK TOOL OPTIONS
Headset wrenches	**HCW-15** 32mm and 36mm Headset Wrench
	HCW-7 30mm and 32mm Headset Wrench
	HW-2 32mm and 36mm Headset Locknut Wrench
Crank Puller	**CCP-2** Crank Puller for square hole crank arms
	CCP-4 Crank Puller for splined hole crank arms
	CWP-6 Crank Puller for square and splined hole arms
Crank bolt wrench	**HR-8** 8mm Hex Wrench
	PH-10 10mm P-handle Hex Wrench
	CCW-14R 14mm Crank Bolt Wrench
Chainring nut wrench	**CNW-1** Chainring Nut Wrench
Chain tool	**CT-3** Heavy Duty Screw Type Chain Tool
	CT-5 Mini Chain Brite Chain Tool
	CT-6 Folding Chain Tool
Chain wear indicator	**CC-2** Chain Checker
	CC-3 Chain Wear Indicator
Pedal wrench	**PW-3** 15mm and $^9/_{16}$" Pedal Wrench
	PW-4 Professional 15mm Pedal Wrench
	HCW-16 15mm Pedal Wrench/Chain Whip
Derailleur hanger alignment gauge	**DAG-1** Derailleur Hanger Alignment Gauge
Cone wrenches	**SCW-13–19** 13mm through 19mm Shop Cone Wrenches
	DCW-1 13mm/ 14mm Double Ended Cone Wrench
	DCW-2 15mm/ 16mm Double Ended Cone Wrench
	DCW-3 17mm/ 18mm Double Ended Cone Wrench
	DCW-4 13mm/ 15mm Double Ended Cone Wrench
Axle vise	**AV-1** Axle Vise **AV-4** Heavy Duty Axle and Pedal Vise

TOOL	PARK TOOL OPTIONS
Freewheel removers	**FR-1** Freewheel Remover for 12-tooth splined Shimano® freewheels
	FR-2 Freewheel Remover for 2-notch Suntour® freewheels
	FR-3 Freewheel Remover for 4-notch Suntour® freewheels
	FR-4 Freewheel Remover for splined Atom®, Regina®, and some Schwinn® freewheels
	FR-6 Freewheel Remover for 4-notch single speed freewheels (1.37 x 24 tpi)
	FR-7 Freewheel Remover for 12-tooth splined Falcon® freewheels
Cassette lockring tool	**FR-5** Cassette Lockring Tool for Shimano® **FR-5G** Cassette Lockring Tool with Guide Pin for Shimano® **BBT-5** Cassette Lockring Tool for Campagnolo®
Chain whip	**SR-1** Chain Whip / Sprocket Remover
	SR-2 Heavy Duty Shop Chain Whip / Sprocket Remover
	HCW-16 Chain Whip/ 15mm Pedal Wrench
3rd hand tool	**BT-5** Adjustable Third Hand Brake Tool
4th hand/cable stretcher	**BT-2** 4th Hand/ Cable Stretcher
Brake toe-in tool	**BT-3** Brake Toe-In Tool
Brake wrenches	**OBW-1** 10mm and 13mm Offset Brake Wrench
	OBW-2 11mm and 12mm Offset Brake Wrench
	OBW-3 14mm and Spring Centering Offset Brake Wrench
Cable/housing cutter	**CN-10** Cable and Housing Cutter
Hex wrench set	**AWS-1** 4, 5, and 6mm 3-way Hex Wrench Set
	AWS-3 2, 2.5, and 3mm 3-way Hex Wrench Set
	AWS-10 Fold Up Hex Wrench Set (1.5mm - 6mm)
	AWS-11 Fold Up Hex Wrench Set (3mm - 10mm)
	HXS-1 L-Shaped Hex Wrench Set (2mm - 10mm)
	HXS-2 L-Shaped Hex Wrench Set (2mm - 10mm) with Holder
	PH-1 P-Handled Hex Wrench Set (2mm - 10mm) with Holder

TOOL	PARK TOOL OPTIONS
Torx wrenches	**TWS-2** Fold-Up Torx Wrench Set (T7 – T40)
	PH-T25 P-Handled T25 Torx Wrench
Torque wrench	**TW-1** Torque Wrench, 0 to 60 inch pounds
	TW-2 Torque Wrench, 0 to 600 inch pounds
Hex bits 4, 5, 6, 8mm	
Sockets 8, 9, 10, 14, 15, 17mm	
$^3/_8$ inch drive ratchet wrench	
Taps	**TAP-6** $^9/_{16}$" x 20 tpi Pedal Tap Set
	TAP-7 3mm x .5 Tap for rear dropout alignment screws
Tap handle	
Frame alignment gauge	**FAG-2** Frame Alignment Gauge
Bench vise, 4 inch	
Air compressor	
Ball peen hammer, 12 oz.	
Rubber/plastic mallet	
Punches, various sizes	
Metric tape measure	
Metric measuring caliper	
Screwdriver, straight blade $^5/_{32}$ inch tip	
Screwdriver, straight blade $^3/_{16}$ inch tip	
Screwdriver, cross tip "Phillips" #1	
Screwdriver, cross tip "Phillips" #2	
Diagonal side cutter pliers	
Long nose pliers (needle nose)	

Big Blue Book of Bicycle Repair

TOOL	PARK TOOL OPTIONS
File - round	
File-10-inch mill bastard	
Hacksaw	
Hacksaw blade, 24 tpi	
Hacksaw blade, 32 tpi	
7 to 17mm combo wrenches	
8-inch adjustable wrench	
12-inch adjustable wrench	
Flashlight	
Scissors	
Lubricant- liquid	**CL-1** Synthetic Blend Chain Lube
Lubricant-grease	**PPL-1** PolyLube 1000, 4 oz.
	PPL-2 PolyLube 1000, 16 oz.
Chain cleaner	**CM-5** Cyclone Chain Scrubber
	CG-2 ChainGang Chain Cleaning System
Solvent	**CB-2** Citrus ChainBrite Chain and Component Cleaning Fluid
Cleaning brushes	**GSC-1** GearClean Brush
	BCB-4 Bike Cleaning Brush Set
Shop apron	**SA-1** Shop Apron
	SA-3 Heavy Duty Shop Apron
Hand cleaner	
Bike polish	
Rags	

Adjustable cup. The left bearing cup of an adjustable bottom bracket.

Adjusting race. A moveable-bearing surface typically mounted to a thread that is used to adjust bearing play and movement.

Allen® Wrench. See hex wrench.

Articulated housing. Brake and derailleur index housing made of small hollow metal segments strung together over a liner.

ATB. All terrain bike, or mountain bike.

Axle nut. A threaded nut that secures wheel to bike. Used with solid axle hubs.

Bead seat diameter. Rim diameter measured where the tire bead is seated.

Bolt circle diameter. Diameter of a circle transcribed by the chainring mounting bolts.

Bottom bracket. The bearings and spindle connecting both crankarms.

Bottom bracket shell. The part of the frame that holds the bottom bracket.

Bottom bracket spindle. The axle in the bottom bracket. It connects both crankarms.

Braided housing. A cable housing made of woven wire around an inner liner.

Brake bridge. The tubing connection between seatstays. Located above tire and used for mounting side pull and dual pivot brake calipers on some bikes.

Brake cable. Braided wire cable that connects brake lever with brake caliper.

Brake cable carrier. Transverse connection between brake caliper arms. Found on cantilever brakes.

Brake cable pinch bolt/nut. Fastener that secures brake cable to caliper arm.

Brake caliper. The lever arms that move brake pads to rim or rotor to apply friction needed to slow and stop the bicycle. Brake centering screw. The screw that changes spring tension between caliper arms, allowing pads to center over wheel rim.

Brake fluid. Either mineral fluid or D.O.T. brake fluid for hydraulic brake systems.

Brake lever. The mechanism pulled by hand to activate brake caliper and pads.

Brake pad. Synthetic rubber block fastened to caliper arm. Pad is forced against moving rim, causing friction, to slow rim rotation and stop bicycle.

Brake pad fixing bolt/nut. Fastener system that holds brake pad to caliper arm.

Brake pad toe. An adjustment to the brake pad used to reduce brake squeal. Pad surface adjusted to strike braking surface at a slight angle, with leading edge striking first.

Brake quick release. Mechanism found on brake caliper to open brake arms allowing wide tires to pass brake pads. The mechanism is sometimes found on the brake lever.

Braking surface. Part of the rim or rotor disc that is rubbed by brake pads.

British Standard Cycle (BSC). A thread standard system used by the British and adopted by much of the world.

B-screw. Body-screw on rear derailleur that changes the placement of the upper pulley (G-pulley) to the rear sprockets.

Cable. Wound, multiple strand wire used for brake calipers and derailleurs.

Cable adjusting barrel. Hollow bolt that acts as housing stop. Adjusts in or out of housing to effectively change housing length and cable tension on brake and derailleur systems.

Cable pinch bolt. Bolt that flattens and holds secure the cut end of the cable. Found on derailleurs and brakes.

Caliper rim brake. A brake system that applies friction directly to the rim for slowing and stopping the bike.

Cantilever brake. Brake system found on many mountain bikes and touring road bikes. Consists of two separate arms pivoting off studs fixed to the frame or fork.

Cassette. Sprocket and spacer assembly mounted to a freehub mechanism on the rear wheel.

Centerline. Mid plane of the bike running in line with wheels.

Chain. A connected series of flexible links used to transfer motion of front chainrings to rear sprockets.

Chain rivet. Small pin that connects two outer chain plates, usually considered a permanent part of chain.

Chainring. Sprocket attached to the crank. Chainring bolt. Special bolts that secure chainring to crank.

Chainring nut. Thin walled nut used with chainring bolt.

Chainring nut wrench. Wrench with two pegs used to hold chainring nut.

Chainstay. Frame tubes connecting the rear dropouts and the bottom bracket shell.

Cleats. Fitting mounted to a cycling shoe that attaches the shoe to the pedal.

Cogs. Sprockets attached to rear hub.

Compressionless housing. Outer plastic and metal sheath that covers derailleur inner cable, allowing it to pass around corners and between moving parts of the frame. Differs from other housing in that outer support wires run longitudinally with inner cable. Also called SIS™ housing by Shimano, Inc.

Cone. A curved bearing race that rides against ball bearings.

Cone wrench. Thin wrench made to fit the narrow wrench fittings of a hub cone.

Crank (Crank arm). The lever arm between the pedal and the bottom bracket.

Crank bolt. Bolt that secures crank to bottom bracket spindle.

Crank puller. Tool used to remove cranks by pulling them from bottom bracket spindle.

Crankset. Rotating mechanism turned by feet, includes chainrings, cranks, & chainring bolts/nuts.

Crown (fork crown). Horizontal portion of fork, located at top of fork blades.

Derailleur. Mechanism used to push chain from one cog or chainring to another.

Derailleur cable. The inner cable of the derailleur cable system. Sometimes called gear cable.

Derailleur capacity. The rated ability of a rear derailleur to take up chain slack from the gear combinations on the bike. Given as the sum of rear sprocket differences plus front chainring differences.

Derailleur hanger. The fitting on a bicycle frame that holds the rear derailleur. On some bikes this piece is replaceable.

Derailleur limit screw. Screw that stops derailleur travel. One screw stops inward travel, a second screw stops outward travel.

Disc brake. Caliper brake system using rotor bolted to hub as the braking surface. Brake caliper attaches to either fork end or frame.

Dishing Tool. A gauge used to measure the centering of the wheel rim over the hub.

D.O.T. brake fluid. Hydraulic brake fluid approved by the US Department of Transportation. Does NOT interchange with mineral brake fluid.

Down tube. Frame tube connecting lower portion of the head tube to the bottom bracket shell.

Drop bars. Curved handlebars made with two bends, with the outermost section being lower than the top and offset 90-degrees. Most frequently used on road bikes.

Dropout. Part of frame and fork slotted to accept wheel axle.

Dual pivot brake. Road type brake with two arms pivoting off separate studs mounted to a center bracket. One arm swings on an arc moving up and the other arm swings on an arc moving down.

E-plate derailleur. A front derailleur design that permanently mounts the derailleur to a plate held by the bottom bracket.

External bearing crankset. Cranksets that integrate the crank and the bottom bracket spindle. Bearings mount outside the bottom bracket shell.

Fixed cup. The right side cup of an adjustable bottom bracket.

Flat bars. A handlebar style where the handlebars bend very slightly from the center.

Foot-pound. A measurement of torque used mainly in the United States.

Fork. Mechanism for holding the front wheel.

Fork blades. Tubes connecting fork dropouts to fork crown.

Frame. Supporting structure for the components and wheels of a bike.

Frame housing stops. Fittings on the frame that hold either brake or derailleur cable housing ends.

Freehub. Ratcheting body bolted internally to hub of rear wheel. Holds cassette cogs. Mechanism does not remove when cogs are removed.

Freewheel. Ratcheting mechanism on the rear wheel fitted with one or more cogs. Cogs and ratcheting body unthread from hub as a unit.

Front derailleur. Mechanism located above front chainrings that pushes the chain from one chainring to another.

Gear cable. See derailleur cable.

Guide pulley. (G-pulley) Uppermost pulley on rear derailleur. Guides chain onto rear cogs.

Gripshift®. Twist shifter manufactured by the SRAM® Corporation.

Handlebars. Connector between stem and cyclist's hands.

Head tube. Tube connecting down tube and top tube, contains headset and steering column of fork.

Headset. Bearing assembly connecting the head tube and fork. Allows fork to rotate.

Hex wrench. Metal wrench of six sides (hex shaped) made to fit inside bolts or other mechanical fittings. Also known as Allen® Wrench.

Housing. The outer plastic and metal sheath that covers brake or derailleur cable , allowing cable to pass around corners and between moving parts of the frame.

Housing end cap (ferrule). Small metal cap that fits over end of housing.

Hub. The center of the wheel, contains bearings and an axle.

Hub brake. Braking system located at the center of the wheel at the hub.

Hydraulic brake. A brake system that uses fluid to transmit power from the rider's hand to the brake rotor.

Hydraulic-mechanical brake. A brake system that combines hydraulic and mechanical systems.

Inch-pound. A measurement of torque used mostly in the United States.

Indexing. Shifting system that uses "clicks" or dwell at each sprocket location.

Inner tube. Rubber bladder inside tire that holds air.

Innermost. Closest point relative to the centerline of the bike.

Interference fit. A method of assembly where one part is slightly larger than it's intended fitting. Parts are held together by the force of assembly.

Internal headset. A headset type that uses a pressed head tube cup that allows bearings to sit inside head tube. Also called Zero-stack or low-profile headset.

International Standards Organization. A group dedicated to setting standards for all industries involved in international trade, such as the bicycling industry.

ISIS Drive®. International Splined Interface System. A crank and bottom bracket spindle interface standard using 10 splines.

ISO. See International Standards Organization

Integrated headset. A headset design where the frame acts as a holder for the bearings. Bearings are held inside head tube. Service or installation does not involve pressing cups.

Kilogram force. A force equal to a kilogram weight or a one-kilogram mass times the acceleration of gravity. Approximately equal to 2.2 pounds force.

Limit screw. Screws on front and rear derailleurs to stop the extreme range of derailleur motion.

Linear pull brakes. A caliper brake with two long arms holding pads. System uses housing stop in one arm, no straddle cable.

Locknut. Nut used to lock a cone, threaded race, or other threaded item to keep it from unthreading.

Low profile headset. A headset that uses a pressed head tube cup that allows bearings to sit inside headtube. Also called Zero-stack or internal headset.

Master link. Linkage system used to join the ends of a chain.

Maximum extension line. A line on a seat post or quill stem indicating the maximum amount the item should be raised above the frame or fork steering column. Also called the "minimum insertion line."

Maximum tooth size. The largest rear spocket size a rear derailleur will be able to shift.

Mechanical disc brake. A disc brake that uses a cable system and has no hydraulic fittings anywhere.

Mineral Fluid. A type of fluid, based on mineral oil, used in some models of hydraulic brakes. Does not interchange with DOT brake fluid.

Minimum insertion line. See minimum extension line.

Mountain bike. Bicycle design intended for rugged, off road use. Also called "ATB,"or all terrain bike.

MTB. See mountain bike.

Nipple. See spoke nipple.

Octalink®. Registered trademark of Shimano® Inc. for a crank and spindle interface standard using 8 splines. Octalink® includes the non-interchangeable V1 and V2 systems.

One-key release. Crank system that allows removal of the crank without a crank puller

One-piece crank. Crank that uses a single piece of metal for the arms and spindle. Also called "Ashtabula" crank.

Outermost. Farthest from centerline of bike.

Pawl. Articulating tooth on a ratcheting system. Used commonly in freehubs and freewheels.

Perdido®. A headset standard from the Chris King® Group, similar in appearance to low profile.

Pipe Billet spindle. A splined bottom bracket spindle from Shimano® Inc. Cranks and spindles do not interchange with square spindles or square holed cranks.

Presta valve. Narrow valve found on inner tubes.

Pulley wheel. Small wheel on the rear derailleur that wraps the chain.

Quick release skewer. Metal shaft and lever with cam, fitted into hollow axle. Allows easy and quick removal of wheel.

Quill Stem. A type of stem the inserts and secures inside a threaded steering column.

Rapid Rise™ derailleur. A registered trademark for a derailleur system from Shimano Inc. The rear derailleur return spring, in a relaxed position, places the derailleur under the innermost rear cog. Increasing cable tension by shifting moves derailleur outward. Other types of derailleurs move inward when cable tension is increased.

Rear derailleur. Shifting mechanism attached to the frame that moves chain from one sprocket to another.

Rear sprockets. The toothed cogs or gears on the rear wheel.

Repair stand. Fixture designed to hold bike while doing repairs.

Retaining compound. Liquid adhesive designed to expand and harden in press fit situations.

Rim. Metal or composite hoop suspended around hub by spokes.

Rim strip. Protective strip covering holes between rim and inner tube.

Rotor. Round disc plate mounted to hub for disc brake caliper.

Saddle. Support for posterior of bicyclist.

Schrader valve. Inner tube valve commonly seen on car tires.

Seat post. Connection between saddle and frame.

Seat tube. Frame tube connecting top tube and bottom bracket. Seat post inserts into top of tube.

Seatstay. Frame tube connecting rear dropout and upper portion of seat tube.

Setscrew. Small screw used primarily for adjustments. Found commonly on brake levers and caliper brakes.

Self-vulcanizing fluid. Special fluid used on an inner tube to adhere patch.

Shift lever. Control mechanism designed to pull cable and control derailleur.

Sidepull brake. Caliper brake using one pivot for both arms, mounted to brake bridge above center of wheel.

Slip fit. Method of assembly where one part slides without force into its fitting.

Spanner. Wrench.

Spindle. Axle for the bottom bracket.

Spider. Arms that hold the chainrings to the crank.

Splined spindle. A tubular shaped bottom bracket axle with ends having machined notches and recesses. The splines mate to splines in the crank.

Spoke. Long thin bolt, connecting hub to rim. Threaded on one end with a hook or fitting on other end.

Spoke nipple. Nut located at threaded end of spoke.

Sprocket. Toothed gear or wheel used to connect with the chain.

Square spindle. A spindle design where the spindle ends are a square shaped stud. Fits into a square hole in the crank.

Star nut (Star fangled nut). A nut designed to press into the inside of the fork steering column. Nut provides method for headset bearing adjustment.

Steering column. Tubing that connects fork crown to stem.

Stem. Connector between fork and handlebars.

Tensiometer. Tool used to determine the amount of tension of spokes.

Tension. Tensile force, pulling along the axis of an object.

Tension meter. See tensiometer.

Thread locker. A special adhesive designed to expand and harden in the threads of a fastener.

Thread pitch. Distance from one thread crest to the next thread crest.

Threadless stem. Stem that fastens to the outside of an unthreaded steering column.

Tire. Rubber and fabric casing which encloses the inner tube and contacts ground.

Tire bead. Wire or fabric molded into the tire edge. Holds tire down onto rim when tire is under pressure.

Tire lever. Lever with smooth, rounded edge used to remove tire bead from rim.

Tire Sealant. A liquid placed in the tire or inner tube. The purpose is to block minor leaks.

Top tube. Frame tube connecting head tube to seat tube.

Torque. Force around an axis.

True. Refers to wheel rim spinning laterally straight and round.

Tubeless tire. Tire and rim system that maintains air pressure without an inner tube. Similar to automotive and motorcycle tubeless tire systems.

Twist grip. Shift lever fitted as part of handgrip that actuates by rotation.

Valve core. Mechanism in inner tube for inflating and deflating tube.

V-brakes®. Registered trademark of Shimano® Inc. for a type of linear pull brake. Pads move on parallelgram attached to caliper arms.

Wheel. A composite of the rim, hub and spokes. May also include tire and tube.

Zero stack headset. A headset type that uses a pressed headtube cup that allows bearings to sit inside headtube. Also called low profile or internal headset.

Zip tie. Thin plastic straps used to secure most anything.

All figures in the table below are inch-pound. Some component companies do not specify torque for certain components or parts. Contact the manufacturer for the most up to date specifications.

HEADSET, HANDLEBAR, SEAT & SEAT POST AREA	
Threaded headset locknut	Chris King® Gripnut type 130-150
	Tange-Seiki® 217
Stem binder bolt- quill type	Control Tech® 144-168
	Shimano® 174-260
Threadless stem steering column binder bolts	Control Tech® 120-144
	Deda® 71
	FSA® carbon 78
	Syncros® cotter bolt type 90
	Thomson® 48
	Time® Monolink 45
Handlebar binder One bolt or two bolt models	Shimano® 174-260
	Control Tech® 120-144
Handlebar binders- 4 bolts face plate models	Control Tech® 120-144
	Deda® magnesium 71
	Thomson® 48
	FSA® OS-115 carbon 78
	Time® Monolink 53
	MTB handle bar end
	extensions
	Cane Creek® 70
	Control Tech® 144

chart continued pp. 218

HEADSET, HANDLEBAR, SEAT & SEAT POST AREA

Seat rail binder	Control Tech®, 2 bolt type 144
	Control Tech®, single bolt 300
	Shimano® 174-347
	Syncros® each bolt 45
	Time® Monolink-44
	Travativ® (M8 bolt: 195-212. M6 bolt: 53-63)
Seat post binder Note: Seat posts require only minimal tightening to not slip downward. Avoid over tightening	Campagnolo® 36-60

PEDAL, CRANKSET & BOTTOM BRACKET AREA

Pedal into crank	Campagnolo® 354
	Ritchey® 307
	Shimano® 307 minimum
	Truvativ® 276-300
Shimano® Octalink XTR crankarm bolts (M15 thread)	Shimano® 357-435
Shimano® Hollowtech II bottom bracket bearing cup	305-435
Shimano® Hollowtech II crank bolt screws	88-132
Shimano® Hollowtech II Left-hand fixing cap	4-6
FSA® MegaExo crank adjusting cap	3.6-6
FSA® MegaExo crank fixing screws	87-100

PEDAL, CRANKSET & BOTTOM BRACKET AREA

Crank bolt (including splinetype cranks and square-spindle cranks)	Shimano® 305-391
	Campagnolo® 312-324
	FRA® (M8 bolt) 304-347
	FRA® (M14 steel) 434-521
	Race Face® 480
	Syncros®240
	Truvativ® 384-420 ISIS Drive
	Truvativ® 336-372 square spindle
	White Ind® 240-300
Crank bolt one-key release cap	Shimano® 44-60
	Truvativ® 107-124
Chainring cassette to crankarm (lockring)	Shimano® 443-620
Chainring bolt–Steel	Shimano® 70-95
	Campagnolo® 84-120
	Race Face&erg; 100
	Truvativ® 107-124
Chainring bolt–Aluminum	Shimano® 44-88
	Truvativ® 72-80
Bottom bracket–Cartridge	Shimano® 435-608
	Campagnolo® 612
	FSA® 347-434
	Race Face® 420
	Truvativ® 300-360
	White Ind.® 240

DERAILLEUR & SHIFT LEVER AREA

STI type shift lever binder	Shimano® 53-69
Shift lever - above-the-bar	Shimano® 22-26
Shift lever - twist grip	Shimano® Revo 53-70
	SRAM® 17
Front Derailleur clamp bolt	Campagnolo® 61
	Mavic® 26-35
	Shimano® 44-60
	SRAM® 44-60
Front derailleur cable pinch	Campagnolo® 44
	Mavic® 44-62
	Shimano® 44-60
	SRAM® 40
Rear derailleur mounting bolt	Campagnolo® 133
	Shimano® 70-86
	SRAM® 70-85
Rear derailleur cable inch bolt	Shimano® 35
	Campagnolo® 53
	SRAM® 35-45
Rear derailleur pulley wheel (idler wheel) bolt	Shimano® 27-34
	Sachs® 44-53

WHEEL, HUB, REAR COG AREA

Spoke Tension Torque is typically not used in wheels. Spokes tension is measured by deflection. Contact rim manufacturer for specific tension recommendations.

Quick release at wheel. Measured torque not typically used. Common industry practice is resistance at lever half way through swing from open to fully closed.

Wheel axle nuts to frame	Shimano® 260-390
	SRAM® 266-350
Cassette sprocket lockring	Shimano® 260-434
	Campagnolo® 442
Hub cone locking nut	Bontrager® 150
	Chris King® 100
	Shimano® 87-217
Freehub body	Bontrager® 400
	Shimano® 305-434

DISC BRAKE SYSTEMS

Disc rotor to hub-lockring models	Shimano® 350
Disc rotor to hub (M5 bolts, six per rotor)	Shimano® 18-35
	Hayes® 50
	Avid® 55
	Magura® 34
Caliper mount	Avid® 80-90
	Magura® 51
	Shimano® 53-69
Hydraulic hose fittings	Hayes® 55
	Shimano® 44-60

BRAKE CALIPER & LEVER AREA

Brake caliper mount to frame, side/dual/center pull	Campagnolo® 90
	Cane Creek® 68-72
	Shimano® 70-85
Brake caliper mount to braze-on linear pull or cantilever	Avid® 43-61
	Control Tech® 100-120
	Shimano® 44-60
	SRAM® 45-60
Brake pad- threaded stud	Avid® 52-69
	Campagnolo® 72
	Cane Creek® 56-60
	Mavic® 62-80
	Shimano® 44-60
	SRAM® 50-70
Brake pad- smooth stud	Shimano® 70-78
Brake cable pinch bolt- linear pull or cantilever	Control Tech® 40-60
	Shimano® 53-69
	SRAM® 50-70
Brake cable pinch bolt sidepull/dual pivot	Campagnolo® 45
	Cane Creek® 68-72
	Mavic® 62-80
	Shimano® 53-69
Sidepull/dual pivot brake pad bolt	Cane Creek® 56-60
	Shimano® 44-60
Cantilever straddle wire pinch (M5 thread)	Control Tech® 40-60
	Shimano® 35-43
Brake caliper wire pinch linear pull/cantilever (M6 thread)	Avid® 52-69
	Shimano® 50-75

The chart below is a quick conversion between inch-pounds, foot-pounds, and Newton-meters. For exact figures, use the formulas below.

Inch pound in-lb	Approx. Foot pound ft-lb	Approx. Newton-meter NM	Inch pound in-lb	Approx. Foot pound ft-lb	Approx. Newton-meter NM
10	0.8	1.1	260	21.7	29.4
20	1.7	2.3	270	22.5	30.5
30	2.5	3.4	280	23.3	31.6
40	3	3 4.5	290	24.2	32.8
50	4.2	5.6	300	25.0	33.9
60	5.0	6.8	310	25.8	35.0
70	5.8	7.9	320	26.7	36.2
80	6.7	9.0	330	27.2	37.3
90	7.5	10.2	340	28.3	38.4
100	8.3	11.3	350	29.2	39.5
110	9.2	12.4	360	30.0	40.7
120	10	13.6	370	30.8	41.8
130	10.8	14.7	380	31.7	42.9
140	11.7	15.8	390	32.5	44.0
150	12.5	16.9	400	33.3	45.2
160	13.3	18.1	410	34.2	46.3
170	14.2	19.2	420	35.0	47.5
180	15.0	20.3	430	35.8	48.6
190	15.8	21.5	440	36.7	49.7
200	16.7	22.6	450	37.5	50.8
210	17.5	23.7	460	38.3	52.0
220	18.3	24.9	470	39.2	53.1
230	19.2	26.0	480	40	54.2
240	20.0	27.1	490	40.8	55.4
250	20.8	28.2	500	41.7	56.5

following formulas will convert other torque designations into inch-pounds (in-lb).

in-lb = ft-lb x 12
in-lb = Nm x 8.851
in-lb = kgf-cm x 0.87